TANTRA ('woven together' in Sanskrit) is the Hindu-based religion which originated 1,200 years ago, when the great erotic temples were built. In the West it is now best known for the inspiration of tantric yoga, and its associated ritualistic forms of sex. But is Tantra just about esoteric sexual practice or does it amount to something more? This lively and original book contributes to a more complete understanding of Tantra's mysteries by discussing the idea of the body in Hindu tantric thought and practice in India.

The author argues that within Tantra the body is a vehicle for the spirituality that is fundamental to people's lives. The tantric body cannot be understood outside the traditions and texts that give it form. Through practice (ritual, yoga and 'reading') the body is formed into a pattern determined by tradition, and the practitioner thereby moulds his or her life into the shape of the tradition. While there is a great range of tantric bodies – from ascetics living in cremation grounds, to low-caste people possessed by tantric deities, to sophisticated high-caste Brahmans expounding the ascetic philosophy of Tantra – all share certain common assumptions and processes. Flood argues that while there is a divergence at different social levels and in different levels of tantric metaphysical claims, these levels are united by a process which the author calls 'entextualisation of the body'. The body becomes the text through the tradition being inscribed on it. This general claim is tested against specific ritual and doctrinal examples, and the tantric traditions are linked to wider social and political forces.

The Tantric Body is a fascinating study that makes an important contribution to the study of South Asian religion, and will have strong appeal to students of South Asian societies and cultures as well as to those of comparative philosophy.

GAVIN FLOOD is Professor of Religion at the University of Stirling and Academic Director of the Oxford Centre for Hindu Studies. He is the author of *An Introduction to Hinduism* (1996) and general editor of *The Blackwell Companion to Hinduism* (2003).

The Tantric Body

The Secret Tradition of Hindu Religion

GAVIN FLOOD

I.B.TAURIS
LONDON · NEW YORK

Published in 2006 by
I.B. Tauris & Co. Ltd
6 Salem Rd, London W2 4BU
175 Fifth Avenue, New York NY 10010
www.ibtauris.com

In the United States and Canada distributed by Palgrave Macmillan,
a division of St. Martin's Press, 175 Fifth Avenue, New York, NY 10010

Frontispiece: Cakra man (Wellcome Ms β511).
With kind permission of the Wellcome Trust.

ISBN 1 84511 011 0 (Hb)
ISBN 1 84511 012 9 (Pb)
EAN 978 1 84511 011 6 (Hb)
EAN 978 1 84511 012 3 (Pb)

A full CIP record for this book is available from the British Library
A full CIP record for this book is available from the Library of Congress
Library of Congress catalog card: available

Typeset in Monotype Ehrhardt by illuminati, Grosmont,
www.illuminatibooks.co.uk
Printed and bound in Great Britain by T.J. International Ltd,
Padstow, Cornwall

Contents

Preface

THIS BOOK represents the application of a general theoretical framework to a body of tantric texts that I have been reading, on and off, for a number of years. That theoretical framework develops the theme of the relationship between subjectivity and text. More precisely, the book offers a description and analysis of the idea that subjectivity is textually mediated within a corpus of tantric texts composed in the medieval period. To give an account of this textually mediated subjectivity is also to give an account of the tantric body. A tradition-specific understanding of self and body is constructed, as it were, through the text. The book therefore does not claim to be a work of Indology as such but draws on Indology to present a particular reading of a range of textual material. This is a reading of the body as represented within those texts, along with a tradition-specific subjectivity that the body entails, and a discussion of the implications of that reading in the context of a broader, historical understanding. The specificity of the claim is that in the Hindu tantric traditions focused primarily on the deities Viṣṇu and Śiva in the early medieval period, the practitioner becomes divine through the internalisation of the text, through the inscription of the body by the text, and learns to inhabit a tradition specific subjectivity. The text is mapped on to the body. The range of texts I discuss is from the Vaiṣṇava and Śaiva tantric traditions, namely the Pāñcarātra, the

Śaiva Siddhānta, and the non-Saiddhāntika traditions often referred to as 'Kashmir' Śaivism that developed particularly from the ninth to eleventh centuries. While the examples I discuss illustrate my general point, a much wider range of textual material could have been presented but for reasons of space. I do not focus on later tantric traditions and do not deal with the Śrī Vidyā, although the general framework I develop would be equally applicable there.

Most of this book was written during a wonderful year as a visiting scholar at the University of Virginia and I should like to thank both staff and students for discussion about the project and their astute observations. The two graduate seminars I conducted were especially helpful in testing ideas and I would like to thank all the students in those classes, including Wijitha Bandara, Suzanne Bessenger, Kristen Calgaro, David Divalerio, Andrew Godreau, Julian Green, Chris Hatchell, Gavin Irby, Sara Jacobi, Slava Komarovski, Karen Lemoine, Bianca Pandit, John Paul Patterson, Matt Rose, Carl Yamamoto, Umeyye Yazicioglu and Yongbok Yi. I would especially like to acknowledge conversations with James Gentry, who coined a felicitous phrase 'variable indexicality' to describe some of this work, Andres Montano, Lynna Dhanani and Craig Danielson. I became a student at the stimulating class on Buddhist tantric traditions across Asia conducted by Professors Paul Groner and David Germano, where I learned much (not least the advantages of team teaching). I also gained a lot from the 'Tantra lunches' organised by Peter Ochs, where 'tantric' topics were opened out for discussion within a wider milieu and in the context of other traditions and other thought worlds. These lunches provided an informal yet rigorous forum and, along with professors Groner, Germano and Ochs, I particularly appreciated the contributions of Jeffrey Hopkins and Jamie Ferriera. This was an extremely engaging experience, true to the dialogic nature that should characterise comparative religion.

There are many debts of gratitude in a book such as this. I should also like to acknowledge those teachers who first introduced me to the study of tantric traditions, Andrew Rawlinson and David Smith at Lancaster, a few conversations with the charismatic Agehananda Bharati, and a dept of gratitude to Alexis Sanderson of Oxford, who has so often responded to my questions with generosity and cordiality and to André Padoux, a great scholar who has done so much to further our understanding of the tantric traditions. The Śaiva texts were very much brought to life for me at the Centre d'Indologie in Pondicherry some years ago, where I had the good fortune to discuss these topics with Dominic Goodall and to read sections of texts with the deeply knowledgeable Śaivasiddhānta Tattvajñā R. Subramanian and Dr T. Ganesan. Frits Staal indirectly introduced me to the tantric tradition of Kerala and to my friend and colleague, anthropologist Rich Freeman, who introduced me directly to that tradition. I should like to thank him for his reflections on our shared interest in linguistic anthropology and for his extremely important theory of ritual possession in the tantric context as the paradigm for the divinisation of icon and priest. His theory has been a strong influence on my own thinking. I remember with fondness the somewhat bizarre situation of reading together, late into the night, sections of the *Īśānaśivagurudeva-paddhati* in an old house in a remote Welsh village. Lastly I should like to thank the I.B. Tauris readers for their encouragement. I trust the publisher's title does not detract from the contents. A grant from the AHRB in the UK allowed me relief from teaching to pursue this book during 2003–04. Unless otherwise stated, translations are my own, although Marion Rastelli's work on the *Jayākhya-saṃhitā* has been a source of guidance at times when the precise meaning of that text has eluded me. An appendix presents the first English translation of one chapter from the published edition of the *Jayākhya-saṃhitā*. Although I trust the translations are accurate, I have tried to err on the side of readability for the English speaker. I was unable to incorporate an important article that only came to my attention as the book went to press, namely Barbara Holdredge's 'Body Connections: Hindu Discourse of the Body and the Study of Religion' (*International Journal of Hindu Studies*, 2/3 (1998), pp. 341–86).

Oui, par le corps
Dans la douceur qui est aveugle et ne veut rien
Mais parachève.

Yves Bonnefoy, 'L'épars, l'indivisible'

PART I

Theory, Text and History

ONE

Introduction: The Body as Text

WRITING at the end of the nineteenth century, the eminent Indologist Monier Monier-Williams was able to say that the Tantras are 'mere manuals of mystics, magic and superstition of the worst and most silly kind'[1] and that with these texts and their traditions 'we are confronted with the worst results of the worst superstitious ideas that have ever disgraced and degraded the human race'.[2] On this view, the Tantras are a far cry from the nobility of Vedānta or the dignity of the Buddha. In complete contrast, almost a hundred years later at the end of the twentieth century, Bhagavan Shree Rajneesh was able to write 'tantra cannot be understood because tantra is not an intellectual proposition: it is an experience. Unless you are receptive, ready, vulnerable to the experience, it is not going to come to you.'[3] On the one hand we have the critical Indologist writing from within the horizon of the values of his own culture about texts and traditions in clear antipathy to them; on the other we have a modern 'mystic' or experientialist writing from within the horizon of values emerging in late modernity.

This book might be seen as corrective reading of both views in that it seeks to understand the tantric traditions in their historical and doctrinal contexts and to offer constructive readings of the texts that are true to Indology and sympathetic to the internal concerns of the traditions, while at the same time offering a 'third-order' discourse about them.[4] More specifically, I wish to understand the tantric body, how the body has been conceptualised by tantric traditions and the use of the body in tantric visions of power and liberation. There are complex problems here and we will need to examine the body in terms of technique, in terms of representation, and in terms of formation. Furthermore, we need to ask how techniques of the body and the representation of the body (in metaphor and textual description) interface with Indian scriptural traditions and socio-political structures. On the one hand we have techniques of the body, methods or technologies developed within tantric traditions intended to transform body and self; on the other we have representations of the body in philosophy, in ritual and in art.[5] Both of these areas – techniques of experience and representation of body and experience – are intimately linked. Representations (particularly icons of deities) are not simply passive texts but are performative, used in 'life transforming practices',[6] and, conversely, techniques of the body themselves entail representations of it, especially in ritual where the body becomes the deity or icon. Indeed, both representation and technique come together in the divinisation of the body which, as we will see, is the hallmark of tantric culture. We need therefore to explicate the interrelated distinctions of representation/technique and doctrine/ritual, which are encompassed by the text/body distinction. One might even say that as text is to body, so representation and doctrine are to technique and ritual; that is the former is expressed in the latter and the latter is articulated in the former. The text is expressed as body and the body articulated in the text.

I therefore wish to present an argument to support three interrelated views. First, in spite of divergent metaphysical claims and different social locations, the conceptualisation of the tantric body and its expression follows certain principles or processes that might be best expressed in the claim that the tantric body becomes inscribed by the text. What we might call an entextualisation of the body occurs in tantric traditions that is specific yet allows a divergence of views and practices. The body is moulded within the constraints of historical tradition, even in its attempt to transcend those constraints. Second, the body, functioning as the root metaphor or topos of the tantric traditions, operates at different levels of practice and discourse. The body is the vehicle for imagining and conceptualising tradition and cosmos such that the structure of the cosmos, forms of language, and text and tradition are themselves understood in terms of the body. Representations of the body occur in texts and in the techniques of the body such as ritual and asceticism; the body itself functions as a representation of tradition, text and cosmos. While I think the claim that the body becomes the text or is inscribed as text is true of all scriptural traditions, this book intends to examine the specificity of the claim within Hindu Tantrism. Third, operating within these claims about the body and tradition is the idea of a tradition-dependent subjectivity; that the index of the first-person pronoun, the 'I', operates within realms of practice and discourse constrained by text and tradition. By 'subjectivity' I do not intend a monad set against the objectivity of the world but rather interiority formed through language and tradition. This linguistic agency is not fixed but in dialogical relationship with others and with social structures and might be called 'variable indexicality'.[7] This is another way of expressing the body as text in that when the body functions within the tradition-specific activities of reading, ritual and asceticism, different notions of the subject come into view. The content of the 'I' is filled out in different ways in these contexts. For example, the tantric practitioner, as we shall see, identifies his body with the cosmos and deity in daily ritual and in yogic practice, identifying himself with something outside of himself that he then becomes.

While my main purpose is to locate the tantric body within the history of ideas, practices and institutions that made up the early formation of medieval India, I would also contend that this reflection raises questions of contemporary cultural and theological relevance. The tantric body is of more than historical interest, as is evident through its mass appropriation in consumerist culture, and raises such challenging cultural questions about the nature of the body, about the relation of the body to language, about human relationships, about the relationship of the human to the wider ecosystem and raises such challenging theological and philosophical questions about the relation of the body to any transcendent reality and about ways traditions construct the self, as to be worth taking seriously as a resource in our response to such questions. While it is important to maintain discourses within the boundaries of tradition in order for them to retain meaning and relevance for particular communities of readers, it is also germane, enriching and challenging to engage theologically and philosophically with thought systems outside of those discourses. Although I do not directly address questions of theological relevance, my third-order reflection nevertheless goes beyond the description of text and tradition established through the mediating, second-order discourse of philology and history.

In the following pages, the reader will find an argument that the tantric body can only be understood in terms of text and tradition. In my local phone book there is an advertisement for '*cakra* balancing' for a reasonable fee (in this respect clearly in accordance with tantric *dakṣiṇā*). Implicit here is a Western appropriation of the tantric body that we might see as a reification of it, and a view that the tantric body is something that can be revealed for those with the means to do so.[8] The argument of this book, on the contrary, is that in its medieval Indian context the tantric body is not a given that is discovered but a process that is constructed through dedicated effort over years of practice. The centres of power or *cakra*s within the body that the phone book advert alludes to can be best understood in terms of entextualisation, the body inscribed as the text, which expresses principles at work within the logic of tantric ideology and practice. Any distinctions between knowing and acting, mind and body, are disrupted by the tantric body in the sense that what might be called imagination becomes a kind of action in tantric ritual and the forms that the body takes in ritual are a kind of knowing. Borrowing a phrase from William Blake (and if the adjective 'tantric' can apply outside of Hindu and Buddhist scriptural traditions, then surely he is a good candidate for its application) the tantric body is a 'corporeal understanding'.[9] This corporeal understanding shows itself in the great emphasis on transformative practices in the tantric traditions, ritual inseparable from vision, the body becoming alive with the universe within it, and vibrant with futurity in the anticipation of the goal of the tantric paths.

Understanding the tantric body in its historical locations is no easy task and it is not simply a matter of contrasting an inauthentic

Western view of the tantric body, outside of tradition, with an authentic tantric view, moulded in accordance with tradition. The very category 'Tantra' or 'Tantrism' is contested and itself must be seen in the context of the history of scholarship in the West and colonialism, as some scholars are doing. Understanding the Western tantric body in relation to modernity and postmodernity is a topic in itself,[10] and the only claim I wish to make about *that* body is that it is modernist in reflecting the reifying tendencies of modernity along with the idea of the practitioner as free-floating individual. By contrast, the traditional tantric body of medieval India is more fluid in terms of its lack of reification and at the same time more conservative in being deeply embedded in traditional understandings and categories. The tantric body is formed in accordance with received tradition, in accordance with scriptural revelation, and in accordance with the somatology of the wider culture. The cultivation of a tantric subjectivity is not the cultivation of individuality (see pp. 12–13).

Tantra, Tradition and the Body

The tantric traditions arose during the early centuries of the common era, developing in Buddhist, Jain and Hindu contexts. The vast body of tantric texts are inseparable from the traditions that gave rise to them. Śaiva, Vaiṣṇava and Śākta Tantras were believed by their followers to have been revealed by Viṣṇu, Śiva, and the Goddess (Devī), and there were even Tantras revealed by the Sun (Sūryā), now all lost, whose followers were called Sauras.[11] There were also Jain Tantras believed to be the word of Mahāvīra and, above all, Buddhist Tantras believed to be the word of the Buddha, which became incorporated into the vast Buddhist canon between *c.* 400 and 750 CE, to this day integral to the living traditions of Tibetan Buddhism.[12] Using the term 'Hindu' to refer to the Śaiva, Śākta Vaiṣṇava and Saura material is anachronistic as the term was used by the Persians simply to denote the peoples of the subcontinent,[13] although there are usages of it as a term of self-description by 'Hindus' as early as the fifteenth century in Kashmir and sixteenth century in Bengal to distinguish people who shared certain cultural values and practices (such as cremation of the dead, veneration of the cow, styles of cuisine and dress, or shared narratives) from Muslims ('Yavanas').[14] It was not a common designation until the nineteenth century. But the theistic Tantras and traditions, those of Viṣṇu, Śiva and the Goddess, are interrelated and share common structures of practice and belief that can be distinguished from those of the Buddhists and Jains by their proximity to the Vedas, orthodox Brahmanical revelation, and their interpreters. The term 'tantric tradition' refers to those religions, or 'ways of life' to use Inden's apposite phrase,[15] that claimed to develop from textual sources referring to themselves as 'tantras', regarded as revelation, the word of God, by their followers. This diverse tantric revelation must be seen in contrast to the ancient, orthodox Brahmanical revelation of the Veda that the Tantras reject completely or accept as a lower level of scriptural authority. In contrast to the Hindu Tantras, the Buddhist Tantras do not respond to the vedic tradition but rather look to Mahāyāna Buddhism and see themselves as a development of it, even though much Buddhist tantric material, the Yoginī Tantras, was probably derived from Śaiva prototypes.[16]

Arriving at definitions of 'Tantra' and 'Tantrism' has been notoriously difficult and has varied between presenting external accounts of a phenomenon named 'Tantrism'[17] and internal accounts of what the term *tantra* refers to. An important indigenous distinction is between *tāntrika*, a follower of the Tantras, and *vaidika*, a follower of the Vedas. This distinction operates across the sectarian divides of Śaivas, Vaiṣṇavas and so on. The former refers to those who follow a system of ritual and teaching found within the Tantras, in contrast to those, especially the Brahman caste, who follow the Veda as primary revelation or *śruti* (and so called Śrautas), or who follow the later texts of secondary revelation called *smṛti* (and so called Smārtas).[18] The issue is complicated, however, by some vedic Brahmans, particularly Smārtas, observing tantric rites and, as Padoux has observed, some texts in the vedic tradition, namely Upaniṣads, being clearly tantric in character, 'which tāntrika authors (Bhāskararāya, for example) consider as confirming the validity of tantric teachings and practices'.[19]

The primary designation of the term *tantra* is a 'loom' or the 'warp' of a loom, with the metaphorical implication of system or framework. It is derived from the verbal root *tan*, to extend or stretch and so, perhaps not insignificantly, is related to *tanu*, 'body'. It came early on to designate a text and there are several examples of the term being used for texts that are clearly not within the tantric tradition, such as the collection of stories the *Pañcatantra* or the famous Mīmāṃsaka work the *Tantravārttika*. The term *tantra* as a noun is a term of self-description that refers to specific texts of revelation and is also a term designating a system of revealed teaching that leads to liberation and power. In this sense the term *tantraśāstra* is used, which, as David White observes, is the closest indigenous category to the English 'Tantrism'.[20] The term *āgama* is used in some Śaiva texts as a synonym for *tantra* with the implication that the text is a disclosure that has come to us. Indeed, Abhinavagupta uses the term to refer to the tantric revelation in general as the 'one revelation' (*ekāgama*) (see pp. 58–60). The term 'tantra' refers not only to texts but to system and, as Padoux observes, *asmin tantre* simply means 'in this system'.[21]

Some scholars have presented Tantrism in terms of a list of characteristics, such as locating a bipolar energy within the body,[22] while others have offered more precise definitions, which are in fact theories, such as seeing Tantra as a quest for power akin to the king's quest for political power. Drawing on Madeleine Biardeau, André Padoux offers the understanding that Tantrism is 'an attempt to place *kāma*, desire, in every sense of the word, in the service of liberation',[23] and David White further develops this in terms of energy.[24] The word 'power' has perhaps a more negative semantic field in English than 'energy', and power relates to the political and historical world in a way that 'energy' does not, although both can be renderings of the Sanskrit *śakti*. One interesting thesis presented by Ron Davidson in the context of tantric Buddhism is that the central 'sustaining metaphor' of the Mantrayāna, or tantric Buddhism, is that the path of the practitioner is akin to the path of the king on his way to becoming an overlord (*rājādhirāja*) or universal monarch (*cakravārtin*), expressed through the forms of consecration, self-visualisation, *maṇḍala*s and 'esoteric acts'.[25] This focusing on the political dimension of the metaphor of power is clearly important, and power suffuses the concerns of the tantric traditions. The Tantras offer their followers power to achieve world transcendence or magical power over supernatural entities in order to achieve worldly success, such as seduction of a desired woman or the destruction of enemies for a king. Sanderson has pointed out that the tantric traditions of power defined themselves against the vedic tradition of purity and saw their power as lying in the transgression of vedic social norms.[26]

Davidson accompanies his claim about the central metaphor of the Mantrayāna with a discussion of 'polythetic' categories that function 'to identify prototypical examples that operate as cognitive reference points'.[27] That is, rather than a 'monothetic' understanding of Tantrism, such as Tsong-ka-pa's definition of Tantra as visualisation of oneself as the Buddha or deity, we need to understand Tantrism in 'polythetic' terms. That is, no one thing can be taken to describe a category but, rather, prototypical examples can be identified which may not share all of the traits within the category. As Brooks observes, 'tantric phenomena need not possess all the defining characteristics of the taxon "tantric" and there is no a priori justification for deciding that any single characteristic is the most definitive.'[28] While perhaps the terms 'monthetic' and 'polythetic' are somewhat unnecessary, the now popular use of prototype theory does have force in the understanding of cultural categories.[29] As discussed by Davidson, a robin (both English and American) is a prototypical bird, whereas an emu is not, but is still within the category. A member of a category does not need to share all characteristics to belong: categories have 'fuzzy' edges.[30] Of course, any inclusion in a category as prototypical will involve judgements which need to be based on careful consideration, comparison and scholarship. Due to scholarly endeavour, especially over the last fifty years, we now know enough about tantric traditions to make some claims about them and to make judgements about prototypicality. One such judgement that I would wish to make is that tantric traditions must be understood in terms of pre-modern scriptural traditions, and another is that they involve the divinisation of the body, which is way of saying that the body is inscribed by the text.

Davidson's account of Tantrism in terms of power is important and it is surely germane to point to the political dimensions of the tantric practitioner that have been generally neglected or ignored (probably partly due to the clear separation of 'politics' from 'religion' that has, rightly or wrongly, characterised Western scholarship). The practitioner, in Davidson's reading of the texts, seeks to assume kingship and exercise dominion. We could, however, read this in a slightly different way, that the central tantric metaphor is indeed, as Tsong-ka-pa identified, divinisation and that the model of kingship – the king undergoing consecration and so on – is in fact the king becoming divine. The divinisation of the king through ritual consecration is directly akin to the divinisation of the icon in a temple and the divinisation of the practitioner in daily ritual (or even the divinisation in possession). More fundamental than the metaphor of kingship is the metaphor of transformation into a deity. The idea that to worship a god one must become a god is a notable feature of all tantric traditions, even ones which maintain a dualist metaphysics.

The empowering of the body, which means its divinisation, is arguably the most important quality in tantric traditions, but a quality that is only specified within particular traditions and texts. Becoming divine is an ancient trope in Indian civilisation. As Hocart observed long ago with reference to the consecration of the vedic king, it is fundamental 'that the worshipper becomes one with the god to whom the worship is addressed'.[31] Divinisation in tantric ritual reflects this general idea but is text- and tradition-specific in terms of content and in the explicit focus on the divinisation of the body as the enactment of its revelation, as this book hopes to demonstrate. The practitioner in ritual contexts becomes divine such that his or her limited subjectivity is transcended or expanded and that subjectivity becomes coterminous with the subjectivity of his or her deity, which is to say that the text is internalised and subjectivity becomes text-specific. This is clearly in line with Tsong-ka-pa's understanding in a Buddhist context and also makes sense in a theistic 'Hindu' one.[32] While the idea of liberation as becoming one with the absolute (*brahman*) has a long history in Brahmanical thinking from the Upaniṣads, the ritual construction of the body as the deity through the use of magical phrases or mantras is prototypically tantric.[33]

In a broader sense, the tantric traditions are examples of forms of practice and reflection handed down through generations which locate themselves historically by reference to a foundational text or group of texts, believed to originate in a transcendent source. This is, of course, true of many traditions including Islam, Judaism and Christianity, as well as vedic tradition. But while this is a general point, it is nevertheless an important one, for processes of identification and entextualisation can be identified within wider scriptural traditions that are also typical of tantric traditions. Scriptural traditions all developed before modernity and before the Kantian understanding of the self as an autonomous agent; an idea that connects with the notion of the citizen who has civic responsibilities yet who remains distinct from the social body and an individuality that comes to stand against tradition. In scriptural traditions, such a notion has been alien, and the self is an index of a tradition-specific subjectivity, formed in particular ways in conformity to tradition.[34] In scriptural traditions, the self is constructed through ritual and the development of a tradition-specific interiority or variable indexicality that is not individual in the contemporary, de-traditionalised sense (characterised by fragmentation and alienation). Scripture-sanctioned rituals serve as identity markers for communities in medieval India, and, although these boundaries can be transgressed,[35] such transgression always assumes their existence. The self in such communities is bounded by text and ritual. Such a tradition-specified self, as MacIntyre reminds us, develops philosophy as a craft or *techne* and needs to develop his or herself into 'a particular kind of person if he or she is to move towards a knowledge of the truth about his or her good and *the* human good'.[36] Tantra can itself be seen in terms of *techne*, and the suffix *tra* expresses the means or instrument of an action expressed by a verbal root.[37] Thus as *man-tra* might be rendered 'instrument of thought'[38] so *tan-tra* might literally be taken to mean 'method or instrument of extension', perhaps with the implication that it is the self or body that is extended to become coterminous with the divine body. I do not intend this etymology (*nirvacana*) to be taken too seriously, but it is nevertheless suggestive.

The specificity of the tantric traditions lies in the ways in which they form a subjectivity, the ways in which the subject of first-person predicates, the 'I', becomes an index of tradition, and the way the body becomes entextualised. Patterns of text are mapped on to the body in ways particular to Tantrism and in response to other ways of mapping texts on to the body, especially vedic ones.

The theory I wish to present is simply this. The tantric body is encoded in tradition-specific and text-specific ways. The practitioner inscribes the body through ritual and forms of interiority or asceticism, and so writes the tradition on to the body. Such transformative practices are intended to create the body as divine. This inscribing the body is also a reading of text and tradition. Indeed, the act of reading is of central importance in the tantric traditions. The fact that the texts were *written* is important and has sometimes been underestimated in focusing on orality/aurality in the transmission of texts. But the texts were written in Sanskrit and in doing so their authors were consciously locating them within what Sheldon Pollock has called the 'Sanskrit cosmopolis'.[39] The texts were intended to be read and heard by those with the requisite authority, to be brought to life, and to be performed. The importance of the written word here is evident from the commentaries upon the primary texts by the later tradition. The importance of reading the texts is further suggested by the presence of ritual manuals (*paddhati*s), 'cookbooks' that served to instruct and remind practitioners about how to undertake particular kinds of performance and about particular tenets of a system. The tantric body, constructed as a public act (even if limited in its public nature through secrecy), is in turn 'read' by traditional practitioners in so far as some tāntrikas wore external signs of their cultic affiliation while others disparaged such signs, retaining their tantric affiliation as 'secret';[40] such secrecy is an overcoding of the body. That is, while some tantric traditions overtly reject vedic tradition and normative, caste and feudal society of medieval India, most must be seen as adding their own writing of the body on to the traditional vedic writing or as reconfiguring the vedic tradition in terms of the tantric. We see this, for example, in the Śaiva traditions of Kashmir so eloquently accounted for by Abhinavagupta (*c.* 975–1025 CE). For him, tantric rites were supererogatory to vedic practice. The body, the vedic body, is overwritten by the practitioner who constructs a tantric body through a further superimposition of rites and the internalisation of a tantric ideology. Thus, in his famous statement (probably a standard saying), Abhinavagupta writes that externally one follows vedic practice, in the domestic sphere one is an orthodox Śaiva, but in one's secret life one is a follower of the extreme antinomian cult of the Kula which involves the disruption of the vedic body through ritual transgression of vedic norms and values.[41]

In locating the tantric body within an account of text, I intend to discuss a clearly articulated cultural form that has developed well beyond its roots. There is much speculation about the origins of Tantrism. On the one hand the origins have been seen in an autochthonous spirituality or Shamanism that reaches back to pre-Āryan times in the subcontinent, yet textual historical evidence only dates from a more recent period. While certainly there are elements in tantric traditions that may well reach back into prehistory – particularly the use of skulls and the themes of death and possession[42] – we simply do not have sufficient evidence to speculate in this way. As Robert Mayer has shown, there is no evidence for a non-Āryan substratum for Tantrism, which must be understood as a predominantly Brahmanical, Sanskritic tradition with its roots in the Veda.[43] In an important book on the origins of Indian civilisation, Sergent has argued that our main resources for understanding the past are linguistic and archaeological.[44] There is no early archaeological evidence for tantric traditions beyond the common era, and while there is textual evidence for a cremation ground asceticism as far back as the time of the Buddha,[45] as well as tantric-like goddesses in the Veda,[46] the specificity of the tantric revelation appears more recently in the history of South Asia. India clearly inherits its earlier Indus civilisation (as shown, for example, by the persistence of common kinds of measurement)[47] but specific tantric elements cannot be located other than in very general ways. Traditions are constantly reconfigured in the light of contemporary situations and there is no reason to think that the tantric traditions are any different. While of course receiving forms of practice and ideas handed down from the past, the Tantras at the time of their composition were a new revelation that transcended the older, vedic texts. While concerned with body and experience, this tantric body can only be accessed via the texts that form it.

Reading Strategies: Text

The argument I wish to present is not historically neutral in the sense that the Encyclopaedist mind-set of Enlightenment modernity, described by MacIntyre, might understand neutrality as a single framework within which knowledge is presented.[48] Nor does it assume that all knowledge is purely subjectively constructed and that history masks a will to power of particular interest groups. Rather, agreeing with MacIntyre's general argument, I take rational inquiry (such as this) to be enabled by traditions of inquiry, and such inquiry is less a discovery of the past and more the construction of the past from a particular perspective or standpoint. The past is constantly reconfigured in the light of new evidence for a given purpose. That there are degrees of accuracy in such reconfigurations is not in question. Clearly there are positions and readings of the past that contain such prior ideological commitments as to distort the past, as we see in more recent reconfigurings of Indian history seen through the lens of a *hindutva* ideology. But this very claim can itself only be based on the presentation of evidence in a different vein, drawing from a rationality of historical method that has developed within the Western academy, a rationality which would, of course, claim a methodological superiority to the *hindutva* reading. But the point is that the presentation and weighing of historical evidence is always within a tradition of inquiry and judgement. Yet this tradition that claims universal truth accessible through an objective, repeatable method needs to acknowledge reflexively that it is itself a *tradition* of inquiry that never attain its own declared universalist goal. The Encyclopaedist claim to objectivity and neutrality is itself a tradition of presentation and assessment according to criteria developed only within that tradition and not, as that tradition claims, the discovery of a single, neutral narrative.[49]

To establish the account of the tantric body I have briefly described above, I am bringing together two primary traditions of discourse,

Indology and what might be described as a post-foundational religious studies. At one level the modernist or objectivist assumptions of Indology are fundamentally opposed to a post-foundational understanding of text as infinitely interpretable. Yet any rigorous post-foundational understanding must assume Indology as the discipline that provides the basic materials from which to develop. Indology is the philological study of Sanskrit texts which is the sine qua non for the study of tantric traditions. Without Indology there can be no study of Tantrism. But while one can understand the claim that philology is the eradication of subjectivity in that the objective system of grammar, the language itself, eradicates subjectivist interpretations, there is nevertheless a further level of reading beyond the philological, which intends to place philological readings in a broader context. We might say that philology is indispensable in establishing the plain sense of the texts, yet we must go beyond philology to establish interpreted senses. If philology creates Nietzsche's pathos of distance, it is nevertheless also the case that a text is nothing until it is read and interpreted.[50]

I shall defer a discussion of the nature of tantric texts to the next chapter, but suffice it to say for now that these texts are set within the context in which they echo and reflect other texts and in which textual agency is complex because often the texts have multiple authors or were composed over a long period of time. In reading these texts we need to be sensitive to the wider textual field in which they are located. To use Inden's phrase, we need to move from philological texts to dialogical texts.[51] There is a useful distinction within rabbinic Judaism between the plain sense of the text (*peshat*) and the interpreted sense (*derash*). The plain sense is the foundation upon which the interpreted sense is built,[52] although even the plain sense is immediately interpreted once read. We might say that the plain sense operates as a constraining force upon the interpreted sense. The interpreted sense should not disrupt the plain sense to the extent that it contradicts it, yet the plain sense is never enough for a particular situation. Interpreted senses are always necessary to bring some meaning to life for some particular community of readers. A post-foundational religious studies develops an interpreted sense of the texts established through Indology, one which takes seriously the implicit and explicit philosophical claims of the texts but does not share (indeed cannot share) the texts' theological presuppositions. This book is no tantric theology but a dialogical reading that stands outside of the texts while partially entering into them in an act of imagination that allows for their reconstruction and reconfiguring in a new mode. That new mode is the account I present of the tantric body as text.

While Indology and post-foundational developments in religious studies are fundamental to my reading strategy, there is also implicit in the book a theory of reading religious texts that I have developed with my colleague Oliver Davies, which needs briefly to be explicated before we proceed.[53] The way in which the body becomes the text in tantric traditions needs to be understood in terms not only of how the content of texts is imposed upon the body, but in terms of the very nature of the texts and how they are received.

Tantric texts can be divided into those texts of primary revelation, the Tantras themselves believed to be the word of the deity, usually in a dialogical form with the Goddess (Śakti) asking questions of the Lord (Bhagavān), although in some texts the relationship is reversed, and secondary works of commentary expounding the meaning of a text, and works describing practice such as ritual manuals. The Tantras at some point in their history, quite early, were fixed in writing. This is not to say that there were not different versions of texts – the Śaiva Siddhānta theologian Rāmakaṇṭha, for example, had a number of readings of the *Kiraṇa-tantra* to choose from[54] (see p. 64) – but it is to say that the work achieved some stability through time. In this sense the Tantras can be contrasted with the Vedas, which were not written but nevertheless acquired a high degree of fixity due to methods of conveying them accurately within schools of recitation. While the Tantras seem to have been written, they were often accompanied by oral teachings and commentary, which is corroborated by the sometimes obscure or pithy nature of the material, and closely linked to systems of acceptance or initiation.

Given that the Tantras achieved some stability through time, we can also say that the meaning of the text and its function became determined by the process of transmission. This is not to go against the distinction between plain and interpreted sense, but rather to say that the text remained alive by being received anew through the generations. The texts of primary tantric revelation probably have multiple authorship and were composed over several generations, which makes agency within the text complex. Indeed, we need to speak of agency within the texts themselves rather than the agency of an individual author. The texts in their intertextuality take on a life of their own. The intentionality of the text, which we might call the 'narrator' and which Bakhtin called the 'author', interfaces with the intentionality of the reader or community of readers who internalise and reconstruct the text in their own lives. As in all texts regarded as revelation, the Tantras were brought to life in the act of reading or reception and in their performance. The receiver of the Tantra, the *tāntrika*, for whom it is divine word, internalises the text through a process of identification which usually involves ritual enactment. The indexicality of the reader interfaces with the indexicality of the text, and the subject of first-person predicates, the 'I', becomes an index of tradition (arguably, Greg Urban has suggested, through the function of the floating signifier itself[55]). The reader also positions himself (and it is usually a he in the tantric traditions) in response to the notional reader assumed by the text, usually an initiate.[56] The reader interprets and internalises the text in the act of understanding and in turn conforms himself to the reader implied within the text. The reader does not simply interpret; the text makes claims upon the initiated reader, which has significant, life-transforming effects.

The sacred text is made 'one's own' through reading and performance, and the 'reader' conforms to the implied reader of the text. This is as true of the tantric traditions as of other scriptural religions. Such a reconstruction of the text in subjectivity is fundamental to the process of textual transmission and religious identity formation. The linguistic anthropologists Greg Urban and Michael Silverstein have identified two processes in textual transmission that they call entextualisation and contextualisation, the taking of a text out of one context and recontextualising it in a new, which are simultaneous.[57] The speech agent retrieves the text back into the living matrix of speech through meaningful acts of reading and performance, through encoding the body with the text. Such acts of reading retrieve a semantic entity from the past, the origin of the revelation, into the present field of meaning. Indeed, commentary upon revealed text is just such a claiming of meaning, the fusion of the world of the text with the reader's own world and the attempted persuading of others of one interpreted sense. Such a reception or reading is communal and tradition-based, only taking shape within communities that have themselves been shaped by prior acts of reading of the same text or group of texts. Radically new or innovative readings might result in new communities being formed and groups questioning the received wisdom of the old tradition. Thus the Tantras of the Śaiva Siddhānta have been received by a community of Brahmans who have themselves been formed by the tradition constrained by the text. But monistic Śaivas in the ninth and tenth centuries offered corrective readings of the old tradition which helped to form a new community of reading. A community reads its own core texts and acts them out, readings that are themselves already governed by the historical life of the community grounded in successive and often corrective readings of the same text or texts. The plain sense of the text gives rise to new meanings in new contexts. The religious reader or community of readers assumes that the voice within the ancient texts, the voice of God in the case of the Hindu Tantras, has present force. This is a fundamentally important point in the transmission of traditions, for only because of the present force of the text for a reader or community of readers does the text have relevance, a relevance principally enacted through ritual.

For tantric traditions the immediacy of this divine voice can only be accessed through the structures of tradition, involving structures or systems of access, namely initiation, which give privileged access to the text's authenticity. As we will see, the Śaiva Siddhānta demands an initiation into the tradition (*samaya-dīkṣā*) to gain access to its texts. This laying claim by the tradition to the space between the reader and the text is to lay claim to the temporal and spatial structures of the world within which the tradition-constrained act of reading takes place. Thus for the tantric reader there is a strongly cosmological dimension to any act of reading and any enactment of the text in daily ritual. The world of the practitioner who acts out the text is itself constructed by the text. There is, then, a complex process of enacting an interpreted sense of the text in relation to the plain sense, and of enacting the injunctive claims of the text on its receivers. The Tantras have a unique intentionality that makes claims on its receivers, who have enacted those injunctions through to modernity.

Reading Strategies: Body

Having given some account of religious or revealed text, the modes of approaching such texts, and a theory of scriptural reading, it remains to make some remarks about what I understand by the term 'body' in my title and how I shall 'read' the body. In what ways could the 'tantric' body be distinct from any other kind of body? Clearly the tantric body is a different order category to 'male' or 'female' body, or 'young', 'beautiful', 'lithe', 'sick' or any number of adjectives that could be placed before the noun. The link I wish to establish between body and text more generally, and the tantric body and tantric text specifically, needs to be placed in a broader context of Western academic concern with the body.

The body has become the focus of many disciplines in the academy including anthropology, sociology, cultural studies, philosophy, literary studies, religious studies, and sub-branches of these, particularly medical anthropology and the related enquiry into pain, sexuality, emotion and agency. The development of interest in the body over the last thirty years and the 'somatisation' of social theory[58] might themselves be of interest for the sociology of knowledge as an index of wider cultural values, values that reflect a concern with gender, the post-existential condition in the West after the Second World War, and the recognition that we are embodied beings. Csordas has observed that the turn to the body in the human sciences is linked to the development of the postmodern condition of fragmented meanings and that this turn reflects an attempt to grasp a stable centre,[59] yet this centre remains elusive because the body is not a static, biological given, but has a history. The body changes through time and across cultures.

I refer the interested reader to essays by Turner[60] and Csordas[61] for a coherent account of the development of interest in the body in the Western academy, especially in sociology and anthropology. To describe these developments here would take us too far from our project, but it is worth pointing out that early interest in the body and body symbolism begins in the Durkheimian tradition of French sociology, particularly with an important paper by Marcel Mauss on techniques of the body[62] and with Hertz's influential work on right and left symbolism.[63] Mary Douglas's *Purity and Danger* (1966) marks a turning point and in *Natural Symbols* (1970) Douglas makes an important distinction between the social body and the natural body. This, along with the publication of Blacking's *The Anthropology of the Body* in 1977, began an interest in the body that developed apace in the human and social sciences, which have demonstrated the diverse ways in which the body is conceptualised and formed.[64]

In parallel to this sociological/anthropological concern, the body became the focus of inquiry for philosophical phenomenology, especially the work of Merleau-Ponty and his *Phenomenology of Perception* (1945), which itself partly draws on the work on body image in the 1930s by a number of psychologists, most notable among them being Paul Schilder.[65] Turner observes that, whereas the French phenomenologists are interested in the 'lived body', Douglas is concerned with the body as a metaphor of socio-cognitive mappings of reality.[66] My concern here is with both, and both are brought together in my argument. On the one hand the tantric body is a metaphor that maps the cosmos, particularly in ritual activity; on the other hand the tantric body is a lived body that performs that mapping, a performance that had and has existential force in the lives of tantric practitioners. The tantric body is both a metaphor of tantric ideas about the cosmos and the human person and the lived body of the practitioner who performs or enacts those ideas.

In arguing for this connection between representation and technique, idea and performance, text and body, the book implicitly and sometimes explicitly draws on the social scientific work on the body carried out over the last century that I have alluded to above. Many writers in the area of cultural theory, such as Donna Haraway, have highlighted the politics of body representation and argued that attempts to essentialise the body operate in the service of a hegemonic discourse that functions to maintain cultural power interests, particularly a biological discourse that links a proposed givenness of the body to (oppressive) social roles.[67] There can be no uncontested nor unpoliticised definition of the body.[68]

This general orientation of theory in favour of a socio-political construction of the body and a suspicion of essentialism is within what can broadly be described as genealogy (which is often subsumed under the – inappropriate – title 'critical theory'[69]). Indeed, much literature and analysis of the body in culture and society have been undertaken within the genealogical tradition of academic discourse, ultimately stemming from Nietzsche and developed by Foucault, that claims that the body is the locus of contested power. The body is inscribed, both hegemonically by the self and by external relationships, in accordance with the power structures of a given society through time. The laying bare of these relationships and forms of inscription through genealogical analysis is an attempt to dissolve them and thereby to offer liberating social critique. Much of the work of feminist scholarship, for example, has been concerned to uncover foundations of patriarchal power upon which particular, limiting constructions of the female body have been built.[70] But generally genealogy offers no positive proposal, only critique and a hermeneutics suspicious of all cultural formations as hiding egregious, oppressive power relations between groups.

While being sympathetic to many claims of the genealogists, I do not cohere with this view. The genealogical account of the body would wish to claim that it is culturally or socially constructed and that the construction of the body is its inscription by particular power relationships. The body is not a given but embroiled in a politics that needs to be negotiated throughout life. But while the body is an 'ambiguous space', in Foucault's phrase,[71] it is nevertheless a contained ambiguity, contained (at least until recently) by its genetic code, by its temporal structure and the inevitability of birth and death. Indeed, it is here that we see one of the limits of the genealogist's social constructivist position. While conceptualisations and practices of the body vary, there is a givenness of temporality in that the body is born, ages and dies. The temporality of being born, aging and dying presents a boundary within which any formation of the body must function. This boundary of temporality therefore means that the body contains inherently within it a narrative structure. To speak of a body is to speak of temporality, and to speak of a body is to speak of narrative. Narrative and the living body are inseparable. The story of a life is the story of a body changing through time, and such a story inevitably entails the stories of others, for, as MacIntyre observes, we are the co-authors of our own narratives.[72] The narrative structure of the body, being born and dying, therefore entails communities of other narrative bodies and the interrelation of bodies through time. Thus the body entails tradition and culture. Furthermore the narrative structure of the body displays a natural affinity with sacred text inasmuch as both are grounded in temporality. The sacred text emerges out of tradition, which constantly reconfigures its narrative through history, and the body in tradition is formed in accordance with this temporality. As I have argued, the narrative of the body is the formation of subjective coherence through the linking of the indexicality of the subject with that of the 'text', an argument that can be fully illustrated as regards the tantric body.

If the first problem with the genealogists' account is their narrative constructionist position and the rejection of a narrative structure inherent in the body, a second related problem is that the only historical *telos* of the body, on this account, has been the will to power. This view is generally at odds with scriptural traditions which maintain, on the contrary, that the narrative structure of the body is teleological in aspiring to some human good beyond the political inscription of power. With regard to the tantric body, while a genealogical-type analysis might reveal the ways in which the tantric body is linked to traditional power structures, to the cult of the king for example, we need to accept the claims of tradition concerning the transcendent goals of the tantric body as having a legitimacy that can be challenged only on a priori grounds. The goods of tradition are fundamentally opposed to a genealogical analysis of late modernity whose goal is ultimately the analysis of power in tradition in order to dissolve that power.

Experience and Asceticism

When speaking about the body the problem of experience must inevitably be addressed. On the one hand we have the body as representation, as symbolic system that encodes a culture's ideas and practices; yet on the other we have the reality of the lived body, that we 'experience' worlds through the senses and body and that for human beings this is our primary mode of functioning (there may be others such as dream or trance states in which there is no awareness of the physical body). Yet we must be cautious of the term 'experience', especially in relation to religion, for its meaning is extremely opaque, and while the English word has a resonance in contemporary culture in that it legitimises particular ways of thinking and behaving, its universal applicability in an unexamined form must be brought into question.

An important current in modern Western thinking about religion, probably stemming from Schleiermacher, who understood religion as a feeling of absolute dependence, and mediated through Otto, has been to emphasise experience as being at the heart of religion. Indeed, many have claimed that beyond differences of doctrine and practice there is an experience common to diverse cultures and histories, and that if we strip away this overlay we will discover a common core experience, variously expressed as a sense of divinity, a sense of the 'numinous', of merging into an ocean of joy, as becoming one with the divine, and so on. Diverse religions are different paths to the same goal of a unified mystical experience. This has been called the 'common core' theory of mystical experience, or, to use Huxley's phrase, 'the perennial philosophy' view.[73] Others, such as Steven Katz, offered strong refutations of this view, claiming that mystical experiences are tradition-specific, strongly linked to language and the linguistic construction of the world.[74] There is no space here to review this literature and assess the arguments, but the argument I present is clearly sympathetic to the critique of perennial philosophy, yet would not wish to dismiss all claims to universality. The Katz position, standing at the beginning of the linguistic turn, highlighted the importance of language in the formation of experience. Language and experience are mutually implicated, as there are no pre-linguistic epistemic givens in this view. All cultural forms are pervaded by language, and we need to know a lot before engaging in the practices of religion, practices that involve sustained learning and internalising of tradition. Inhabiting a religious tradition is more like learning a skill than acknowledging propositions. I think this needs to be complemented by the idea that it is not only language but also somatic patterns of narrative and the enactment of traditions that are deeply formative of experience, and indeed that all human experience is within those boundaries. The anthropologist of Nepal Robert Desjarlais, for example, describes his own trance states as being parallel to those of his Nepali informants, yet these experiences, his own 'shamanic visions', are regarded by those informants as being 'culturally irrelevant'.[75] Experience is meaningful only within a cultural narrative and the complexity of experience created within the complexity of the interlocking cultural narratives that we inhabit.

If we understand 'experience' not as a timeless mode outside of language and conception, but as a way of speaking about the narrative of a human life, as Oliver Davies does,[76] then the term has relevance, especially when speaking about the body. There is an argument for the resurrection of experience in a new mode. Indeed, experience in this sense is integral to the body as a way of being in the world, what Csordas has usefully called 'embodiment', a central feature of such embodiment being its indeterminacy.[77] The body is the precondition for experience and at this level functions in a precognitive way. The body as experience, as lived body, is arguably a precognitive condition for all cultural and religious expression. Drawing on the work of Merleau-Ponty, Drew Leder argues that the body is experienced as an absence, the disappearance of the body from our awareness while yet functioning as the precondition for awareness.[78] Such disappearance from awareness of the lived body is linked to the body as representation in that representations of the body into which we are habituated become inseparable from our experience. There is a reciprocation between the body as lived and the body as pre-cognitive experience: the experience of the body is fundamentally constrained by the body as symbolic order, and the symbolic order of the body only comes to life because experienced, and this can be at a deep level in a non-cognitive way. To refer ahead somewhat, the experience of oneself as being identical with the supreme deity Śiva is an internalisation of the Śaiva symbolic order such that subjectivity is engulfed or overwhelmed by the experience of Śiva. The body as symbolic system for ordering the cosmos becomes an existential location for a subjectivity expanded to a tradition-constrained limit. That is, the practitioner achieves a corporeal understanding of the vibrant goal.

In the context of religion, rather than a pristine 'experience' expressed and approached in different ways, we need a much more nuanced argument in which the body is seen in terms of text and the subjective appropriation of tradition. The narrative of the practitioner's life conforms to the narrative of tradition and the body is encoded in text-specific ways. This encoding, this mapping of tradition on to the body, is also the experience of tradition and the fusion of the lived body with the symbolic order of the tradition. Another way of saying this is that the extra-textual subject, what is called the indexical-I, is filled out with tradition and text-specific content and that this is indeed 'experience'.

In an important book on Tibetan Buddhism, *Civilized Shamans*, Geoffrey Samuel has argued for a distinction between shamanic and clerical Buddhism, where 'shamanic' refers to 'the regulation and transformation of human life and human society through the use (or purported use) of alternate states of consciousness by means of which specialist practitioners are held to communicate with a mode of reality alternative to, and more fundamental than, the world of everyday experience.'[79] On the one hand we have the practitioner focused on somatic experience in contrast to the monk–scholar concerned with monastic discipline and philosophy. In the context of Hindu Tantrism the shamanic practitioner might be seen in the *tāntrika* cremation ground ascetic seeking ecstatic experience through yogic techniques, ecstatic sexuality and intoxicating substances in contrast to the tantric Brahman temple priest or practitioner still within the sphere of orthoprax injunction. This distinction could be reflected in the distinction between the *sādhaka*, the practitioner desiring pleasure and power in higher worlds (*bubhukṣu*), and the *ācārya*, the teacher desiring liberation (*mumukṣu*). However, the argument of this book is that both ecstatic and formalised Tantrism must be understood as the encoding of the body with the text. The tradition forms the body of both 'ecstatic' and 'formal' practitioner and neither idea can be understood outside of a textual revelatory tradition.

In the following pages we will see how the entextualisation of the body operates in the tantric traditions in terms of the identification of embodied self with that assumed in the texts, in terms of reading, and above all in ritual and asceticism. In ritual, tradition and text are mapped on to the body through a series of procedures such that the body becomes divinised. In a parallel way this process occurs in what might be called asceticism, where through ascetic practices the practitioner inhabits worlds given in the texts of tradition. Through ritual and ascetic practices, the tantric adept seeks to expand his subjectivity such that he experiences different worlds within the system until he attains liberation, which is understood as the divinisation of self and body. Implicit here is an understanding of ritual as a form through which culture is replicated, that enacts cultural values, and embodies the memory of tradition. Rituals are systems of signs that establish a continuity of identity and through non-identical repetition.[80] The lived body and the symbolic representation of it merge together. This merging of symbolic representation and lived, experienced body is a corporeal understanding of text. A corporeal understanding of the text is a way of inhabiting the text linked to a 'religious reading' rather than a non-corporeal 'consumerist' reading, to draw on a distinction by Paul Griffiths,[81] although in contrast to Griffiths what constitutes religious reading is not the quality of attention but the indwelling of the subject in the text and the text in the subject. This book clearly does not itself represent a corporeal understanding, but does bear witness to such an understanding in the tantric case and claims that such corporeal understanding is always, illimitably, textual.

The Argument of the Book

The book is divided into two parts. Part I, 'Theory, Text and History', outlines the argument and describes the tantric texts and traditions I shall be concerned with in their historical context. In

Part II, I show by some detailed examples how the body is inscribed and the self mapped by the texts within a diversity of metaphysical viewpoints. Some tantric traditions are dualistic in maintaining an eternal distinction between the true self, a transcendent God, and the world, while others are monistic in maintaining their ultimate identity. While some texts are synthetic in claiming that ritual can be done according to a variety of texts or that rituals from one group can be absorbed by another, as Granoff has shown,[82] other texts are clear that ritual must be performed according to the procedures outlined in a specific scripture. The *Rauravāgama*, for example, explicitly says that rites being performed prescribed by one Tantra should not be mixed with rites from another. Mixing texts in ritual is harmful to the king and kingdom.[83]

In spite of this diversity, the desire for traditions to distance themselves from each other and their often rigorous argument, the divinisation of the body is a theme and process shared by different traditions. The body becomes the uniting metaphor of these systems and processes at the level of practice and demonstrates a shared substrate of ritual and cosmology in spite of divergent metaphysical claims. In particular, I would wish to identify two processes or fundamental principles (which are also themselves metaphors) that form the tantric body. The first is a hierarchical and emanationist cosmology in which lower levels emerge from higher: a movement from the refined and pure to the coagulated and impure, from refined matter to physicality. In the second, the body recapitulates this hierarchical cosmos; the body becomes a cosmography, a writing of the cosmos. The structure of the body reflects the structure of the cosmos and is itself thought to be an emanation from a higher level. What follows from these two fundamental principles articulated in our texts is: (a) to achieve salvation is to trace a route back through the cosmos to its divine source or the point at which the disembodied self became entangled with matter, which is also conceptualised as a journey through the body; (b) this pathway back to the source is the mapping of the body in tradition-specific and text-specific ways through ritual and interior practice. This is the entextualisation of the body, which we can also speak of in terms of subjectivity having variable linguistic agency in which the boundaries of the subject of speech change through the internalisation of text. Thus, for example, the tantric tradition focused on the god Viṣṇu (the Pāñcarātra) envisions the universe in terms of three broad categories: the pure creation, the mixed creation and the impure creation. The mixed is an emanation from the pure, and the impure an emanation from the mixed through God's power or energy. 'Pure' means devoid of physicality and 'pollution', which are features of impure creation. The goal of life, on this account, is to progress through the levels of the cosmos from the impure to the pure, a journey which is reflected in the body; the body becomes an image or icon[84] of the universe and the structure of one is recapitulated in the other. Much of the present book will be an illustration of this fundamental concept.

The consequences of this argument in terms of the history of ideas are first that the tantric body entails an emanationist cosmology which is implicitly (and sometimes explicitly) pluralistic. Rather than monism, often associated with the Indian religion, the tantric traditions inherit the ancient systems of speculative thinking that we can refer to as Sāṃkhya. Second, developed metaphysical interpretations of an idealistic nature about the unity of consciousness are a later, secondary overlay on to the basic ritual and cosmological structure, evidence that supports Sanderson's view about these texts. Indeed, metaphysical speculation sits on top, as it were, of a ritual substrate and we have what Beyer has called, in a Buddhist context, the 'ritualisation of metaphysics'.[85] Third, tantric traditions must be seen not as being generated out of a non-dual, spontaneous religious experience which takes on different cultural and doctrinal forms, but as developments of ancient traditions of speculation and practice closely linked to Brahmanical imagination, vedic practice and institutions. Along with ritual, the tantric *imaginaire* is less concerned with the usual activities of Indian philosophical discourse, namely epistemology and logic, and more concerned with a poetics of imagination and aesthetics articulated in texts and commented upon by a second-order discourse within the tradition. There is thus a devotional or *bhakti* dimension to many tantric textual traditions.[86] Fourth, the politicising of the tantric body means that traditional power relationships are maintained in the wider social body. The tantric body is a pre-modern, 'conservative' body that conforms to the structure of tradition and confirms the matrix of social power even in its ritualised flaunting of it.

In the following pages I intend to illustrate and develop the argument of the textual inscribing of the body and its linguistic agency. The tantric body cannot be understood without some account of the vedic body, and the next chapter gives an account of different historical discourses, namely legal, political, and philosophical, that have contributed to formation of the tantric body either positively by being appropriated or negatively by being rejected. Part II develops the argument of body as text with detailed examples from the Pāñcarātra and Śaiva traditions. Here we shall include an account of the breaking of vedic prohibitions in caste-free sexual ritual of ecstatic Tantra intended to realise the goal of uprooting desire. We examine in more general terms the tantric 'imagination', showing how the body becoming divine is the central trope of Tantrism: entextualisation is a topos operative from the king to the village washerwoman. An appendix offers a translation of the divinisation of the body through *nyāsa* from the *Jayākhya-saṃhitā*, which has provided much illustration of the tantric body in this book.

TWO

The Vedic Body

AN IMPORTANT characteristic of scriptural religious traditions is the ability to recognise in the past what could be and what could not be a guide for the future and the ability to identify resources in the past necessary for the construction of the future.[1] Although 'new' in the early centuries of the common era, the tantric traditions nevertheless had a sense of themselves as having a continuity with the past, of being *traditions*, a sense of receiving something handed down and passed on. Indeed, this heritage is of central importance in the formation of the tantric traditions, which can only be understood in relation to it. The tantric traditions are the inheritors of systems of thought and techniques of the body whose origins lie in the ancient past and which had achieved a high degree of reflexive awareness at the time of the emergence of the tantric systems. In order to understand the tantric body we must offer some account of what we might call the vedic body. These abstractions, the 'vedic body' and the 'tantric body', are intended simply to be a condensed shorthand for representations and techniques of the body in what might broadly be called the vedic and tantric traditions. Both bodies function as symbolic systems and metaphors through which the social world and wider universe are conceptualised; both bodies are the product of deeper cultural forces and structures of power; and both bodies were also the lived bodies of practitioners in the traditions, the existential modes by which human beings inhabited their world. The vedic body is a vast topic in itself, but for our purposes we need to focus on important dimensions of Brahmanical discourse that affected the practices of being a Brahman, that affected the techniques of the vedic, Brahmanical body. Brahmanical representations of the body are closely related to different realms of value in the Brahmanical universe and different conceptions of the good for an individual and community. These values are articulated in different genres of text and we shall here focus on legal discourse, political discourse, and a philosophical discourse concerned with the highest good. All of these impact upon the tantric conception of the body and practices either through being absorbed by the tantric traditions or through their rejection. Apart from legal, political and philosophical discourse about the body, there are also two further areas of discussion and practice that have a direct bearing, namely medicine and an erotics that interfaces with aesthetics. But first we need to offer a brief description of the political and social context within which vedic and later tantric discourse emerged.

The Political and Social Context

As Sanderson has observed, by the early medieval period Brahmanical traditions of thinking and practice (and such systems were only Brahmanical) were mutually aware of each other[2] and defined their boundaries in response to each other's philosophical positions, often arranging these views in a graded hierarchy. Some schools accepted the Veda as revelation, regarding it to be the source of their tradition; others rejected them. In philosophy we see the development of exegesis with the Mīmāṃsā tradition, various forms of monism in Vedānta, particularly the Advaita tradition developing from Śaṃkara (788–820 CE), to later Vaiṣṇava forms, the dualism of Sāmkhya, the heterodox systems of the Buddhists and Jains, along with the development of the tantric traditions. The philosophical positions of many schools also express traditions of practice and the doctrines of wider communities which arose within particular social and political contexts.

The problem with the history of India is that it has so often been difficult to date texts and to place philosophical texts in a social history, but this becomes easier once we enter the first millennium CE. While the early medieval period saw the mutual clarification of philosophical positions, it also witnessed much political turbulence. The comparative political stability of the Gupta and Vākāṭaka empires (c. 320–550 CE) was replaced by a period of some complexity, with different kingdoms and tribal lords coming to political dominance and then passing away. In historically locating the social history of tantric Buddhism, Davidson has laid out the political developments from around 500 to 1200 CE in a meticulous and clear way, making the point that while this period has been neglected by historians – often because the post-Gupta period was associated with decline and decay – the empires of the Gurjara-Pratīhāras (*c.* 725–1018 CE) and the Pālas (*c.* 750–1170) lasted longer than the Guptas.[3] With the destruction of the Guptas and Vākāṭakas there is increasing decentralisation, with an emphasis on the region and a rise in the status and concept of kingship. Echoing the ideal of a previous age, the early medieval period witnessed the rise of the ideology of the 'universal ruler' (*cakravārtin*) and the strengthening of the court as the locus of cultural activity, such as the development of schools of Sanskrit poetry and drama. Alongside the development of the region, Davidson shows how the king becomes divinised and in the new feudal kingdoms divine; royal power is expressed in the regional temples, which 'became showpieces of royal self-representation'.[4]

These kingdoms formed a complex network, which Inden has called an 'imperial formation' and Stein has called a 'segmentary state', in which a ritual hegemony operated where a lesser king or tribal lord would pay ritual obeisance and taxes to a more powerful king, as in the case of the Cola state.[5] This model would seem to have been operative at least up to the period of the Vijayanagara empire (1336–sixteenth century) in which the king would on the occasion of the Navaratri Festival receive ritual obeisance, deriving his power from the Goddess herself.[6] It would seem that the model of kingship promoted in Kautilya's *Arthaśāstra*, which was composed some time during the first few centuries of the common era, had some currency and reflected the practices of belligerent kings who waged war on their neighbours while attempting alliances beyond them on the principle that one's enemy's enemy is one's ally.

During this period, different religious groups fared differently at different times. The Buddhists were successful in India up to a point, with large, elaborate monastic institutions such as Nalanda becoming wealthy and attracting royal patronage. The Śaiva Pāśupata tradition, a renunciate order that rivalled the Buddhists, seems to have become highly successful, attracting royal patronage, as Davidson documents, and becoming associated with royal temple construction in the seventh to tenth centuries.[7] The Pāśupatas were in control of the famous and wealthy temple at Somanath, for example, before its ransacking by Mahmud of Ghazni in 1026.[8] Indeed, Mahmud of Ghazni had previously plundered the Kashmir valley in 1014 CE, presaging a destruction of 'Hindu', especially tantric, discourse in the years that followed with the advent of Muslim rule. As Dyczkowski observes, the consolidation of Muslim rule in north India witnesses, and is partly responsible for, the disappearance of tantric traditions. Āgamic Śaivism retreated to the south, where it survives in Tamil Nadu, and a tantric tradition also continues in Kerala. Similarly the tantric cult of the Goddess Kubjikā retreated and was given royal protection in Nepal.[9] As a result of these historical developments, namely the Muslim conquest, there are very few tantric manuscript sources from northern India, outside of Nepal. Indeed, the tantric tradition in the north more or less completely disappeared, although after the Śaiva Tantras or āgamas there was a second, later development focused on the Goddess or Śakti rather than Śiva, which became especially important in Bengal.

It is not unreasonable to suppose that the political structure that developed had some impact on the conceptual schemes, images and practices of different traditions. As the kings had become gods, the gods became like kings and the royal court became the model for the gods' court in the heavens. Cosmology, so central in the religions of India as a hierarchy of worlds, comes to resemble the social and political hierarchies of the wider social order, and those hierarchies come to resemble the Hindu cosmos: a social order in which everything had its place with a high degree of deference, and which was believed to reflect the natural order. But while the religious traditions developed in this highly politicised context, and it is important to locate traditions within social and political history where possible, this alone is not enough to explain or understand them. Tradition cannot be reduced to its political environment, and the meaning and significance of a textual history cannot be explicated in terms of social and political history, for the meanings of texts with semiotic density exceed social and cultural particularities and are reconstituted in traditions re-imagined throughout history. The question is open concerning the extent to which the political conditions that favoured Śaivism in Kashmir in the late tenth century, royal patronage being a key factor in its dissemination, impacted upon the forms of interiority promoted by the tantras. Indeed, traditions of textual transmission and commentary are fairly oblivious to external political forces, as Halbfass has observed with regard to Brahmanical representation of the 'foreigner',[10] and traditions have often shown remarkable resilience to erosion by external, political forces. The famous Śaiva philosopher Abhinavagupta had royal patronage and his non-dual doctrine was highly influential in courtly circles, but one suspects that part of this success was the appeal of the tradition itself and the forms of inwardness is promoted. Abhinavagupta's *Tantrāloka* reflects a rich tradition – or range of traditions – that became successful not simply due to reasons of political patronage, but because the content of the teachings had resonance among an educated Brahmanical elite. Scripture and tradition have an internal coherence or structure of meaning that operates with varying degrees of success outside of particular political and historical circumstances: a coherence which itself partly accounts for the survival potential of any one tradition.

In studying the history of ideas in India we are mainly studying the self-representations of the educated, Brahmanical class who composed the treatises and guarded the transmission of tradition through the generations. Within the vedic tradition the Brahmans were concerned with establishing and maintaining their position as the upholders of moral virtue and social order, namely *dharma*. Taking our cue once again from MacIntyre (although in a very different context) we might claim that scriptural traditions focus on three areas.[11] First, there is a concern with the body as a marker of personal identity. Throughout the history of Indian society (and arguably of all human societies) the body is a sign of social location. The subject of first-person predicates not only has but is a body for the traditional Brahmanical community within the sphere of vedic teaching; a body that marks a person as belonging to a particular endogamous social grouping or caste, the property of the body one is born with.[12] While some tantric traditions believed that initiation could eliminate caste, the body nevertheless remains an index of social identity through the marks of one's cult, one's gender and one's practices. Second, there is a concern with agency. Part of belonging to a community and tradition is being able to account for one's thoughts and behaviour to others. Although this is complicated by questions of reincarnation and karma for the broad vedic tradition (which does not unequivocally accept the doctrine of *saṃsāra*), people have moral and legal responsibility to uphold the values of the social order. For Brahmans this meant above all upholding the rules of ritual purity, but it also meant legal obligations on all strata of society, including the king. Third, the life of the body/self must be seen in terms of a quest.

That life is limited by birth and death is clearly recognised in the vedic tradition with its emphases on the construction of a person through rites of passage (*saṃskāra*s) and in the sense in the philosophical traditions that there is a continuity beyond life and that what preceded a particular life has a bearing and constraining influence upon it. In MacIntyre's phrasing, 'my life has the continuity and unity of a quest, a quest whose object is to discover that truth about my life as a whole which is an indispensable part of the good of that life.'[13] Although MacIntyre is writing about a very different tradition, his statement holds true for the vedic tradition. Indeed, the Brahmanical tradition thematised the narrative dimension of life and claimed that three and later four goods were crucial to it, namely the values of social responsibility (*dharma*); material, political and symbolic prosperity or success (*artha*); and pleasure (*kāma*) within the boundaries of social responsibility. Later the fourth goal of salvation or liberation (*mokṣa*) as an ultimate goal or good for a life was added to the list.[14] Of course, the goods of a life in its narrative course are inseparable from the personal identity of the body and the agency assumed to achieve those goals. The Brahmanical discourses and prescriptions for social-identity-forming practices, for technologies of the body, can be roughly mapped on to these goals. By the early medieval period, rich textual traditions had developed loosely connected to the goals of *dharma*, *artha* and *kāma*, namely legal material (*dharma-śāstra*), political discourse (*artha-śāstra*) and erotics (*kāma-śāstra*). All these discourses have something to say about the vedic body, although not necessarily in agreement, and the tantric body must be seen in the light of these formations. The tantric traditions are informed by Brahmanical discourse, not least in their rejection of it. The Tantras and their concerns can in many ways be understood as a response to Brahmanical 'legalism' and the sexualised ritual of some tantric traditions as being quite distinct from the erotic discourse of the *kāma-śāstra*. The tantric traditions, as we shall see, accept the narrative of life as a journey but reinterpret or even reject the vedic configuring of this journey. They often reject that the goal and ultimate good must be determined within the boundaries of vedic social values and break the link between the highest good for a life and an identity determined by brahmanical discourse and power. Rather than a person's highest good being found within the vedic tradition, on the contrary it must be located outside of that tradition in sets of values that are supplementary to the vedic, or, in more extreme traditions, reverse them. Indeed, many tantric representations of the body serve to disrupt that sense of vedic identity, as we shall see. To gain some leverage on representations of the vedic body linked to the scheme of values, we need to examine legal discourse, political discourse, and a philosophical discourse about the self.

Legal Discourse

Brahmanical understandings of bodily identity, agency and goal are articulated in legal texts and commentary upon them. The legal treatises technically known as *smṛti*, 'remembered tradition' that can be responsibly rendered as 'secondary revelation'. The earliest is the famous Laws of Manu (*Manusmṛti*) composed some time between the second century BCE and the second century CE; and the *Yajñavalkyasmṛti* composed probably during the Gupta era are the most important texts in the sense that they both have 'a stream of commentators'[15] and formed the basis of jurisprudence in later colonial India, although they go beyond simply legal concerns.[16] In some ways they might be seen as the very opposite of the Tantras, although a later text, the *Mahānirvāṇa-tantra* contains legal material derived from British law, making the text a 'juridical hoax' composed no earlier than the mid eighteenth century.[17]

Dharmaśāstra comprises texts that are legal treatises in a very wide sense, for they include material on daily purification practices, rites of passage, atonement for omitted rites and so on. Mainstream tantric texts of the Pāñcarātra and Śaiva Siddhānta maintain a close proximity to the vedic tradition and prescribe a whole way of life that incorporates vedic rites of passage (birth, vedic initiation, marriage and death) along with the supererogatory, tantric rites of their tradition. They supplement vedic ideals with their own accounts of the highest good for a life and while they claim to supersede vedic views, they are nevertheless influenced by the dharmaśāstra, not only in their incorporation of the general pattern of ritual life but also in the use of terminology. As observed by Bühnemann, for example, in relation to the *Kulārṇava-tantra*, impurities that arise at the beginning and end of mantra recitation need to be removed. In analogy to the dharmaśāstra the text refers to these impurities as *jātakasūtaka* and *mṛtakasūtaka*, pollutions that need to be purified in connection with birth and death.[18] The *Jayākhyasaṃhitā* also refers to this purification in relation to expiation for omitted rites (*prayaścitta*).[19]

The general view of the body promoted in dharmic literature is ambivalent. On the one hand great care is taken over the body, a guarding and control of the body's functions in accordance with highest moral duty (*parama dharma*) for a life; on the other the body is the location of the passions and is inherently impure through its desires, instincts and effluvia. Not only this, in most philosophical systems, which are generally addressed to male adherents, the body's sexuality is itself a distraction from the path of liberating knowledge. As Doniger discusses, the understanding of the body as impure, along with a distrust of desire, is linked to a radical misogyny in ancient Brahmanical culture and male anxiety in the face of the female body and sexuality.[20] This anti-body rhetoric generally takes the form of listing body parts and functions and drawing the reader's attention to each with a view to highlighting a repulsion generated in this kind of objectification. Roberts insightfully observes that this 'semiotic deconstruction of the body and its organs is the price paid for the tolerable cultural management of sexuality'[21] and it is clearly the case that negative representations of the body are linked to negative views of sexuality and often to a misogyny that identifies women with the body. An example of the objectification of the body in Manu, discussed by Doniger, is as follows:

> [A man] should abandon this foul-smelling, tormented, impermanent dwelling-place of living beings, filled with urine and excrement, pervaded by old age and sorrow, infested by illness, and polluted by passion, with bones for beams, sinews for cords, flesh and blood for plaster, and skin for the roof.[22]

This passage occurs in the context of a discussion about the circle of reincarnation (*saṃsāra*), which one who does not have a vision of the supreme self or absolute (*paramātma-darśana*) will re-enter again and again.

Yet while there are undoubtedly passages such as this that at the plain sense level of the text present an extremely negative attitude towards the body, this cannot be taken as a sign *tout court* of Brahmanical attitudes. The picture is more nuanced and complex. According to the commentator Bhāruci, we must understand the passage in the context of a discussion about the dharma of the renunciate (*pravrajita*) or ascetic (*tāpasa*) whose meditation practice gradually allows a detachment (*vairagya*) from the body to this higher vision.[23] This negative representation of the body occurs in the context, according to Bhāruci, of the particular good or value (*viśeṣa dharma*) of the renunciate who seeks to transcend the social order in the stages on life's way beyond that of student and householder. The renouncer who seeks liberation has gone beyond the world of social transaction and legal responsibility[24] and seeks to go beyond the body in a 'spiritual' (*ātmaka*) liberation. Although renunciation is excluded from the householder, it is still within the overarching, total scheme of the orthodox, Brahmanical world-view, and in a sense is included by its exclusion. Even the rejection of householder values is incorporated into Brahmanical representations.

While the body of the renunciate is seen by Manu in the negative terms described above, the body of the student and householder is represented not in such stark terms, but in terms of the need for its control and purification. The householder and student operate by a different set of values to the renouncer, those of moral and legal responsibility to the wider social body, which are different in not displaying disgust for particular body parts or functions, but rather displaying a need to control the body through rigorous purification.[25] The body is the vehicle for a successful life, but only through its strict control and avoidance of impurity and spontaneous desire. Some of the rhetoric in Manu concerning the restraint of the senses and body is derived from the general yogic discourse that control of the senses leads to a higher knowledge. For example:

> A wise man should strive to restrain his organs which run wild among alluring sensual objects, like a charioteer restrains his horses. (Manu 2.88)
>
> Desire is never extinguished by the enjoyment of desired objects; it only grows stronger like a fire [fed] with ghee. (94)
>
> But when one among all the organs slips away [from control] thereby wisdom slips away from him, like the water flows through the one foot of a [water carrier's] skin. (99)

For the dharmaśāstra the body is not only subjected to rules of ritual purity, but is the subject of legislation; an index of the whole society that reflects social stability and the need to maintain caste boundaries, thereby maintaining power relationships within the community. The vedic body is a controlled body, a control that seeks to keep the body under the sign of Brahmanical authority in formulating the limits of legal transactions, such as inheritance law, and in seeking to control actions from rising in the morning to elaborate rules for cleansing procedures around bodily processes.[26]

A large part of this process is the control of women's bodies in legal procedures and in discourse. Although the Hindu legal treatises were probably the first in human history to recognise women's property rights, by twenty-first-century standards they are inevitably open to critique. Generally women are subject to male authority throughout dharmic literature. For example, there is a debate in the dharmaśāstra about whether a widow should inherit her husband's property, some texts saying that she should inherit it totally, as the wife is half of her husband's body, and so as long as half of his body lives, how could anyone else gain his property? Another set of texts, however, supports the view that a man's property should go to his male relatives.[27] The eleventh-century Jīmūtavāhana suggests a compromise, arguing that a widow should inherit if there are no sons, although not be able to dispense with the property.[28] Other examples could be cited to illustrate the general Brahmanical idea that women are subject to male authority, to father as a daughter, to husband as a wife, and to son as a mother.[29] Indeed, according to Manu woman is the field (*kṣetra*) in which the man sows his seed to produce (ideally male) offspring.[30]

The vedic body is thus inscribed with vedic values through the ritual processes of rites of passage through which it is constructed (*saṃskāra* means 'put together'), controlled through rules of ritual purity, and controlled through legal procedures. Both men and women are subject to these controls in ways which go against contemporary Western values, but which were also challenged at the time of their predominance by both renunciate traditions and by the tantric traditions. The Brahmanical control of the body was rejected in many cases by the Tantras and their followers, sometimes in a mild way through their subversion by overwriting the vedic body with tantric rites, sometimes in an overt way by its complete transgression in ecstatic bodily experience. While the discourse of women's bodies remains ambiguous in the tantric corpus (all texts so far as we know were written by men), there is often an explicit rejection of the Brahmanical control of the body and a reconstruction of it in other ways, even in tantric traditions such as the Śaiva Siddhānta that align themselves with the vedic tradition. The body is not simply subject to control by purity laws and is not only the object of legal transactions to maintain the social order, but rather the traditions of the 'left' contain the potential for extreme, ecstatic, experience that shatters vedic, conformist structures. But the spontaneous rupture of the vedic body in any ecstatic Tantra is a spontaneity nurtured and facilitated only within the specificity of tradition (see pp. 166–9).

Political Discourse

Closely linked to legal (and moral) discourse is a political discourse about the state and the nature of kingship, the *rāja-dharma*. Although integral to the dharmaśāstra itself (Manu, for example, contains important sections on it) *rāja-dharma* came to be treated in independent treatises,[31] the most famous of which is Kautilya's *Arthaśāstra*, the 'science of government' (first–second century CE) concerned with the two aspects of *rāja-dharma*: the development of prosperity (*artha*) defined as education and riches[32] and government defined as punishment of offenders (*daṇḍa*) or, more broadly, the exercise of law. Kautilya's work is a theoretical discourse, deeply concerned with the maintenance of power within the segmentary state and the control of populations, not simply as a consequence of brute political force, but because the control of the people by the king is integral to the order of the cosmos, to dharma. Property rights are ruthlessly maintained, including rights over women, through the punishment and torture of thieves, and adulterous liaisons across caste are punished by disfigurement or even death.[33] Kautilya is keen to point out the powers of the king to disfigure, maim and execute for the maintenance of the social body, the upkeep of the segmented hierarchy of the medieval Indian kingdom.

As in medieval Europe, we have in the Indian material a link between the state or the body of the kingdom and the body of the king.[34] According to Kautilya and others, the state (*rājya*) is made up of seven elements (*saptāṅga*): the ruler or sovereign, the minister, the territory of the state itself (*rāṣṭra*), the fortified capital, wealth in the treasury, the army and friends.[35] These are called constituents (*prakṛti*) or limbs (*aṅga*), with the implication that they are the limbs of the social body. While there are very few textual references that directly compare the state to a body, one or two make this explicit connection. Jīvānanda's *Śukranītisāra*, a digest on governance, compares the state and specifically these seven constituents to the organs of the body: the king is the head, the ministers are the eyes, the ally is the ear, the treasury the mouth, the army the mind, the capital the hands, and the territory the feet.[36] This idea of society as a body, and by extension the kingdom, is quite ancient in India and is common in modern popular discourse.[37] The *Ṛg-veda* contains a famous hymn to the cosmic man from whose sacrifice the cosmos is formed, including the social order, with the Brahmans coming from his mouth as the voice of society, the nobles from his arms as the strength of society, the commoners from his thighs as the support, and the serfs from his feet.[38] For the body to function all elements must work together in harmony, although according to Manu each one is superior to the preceding. Manu compares these limbs to the senses (*indriya*) restricted to their own domains (*viṣaya*),[39] thereby highlighting the conception of the state as a body. Manu's commentator Bhāruci observes that a vice (*vyasana*) in any of this group is likely to destroy the policies of the kingdom, so the king's function is to maintain the health of the social body through the exercise of power in accordance with dharma.

The social body is identified with the body of the king. Kautilya says that the sum total of the constituents of the kingdom is the king and that which he governs.[40] Indeed, because of this link, the moral virtues of the king have a direct impact upon the kingdom and there is a correspondence between the body of the king and his kingdom. Through controlling his senses and behaving like a kingly sage (*rājārṣi*) by eliminating the vices of lust, anger, greed, pride, arrogance and excitability, the king will succeed in a long and prosperous rule.[41] The body of the king reflects the body of the kingdom and vice versa. Furthermore, the king is identified with a deity or deities. Manu, for example, says that the king comprises fragments of the gods[42] and so there is a correspondence between the bodies of the deities, the king and the kingdom. Given this intimate connection, it is no wonder that some thinkers in medieval India, notably Jayantha Bhaṭṭa, thought that royal interest in extreme tantric practices would have a detrimental effect on the kingdom. If the king goes against dharma, defined in terms of orthodox, Brahmanical practice, then all the people will suffer because of the connection between the two bodies, although, in spite of the identification of the king with the divinity, the law books do advocate the forcible removal of a bad king 'like a dog afflicted with madness'.[43]

We have seen in the dharmaśāstra that the ambivalence towards the body lies not in its rejection, but in the need for the body to be controlled and restricted within the value system of dharma. Even, or perhaps especially, the king's body was not exempt. The body is good in so far as it is a means of purifying the self and keeping the dictates of tradition and probity, but bad in that if left uncontrolled it will turn towards vice and the kingdom will suffer. All bodies are interconnected in this world and the higher the status of the body the wider the consequences of action. Marriott is surely correct here in emphasising the transactional nature of personhood.[44] An outcaste (*caṇḍāla*) living beyond the cremation ground with 'heretics' (*pāṣaṇḍa*)[45] is far less consequential than the high-caste member of the social body. In one sense, the higher the degree of ritual purity to be maintained, the more the social restriction, and the more damage done to the social body in transgression.

This presentation of the body and its function within the wider culture assumes the validity of the distinction, highlighted by Dumont, between purity and impurity, qualities, and indeed values, reflected in the ritual construction of the body and its gendered role. It is, of course, very difficult to access the social reality of ancient and medieval India other than in its representations, often ideal, such as Kautilya's text. Although Dumont has been criticised,[46] that the purity–impurity (*śauca–aśauca*) distinction is historically valid would seem to be the case from explicit textual references concerning it. While the whole complex web of Indian social history cannot be reduced to this basic division, which itself must be seen in the context of power and social classes vying for position, it is nevertheless of fundamental importance in understanding the vedic body and, as we will see, the tantric body. Other cultural dynamics have been identified in the social field, especially the auspicious and inauspicious by Marglin[47] and the importance and loaded nature of prestations by Raheja,[48] a discussion of which would take us too far from our topic. But it is important to remember that in dealing with the textual history of ideas we are dealing with representations and the ways in which different groups, mostly of Brahmans, wished to present themselves to their community of readers. An important representation was of the body controlled by purity and impurity and the social body that reflected this distinction. In medieval India Brahmanical men and women were severely constrained by the endogamous group they were born into. One way to escape some of these constraints, and to take on new constraints, was through the institution of renunciation, the formal seeking of the highest good, the goal of liberation from the body and social world to a goal defined in various ways by different traditions of renunciation.

The Highest Good

While the rather artificial scheme of the human goals, the *puruṣārthas*, has the disadvantage of the oversimplification of competing values available within the social body, it is significant for the very fact of attempting, fairly successfully, to integrate them into a coherent scheme. The world-affirming values of social responsibility, success and pleasure have sometimes been contrasted with the world-denying value of liberation from the world. That these two realms of value exist and are held together does not reflect a contradiction but does reflect a tension in the history of Hindu traditions that is a characteristic of them. It not simply a matter of history that a dominant social group, the Brahmans, that maintained one group of values came to integrate another, contradictory, value. While there is evidence for this in the sense that the three goods of *dharma, artha* and *kāma* as a coherent group are earlier than the four which adds *mokṣa*, the tension between the positive affirmation of social values that emphasises duty, success and pleasure, along with their negation in renunciation, has been there from extremely early on in the tradition. The Upaniṣads, which reflect this tension, are certainly being composed by 800 BCE.[49] We must resist any oversimplification of contrasting a world-affirming arena of vedic values with a world-negating arena of non-vedic values, in favour of a more complex picture of historical development in which the tradition draws life from the tension. On the one hand there are claims that what is most important in the world is power or pleasure, while on the other there are claims that liberation transcends all worldly values.[50] The tension is seen in Manu, which advocates the importance of dharma and Brahmans fulfilling their social obligations, yet also looks to the transcendent goal of liberation.

The tension between competing goods in the Brahmanical tradition is partially resolved through the institution of the 'stages of life' (*āśrama*) in which the householder can pursue the goods of social obligation, success and pleasure, leaving the world-transcending liberation to the renouncer. This is clearly an affective strategy within the tradition, but one that is not wholly satisfactory to many within it, and some texts, rather than encourage a disjunction between competing goods, try to integrate them. The famous *Bhagavad-gītā* is an example of this. Here the god Kṛṣṇa advocates the necessity of doing one's social and moral duty, yet at the same time claims that there can be liberation from the world of action through acting with detachment from its fruits (*asakta karma*).[51] The goods of worldly morality and a world-shattering transcendence are placed side by side, and the human condition exemplified by Arjuna is to struggle with the tension.

The vedic body, then, is inscribed by a number of discourses and traditions that the tantric traditions respond to. First, we have the Brahmanical writing of the body in accordance with the highest social good of correct action in accordance with scripture. This is a tradition of ritual that maintains the integrity of the body and the clear differentiation of social and gendered roles that provides the basis for all further speculation. Accompanying this level of ritual action fundamental to the culture, we have a discourse about the nature of ritual action as enjoined by scripture, namely the Mīmāṃsā, which furthermore directly feeds in to a discourse about law, kingship, and the nature of society as a whole. Second, we have at the level of discourse a dualist metaphysics in the Sāṃkhya tradition, which is more concerned with what it sees as the highest value of liberation from the world. Third, we have a monistic metaphysics in the Advaita Vedānta that sees the highest goal as realisation of the self's identity with a featureless, unbounded absolute reality. By the time of the early medieval period and the rise of the tantric traditions, the picture is more complex, with theistic traditions developing discourses of transcendence, some of which attempt to integrate this with the culture of Brahmanical ritualism. The tantric traditions emerge at a time when the cultural baseline of Brahmanical orthopraxy, with its adherence to the values of caste and stage of life (*varṇ āśrama-dharma*), were strong yet becoming overlaid with theistic systems of ritual and devotion (to Viṣṇu and Śiva). These systems, along with competing discourses about the highest good, are reflected in the tantric traditions and the tantric transformation of the Brahmanical patterns.

THREE

The Tantric Revelation

Writing from his prison cell in Kashmir some time during the closing years of the ninth century, the Nyāya philosopher Jayantha Bhaṭṭa defended the authenticity of tantric revelation, but within the boundaries of vedic reason. If the Tantras offer teachings that are acceptable to learned people and if they do not go against dharma, then he can see no reason why they should not be adopted. However, if they proffer immoral teachings then the king should certainly prohibit their continuance. This was indeed the case with the sect of the blue clad (*nīlāmbara*), who practised on festival occasions, says Jayantha, unconstrained group sex in public places, simply covered with a blue garment![1] For Jayantha such behaviour was against the public good and against the scriptures. While Jayantha locates himself within the vedic tradition and espouses its values, he is living in a time when the mainstream, orthodox and orthoprax tradition is being challenged by unorthodox forms of practice and texts that claim to be from a divine source. Jayantha is clearly an intelligent and humorous man, deeply concerned about social values and the possible threat to those values caused by new ideas. He wrote his famous text of philosophy 'The Bouquet of Logic' (*Nyāyamañjari*) in prison to keep himself amused (truly an Indian Boethius!); in it he defends orthodox revelation, the Veda, but is nevertheless open to the possibility of new revelation and is a realist in understanding that his community needed to adapt to the new challenge. But when that challenge threatened what he saw as the fundamental values of his society, then he strongly defended the old morality. Indeed, after his release from prison he wrote a comic play, the *Āgamaḍambara,* which Sanderson renders as 'Much Ado About Scripture', highly critical of extreme tantric ascetics in his country.[2]

Jayantha's writing shows a tension in early medieval Kashmir between Brahmans who regarded the Veda as revelation that should provide and govern values and others who were offering different ways of life and thinking, such as the Buddhists, Jains and those who were propagating different kinds of writing as revealed knowledge, such as the tāntrikas. Before proceeding to a fuller account of the body as text in tantric traditions we need some discussion of what the tantric tradition understood by 'scripture' or 'revelation' (*tantra*, *āgama*) and how scripture related to other traditions of the time. It is highly significant that tantric traditions are scriptural. Like other Indian religions, they take their doctrine and ritual from scripture and formulate their goals wholly in conformity with the text. If the vedic revelation provides, in Oberhammer's terms, the authority for a tradition passed down the generations (*Überlieferungsautorität*),[3] then so too do the Tantras. This is often overlooked or underestimated, for to see tantric traditions as scriptural is to emphasise their traditional and conservative nature, even when they fly in the face of orthodox vedic values. Tantric practices are always textually substantiated and the origin of those texts claimed to be beyond the world in a transcendent source. The Tantras of all traditions locate their origin from the mouth of their God (or the Buddha or Mahāvīra) and claim that through a process of dilution, simplification and shortening, they have come to the human world via intermediaries, usually sages who have often undergone great penance to gain the scripture. Their purpose is guidance, liberation and pleasure or power for those lost in the ocean of birth, death and rebirth.[4]

We need to understand the Tantras in the context of scripture in India. First, text is inseparable from tradition and formed within tradition, although a text can have such consequences as to change tradition completely (as in the case of the New Testament in Christianity). Second, the tantric traditions are regarded as a revelation from a transcendent source and the texts describe the 'descent of the Tantra' (*tantrāvatāra*)[5] from a pure, divine origin but becoming eroded in the course of its descent to the human world, where it is sometimes presented as a particular (*viśeṣa*) or esoteric revelation for the few with the qualification (*adhikāra*) to receive it, in contrast to the exoteric, vedic scriptures. Third, the Tantras need to be seen in what Inden, following Collingwood, has called a 'scale of texts' in which a text is positioned in relation to others usually in a hierarchy such that '[t]exts at each level in the scale supplement and comment on the levels below.'[6] This is clearly the case with the Tantras, which present themselves in a scale of revelation, relegating other traditions to lower levels of this revelation and reading the earlier traditions through the lens of their own revelation. There is a high degree of intentionality in the scale of Tantras such that if a text does not deal with the details of a particular topic, it is assumed that this is covered elsewhere. Finally, following Inden, we need to understand the anonymous Tantras (and some related texts with named authors) as having a composite authorship,[7] and so when speaking about the intentionality of a text or 'author' of a text we are not speaking in terms of authorial intention in the usual sense. Thus an account of scripture in Tantrism needs to be placed in an account of the vedic understanding of the scripture and revelation that were current at the time of the rise of the Tantras. There is no space to develop this here, but we can say that according to vedic exegesis, the Mīmāṃsā, revelation is a system of signs that points to a transcendent meaning. This revelation has no author, and so that transcendent meaning must be understood in terms of its inner intentionality and is therefore self-validating. Nyāya, by contrast, refuted the atheism of Mīmāṃsā and proposed God as the author of the Veda. The Tantras are closer to the Nyāya perspective and are interestingly defended by the Nyāya philosopher Jayantha Bhaṭṭa.[8]

The Validity of Tantric Revelation

Rigorously defending the Veda against sceptical and Mīmāṃsaka critics, Jayantha offers proofs that the author of the Veda is God on the grounds that Prajāpati, the Lord of creatures, says that he is the author, the Veda is composite like other objects in the world such as cloth, and so, like cloth, must have a maker, and the validity of the Veda is furthermore ensured by their being spoken by trustworthy people.[9] In a parallel way Jayantha defends the authenticity and authority of the tantric revelation. As a theist he accepts the possibility of further revelation from a divine source and as a philosopher maintains criteria for their acceptance or rejection, namely their accordance with received, orthodox scriptural tradition and their wider acceptance by knowledgeable persons. For him scriptural revelation is not a closed canon. There are five criteria of authenticity that Jayantha uses: they must have been accepted by an assemblage of great persons (*mahājanasamūhe*), by a large number of learned persons (*śiṣṭa*); they should not appear unprecedented (*nāpūrvā ... bhānti*) even if only recently composed; they should not be motivated by greed; and they should not cause people agitation (*nodvijate*).[10] The Śaiva Tantras (he uses the term *āgama*s) meet these conditions in that they do not contradict the truths offered in the Veda, being pervaded by Upaniṣadic teachings about liberation, and do not go against the caste system. Indeed, they only add new rituals. Even the Pāñcarātra revelation is authentic in Jayantha's eyes, authored by Lord Viṣṇu, who is God, the creator, preserver and destroyer of the world. He cannot imagine that the Śaiva and Pāñcarātra Tantras are composed from motives of greed or delusion, although this is not the case with Buddhist scriptures since they are not affiliated to the Veda and advocate the abandoning of traditional values and the institution of caste. Furthermore, the Buddhists are morally inferior, being indifferent to the world and addicted to animal slaughter.[11] It is not precisely clear which 'wicked Buddhists' Jayantha means, although he is referring to tantric Buddhism and perhaps the more extreme antinomian practices that go against caste and Brahmanical mores, taught in the Yoginī Tantras.

Nor is Jayantha completely convinced about the authenticity of all the Śaiva Tantras. In very humorous vein in the *Āgamaḍambara*, Jayantha raises his doubts about the legitimacy of certain groups. In Act 2 of the play, the central character, a Brahman, is astonished (*vismaya*) to witness a man and woman entwined together in a single blue garment (*nīlambara*), exclaiming 'Oh alas, such asceticism [I have never seen] before!'[12] They are singing very tenderly (*atipeśala*) but many more come into view, singing songs of their sect (*carcarī*) in the vulgar tongue, drinking spirituous liquor, and behaving in a very excited and dissolute way (*ativipluta*), their observance (*vrata*) involving sex that disrupts correct, vedic behaviour with regard to caste and stage of life.[13] The Brahman Saṅkarṣaṇa observes that this *nīlambara* 'asceticism' is a new practice (*nūtanamadyapravṛtta*) that is a form of the great vow (*mahāvrata*) that the Lākula Pāśupata ascetics followed. He is fearful of pollution and so shocked by such extraordinary ascetic behaviour (*tapaścaryāścaryam*) that he resolves to tell the King and to ensure that such people are banished from the land. Jayantha tells us in the play, and in the *Nyāyamañjari*, that King Śaṅkaravarman (883–902 CE) does indeed ban the *nīlambara* sect.[14] Jayantha is also sceptical of the Kāpālikas who beg from a cranial begging bowl and who appear in the *Āgamaḍambara* as two cremation ground ascetics fearful for their future having heard how the king is cracking down on such sects.[15] Other ascetics are also fearful of the king's wrath, but our hero assures them that sects such as the Śaivas, Pāśupatas and Kālāmukhas have nothing to fear as they are in line with vedic values and practices, as is the Bhāgavata sect that reveres the Pāñcarātra scriptures dealt with in the final act.

That Jayantha is writing about the Tantras probably before 900 CE, a hundred years before the Śaiva polymath Abhinavagupta, is significant for it shows that these traditions had achieved a strong degree of development by his time. It also shows that these traditions are indeed still developing with new texts being produced with such appeal that thinkers like Jayatha feel the need to make judgements about them. Indeed, Dyczkowski observes that the Śaiva Tantras proliferated at an extremely rapid rate in the centuries before Abhinavagupta.[16] Jayantha specifically mentions Śaiva and Pāñcarātra texts, and it is this broad distinction that we need to give some account of, for this is the body of material that provides us with the ritual foundations that define the tantric traditions and become so influential. This is not the place for a systematic exposition of the main textual developments in the traditions; for that I refer the reader to the excellent essay by Alexis Sanderson.[17] The intention is, rather, to provide some orientation and to give some broad indication of their historical location. The entextualisation of the body in the tantric traditions is the entextualisation of specific texts, written in specific times and places.

The Tantras are dialogues between the main deity of the tradition and his/her spouse or a sage. Tantras focused on Śiva are presented as a dialogue between him and his Goddess or Śakti, Tantras of Viṣṇu between him, particularly in his form as Nārāyaṇa, and his consort Lakṣmī, or with a sage such as Nārada and in some Tantras focused on a form of the Goddess; it is Śiva who asks questions of her. These texts are traditionally divided into four sections, knowledge (*jñāna*), yoga, acting (*kriyā*) and behaving (*caryā*). Very few are actually constructed like this and those that are tend to be later, although this nevertheless provides a useful way in which to approach the texts. Most Tantras are primarily concerned with *kriyā* and *caryā*, with daily ritual, with temple construction and the consecration of images. The Tantras themselves are generally little concerned with philosophy in the sense of presenting arguments about the nature of being and knowledge, but they do contain metaphysical speculation about the structure of the cosmos. Indeed, this is fundamental to many texts and, even if not explicitly stated, informs descriptions of ritual.

The Pāñcarātra Revelation

Along with Jayantha, other orthodox thinkers took up the defence of some of the Tantras. Within the Vaiṣṇava tradition Yāmuna (*c.* 918–1038 CE), the grand teacher of the famous theologian Rāmānuja, wrote the *Āgamaprāmāṇya*, a defence of the revelation of the tantric Vaiṣṇava or Pāñcarātra tradition. The Pāñcarātra sources provide a large body of texts concerned with the usual tantric topics of cosmology, initiation, daily and occasional ritual, mantras and the construction of temples. Yāmuna defends this body of texts as being on a par with the Veda: 'The Pāñcarātra Tantra is authoritative like the vedic sentences ordaining sacrifice (*jyotiṣṭoma* etc.) on the grounds that it is based on knowledge free from all defects.'[18]

Indeed, Yāmuna agrees with Jayantha and the Mīmāṃsakas that scripture is self-validating, that its authority is not questionable because the texts are the utterance of the Lord of the Universe, Vāsudeva. According to another Pāñcarātra defender, Amalānanda, the Āgamas do not have the same self-authenticating validity as the Veda, but their authenticity is nevertheless assured because the Veda bear witness to the omniscience of Vāsudeva.[19] Evidently Yāmuna's defence was successful in so far as Rāmānuja accepts the authority of the texts (although perhaps with some diffidence) and Pāñcarātra rites become central in the Śrī Vaiṣṇava tradition that became the dominant form of Vaiṣṇavism in the South.[20]

Two traditions within Vaiṣṇavism lay claim to the designation *tantra*: the Vaikhānasa tradition and the Pāñcarātra. The Vaikhānasa regards itself as wholly orthodox and in line with vedic revelation, although it has its own texts, the fourth-century CE *Vaikhānasa-sūtra* that described daily worship of Viṣṇu and a collection of Saṃhitās which describe offerings to the emanations of Viṣṇu or Vāsudeva, Puruṣa, Satya, and Acyuta, that we also know from the Pāñcarātra *Jayākhya-saṃhitā* (see p. 102). The Vaikhānasa texts, as Colas shows, divide what they call *vaiṣṇava tantra* into the Vaikhānasa and Pāñcarātra, where the former is the principal (*mukhya*) tradition and the latter the complementary (*gauṇa*) to protect it. Yet the tradition also claims to be *vaidika* and of gentle (*saumya*) quality, in contrast to the Pāñcarātra, which is *tāntrika* and non-vedic (*avaidika*).[21] Clearly the Pāñcarātra must be seen as an independent tradition not subordinated to the Vaikhānasa, but the connections between the two traditions show the complexity and overlapping nature of the terms *tāntrika* and *vaidika*.

The Pāñcarātra Saṃhitās form a massive body of texts which have received comparatively little scholarly attention, although Otto Schrader's *Introduction to the Pāñcarātra* (1916) remains an exemplary work.[22] There are three texts regarded as key, namely the *Sāttvata-saṃhitā*, *Pauṣkara-saṃhitā*, and the *Jayākhya-saṃhitā*, known as the 'three gems'.[23] These texts are believed to be the revelation of Viṣṇu or Vāsudeva, also called Nārāyaṇa but are clearly within the general category of tantra and dealing with the general topics of cosmology, mantra and ritual. The dating of these texts is difficult to establish, but the *Jayākhya* is quoted by the Śaiva thinker Utpaladeva (*c.* 925–975 CE) and so predates him.

The Śaiva Revelation

Orthodox thinkers such as Jayantha Bhaṭṭa and Yāmuna are keen to establish the legitimacy of much of the tantric revelation, or part of it, by asserting its vedic inheritance and claiming that the teachings of these texts do not contravene vedic injunction. Another strategy, however, was very different, and this was to proclaim boldly the superiority of the tantric revelation over the vedic. The Veda are for an earlier time and for a lower level of understanding, but the tantric revelation is the truth of God opened out in a graded hierarchy for the initiate. This was the view of the non-dualist Śaiva thinkers of Kashmir, particularly Abhinavagupta (*c.* 975–1025 CE), who argued not only for the legitimacy of the tantric revelation but for its superiority, especially in his monumental *Illumination of the Tantras* (*Tantrāloka*). While theologians of the Śaiva Siddhānta, such as Rāmakaṇṭha, wished to align their scriptures and practices with vedic orthodoxy, theologians of the non-Saiddhāntika traditions – commonly referred to as 'Kashmir' Śaivism – on the contrary wished to distance their scriptures from what they perceived to be the restrictive and limited nature of the vedic scriptures. While clearly being well versed in the orthodox texts, Abhinavagupta and his followers saw these merely as 'external' scriptures and as inflows into a higher expansion of consciousness articulated through the Śaiva revelation.

The structure of the Śaiva canon and the traditions that it expresses are complex.[24] Much of the voluminous tantric corpus arose in the context of yogic and visionary practices, particularly the Buddhist 'pure vision' texts and the 'treasure system' or discovering hidden treasure (*nidhi*, *gter-ma*) such as sacred texts found in both Buddhist and Hindu tantric traditions.[25] While such texts are in one sense new, they are nevertheless part of an ongoing tradition of revelation and a canon that is not fixed in the early medieval period. For now it is important to understand the tantric Śaiva view of revelation in order to comprehend the ways in which these texts become internalised by the practitioner. The body of the practitioner reflects the body of the text. For the non-dual Śaiva theologian Abhinavagupta, revelation is divine speech; the making known to human beings the nature of transcendent reality, the processes whereby that reality takes on form as, and in, the world, and the methods for its realisation. Abhinavagupta sees scriptural revelation as the disclosing of divine reality, which for him is pure, universal consciousness (*caitanya*, *cit*, *saṃvit*), the highest expression of which is articulated in the Tantras of non-Saiddhāntika tradition called the Trika and the related tradition of the Krama. Indeed, there are different levels of revelation linked to different levels of understanding, which are further linked to the levels of a hierarchical cosmos. For Abhinavagupta the highest revelation is a text called the *Mālinīvijayottara-tantra*, on which he wrote a commentary (*ślokavārttika*) and on which his *Tantrāloka* is a practical text of exposition or manual (*paddhati*) along with its summary, the *Tantrasāra*.[26] While the *Mālinī* itself appears to follow a dualist metaphysics, as Sanderson has demonstrated, Abhinavagupta projects on to it the monism derived from his Krama sources and from his own lineage in the 'recognition' or Pratyabhijñā school.[27] For Abhinavagupta, revelation, consciousness and cosmology entail each other. Thus he saw the texts of the Śaiva Siddhānta, the dualist tradition of Śaivism that aligned itself with vedic orthodoxy, as being a lower level of divine disclosure than the texts of his own Trika and Krama traditions, which, according to him, revealed the true nature of reality as non-dual; that ultimately there is no distinction between self and Śiva, nor between self and world. The truth of scripture, its esoteric heart, reveals the nature of self and world as dynamic, vibrating consciousness (*spanda*).

Abhinavagupta classifies the tantric revelation into three divisions in his commentary on the *Mālinī*: the division of Śiva (*śivabheda*), comprising ten Tantras; of Rudra (*rudrabheda*), comprising eighteen Tantras; and of Bhairava (*bhairavabheda*), comprising sixty-four Tantras.[28] These categories of text express the metaphysical positions of dualism, dualism-cum-nondualism, and non-dualism respectively, of which the latter is the superior for Abhinavagupta. Certainly the Śaiva Siddhānta accept twenty-eight Tantras as authoritative (the ten Śiva and eighteen Rudra), although the lists vary in different texts and there are also complementary texts or Upāgamas associated with them.[29] This fairly simple division is complicated by Abhinavagupta, in that he needs to relate it to the classification found in the Tantras of a division into five streams flowing from the five mouths of Śiva in his form as Sadāśiva. The form of Sadāśiva with five faces is primarily a body of power (*śākta vapus*) made up of mantras. On this account the source of the scriptures is the mantra body of Śiva, the body of power and sound. Abhinavagupta describes the Sadāśiva as having five mantras as his body, namely Īśāna, Tatpuruṣa, Aghora, Vāmadeva and Sadyojāta, each of these facing a direction in which the revealed tantric corpus flows.[30] The mantras of these five, as found, for example, in the *Mṛgendrāgama* following the *Kāmikāgama*, are as follows:[31]

Oṃ hoṃ īśānamūrdhne namaḥ
Oṃ heṃ tatpuruṣavaktrāya namaḥ
Oṃ huṃ aghorahṝdayāya namaḥ
Oṃ hiṃ vāmadevaguhyāya namaḥ
Oṃ haṃ sadyojātamūrtaye namaḥ

Each of these is associated with the directions and other pentads in Śaiva theology, particularly the five acts of Śiva of creation, maintenance, destruction, concealing and revealing and with classes of scripture and teachings. Thus we have the following correspondences detailed by Hanneder:[32]

Face	*Direction*	*Scripture*	*Teaching*
Sadyojāta	West	Ṛg-veda	worldly knowledge (*laukikavijñāna*)
Vāmadeva	North	Yajur-veda	vedic teachings (*vaidika*)
Aghora	South	Sāma-veda	teaching about the supreme self (*adhyātmika*)
Tatpuruṣa	East	Atharava-veda	the higher path (*atimārga*)
Īśāna	Zenith	'comprising all knowledge'	path of mantra (*mantramārga*)

Hanneder explains that the scripture 'consisting of all knowledge' (*sarvavidyātmaka*) refers to the next set of correspondences, namely the scriptures of the path of mantras. Some later sources complicate the scheme further by categorising the tantric scriptures into twenty-five streams (five times five faces).[33]

Tantric Śaivism is therefore the path of mantras which flows from the upper face of Sadāśiva. This Īśāna face is further divided into five currents of groups of Tantras, as follows:[34]

Direction	*Face*	*Tantra*
Zenith	Īśāna	Siddhānta
East	Tatpuruṣa	Garuḍa
North	Vāmadeva	Vāma
West	Sadyojāta	Bhūta
South	Aghora	Bhairava

Relating this to Abhinavagupta's threefold classification, the *śivabheda* and *rudrabheda* flow from the Īśāna face while the *bhairavabheda* fuses the northern and southern faces.[35] Abhinavagupta further complicates the scheme by reference to a lower, hidden face turned towards the subterranean worlds (*naraka*). The Siddhānta Tantras are the twenty-eight dualist texts, and the Bhairava Tantras are those of the non-Saiddhāntika tradition that forms the scriptural basis of Abhinavagupta's Trika. Hanneder quotes a text, the *Śivatattvaratnākara*, that describes the four streams below the Īśāna face, saying that the Garuḍa Tantras teach the Tatpuruṣa mantra as the antidote for snakebites and poisoning; the Bhairava Tantras teach the destruction of enemies; and the Bhūta Tantras teach mantras and herbs for the pacification of ghosts and demons.[36]

Abhinavagupta has the highest regard for revelation (*āgama*), which, he says, forms the basis for one's life (*upajīvya*)[37] and which should be followed in order to reach perfection. This perfection is achieved quickly through pursuing the teachings in the scriptures of the left stream (*vāmaśāsana*) and transcending the vedic scriptures, which rest in the 'womb of illusion' (*māyodarasthitam*).[38] These scriptures lead to the highest perfection of consciousness (*saṃvitsiddham*), a perfection to be realised in one's own experience (*svānubhavasiddham*) beyond the mere ritual action declared in the Veda that should be forsaken.[39] Relying on Śaiva scriptures allows us to go beyond apprehension or fear (*śaṇkhā*) characteristic of the

The Tantric Revelation
(based on Sanderson's mapping of the traditions)

Veda	**Purāṇa**		**Tantra**	
Mīmāṃsā, Nyāya interpretation	Smārta worship of Śiva and Viṣṇu	non-Puranic worship of Śiva		
		atimārga (Pāśupata Sūtras)		
		mantramārga		
		Śaiva Siddhānta (dualist Tantras)		
			non-Saiddhāntika groups (Bhairava Tantras)	
				Kaula Tantras

‹ + ——————— **Degree of conformity to vedic values** ——————— - ›

Veda and orthodox Brahmanical teachings, for the Śaiva teachings are their reversal (*viparyaya*).[40] Abhinavagupta further subdivides the Bhairava Tantras into four 'seats' or 'thrones' in ascending order of importance, that of maṇḍala (*maṇḍalapīṭha*), mudrā (*mudrāpīṭha*), mantra (*mantrapṭīha*) and the throne of vidyā (*vidyāpīṭha*), where *vidyā* doesn't simply mean 'knowledge' but is a kind of mantra associated with female deities. This is a feature of the distinction, the *mantrapīṭha* being connected to male deities, the *vidyāpīṭha* to female ones.[41] The *Svacchandabhairava-tantra*, a text popular in the Kashmir valley at the time of Abhinavagupta, is an example of the former, while the *Siddhayogeśvarīmata* is in the latter category, with the *Mālinīvijayottara-tantra* as its essence.[42] It is this text, itself part of the longer scripture (the *Siddhayogīśvarīmata*) that forms the basic scriptural authority for Trika Śaivism, which Abhinavagupta regarded as the highest revelation of Śiva. It describes itself as having been a small part of the much larger scripture but reduced for the understanding of those possessing only weak intellects (*alpadhīhita*).[43] Thus for Abhinavagupta we have a graded hierarchy of revelation, with the wholly external Veda being transcended by scripture focused on male power (the *mantrapīṭha*), being superseded by the most esoteric focused on the power of the feminine divine (the *vidyāpīṭha*).

Text and Tradition

The precise relationship between the indigenous classification schemes outlined above and the social-historical development of the tantric traditions is not clear, but the schemes do arguably represent forms of self-description that corresponded to specific traditions, although the relationship between text and tradition is complex in the Śaiva case. Sanderson has mapped out this relationship in some detail; what follows is a simplified reading of his mapping.[44] If we understand this revelation in terms of proximity to orthodoxy and vedic revelation, then on the one hand we have worshippers of Śiva wholly in line with Smārta brahmanical orthodoxy who follow rites of worship expressed in the Purāṇas, while on the other hand we have non-puranic worship of Śiva. These Śaivas were ascetics known generally as the Pāśupatas, who thought of themselves as following a higher or outer path (*atimārga*) and fulfilling a fifth stage beyond the four orthodox stages or ways of life (*āśrama*).[45] Although they were ascetics, they became highly successful in terms of control of temples and with a great deal of political influence. Indeed, they displayed martial qualities which aligned them with the later naked ascetics, the Nāgas, who defended orthodox dharma.[46] One branch of the Pāśupatas, the Lākula, advocated practices threatening to Brahmanical orthodoxy, namely the carrying of a cranium begging bowl and skull-topped staff, and taking the great vow (*mahāvrata*) or penance prescribed in the dharma literature for killing a Brahman of wandering as a mendicant carrying his skull for twelve years.[47] In carrying a skull these ascetics imitated Śiva, who in myth followed this 12-year penance for decapitating one of Brahmā's five heads with the thumb nail of his left hand. In the twelfth year the skull fell from his hand at Kāpālamocana in Benares.[48]

Technically the puranic followers of Śiva were Maheśvaras concerned with ritual purity and following orthodox, puranic worship of Śiva, while those who had undergone an initiation, such as the Pāśupatas, were Śaivas. So, worship of Śiva can be classified into the Maheśvaras and the Śaivas. The Śaivas themselves can be classified into the higher or outer path (*atimārga*), flowing from the mouth of Tatpuruṣa, and path of mantra (*mantramārga*), flowing from the mouth of Īśāna, which follows the revelation of the Tantras. This classification scheme further breaks down the *mantramārga* into the Śaiva Siddhānta, whose focus is the deity Sadāśiva and whose followers saw their revelation as not disruptive of the Veda and Brahmanical social norms, and non-Saiddhāntika groups. The Śaiva Siddhānta is normative tantric Śaivism, the basic system of the non-Saiddhāntika traditions, which sees itself as in line with vedic revelation and the teachings of the orthodox Brahmans. At the other extreme we have non-Saiddhāntika Tantras, whose focus is the ferocious form of Śiva, Bhairava, and whose followers situated themselves within the culture against Brahmanical orthodoxy. These Bhairava Tantras were the revelation of traditions which propagated practices that went against orthodox values, particularly expressed in making offerings of meat, wine and sexual substances to appease their ferocious gods (see pp. 165, 169). The followers of these texts, and their originators, were the Kāpālika ascetics who inherited the Lākula practice of the great vow. They used a skull begging bowl, covered themselves with the ashes from cremation grounds, and carried a skull-topped staff (the forerunners of the modern Aghorīs).[49] In the early medieval period, texts produced in their milieu became the main scriptural authority for the monistic Śaivism of Kashmir, focused on the ferocious Bhairava or Śakti as Kālī in one of her forms. Indeed, Tantras devoted to the Goddess became important especially in the later tradition, and we need to mention here one last classification scheme, that of the revelation of the Kaula Tantras.

While the Bhairava Tantras are an early, prolific and most important development within Śaivism, a further group of texts was developing at the same time which saw themselves as being within a tradition that emphasised the Goddess or Śakti, the power of Śiva. These traditions called themselves the 'family' (*kula*) or those traditions related to one of the families of goddesses (*kaula*). But while there is an emphasis on Śakti, the Kaula Tantras nevertheless regard themselves as Śaiva and worship Bhairava as their supreme deity. In complete contrast to the Tantras of the Śaiva Siddhānta, the Kaula Tantras are mostly concerned with private ritual in secluded places and making offerings of meat, wine and sexual substances (*kuṇḍagolaka*) to ferocious Bhairava and his consort Bharavī. An important classification of this group of Tantras is found in texts such as the *Yoginīhṛdaya*. This text divides scriptural transmission into four currents: the eastern or primary (*pūrvāmnaya*), containing texts of the Kaula tradition and worshipping Śiva and the Goddess as Kuleśvara and Kuleśvarī; the upper transmission of the ferocious Goddess Guhyakālī pertaining to the Krama tradition; the Western transmission of the crooked Goddess Kubjikā associated with Kuṇḍalinī; and the southern transmission forming the Śrīvidyā tradition focused on the gentle, erotic Goddess Tripurasundarī.[50] The Śrīvidyā in particular grew and developed in South India, where it exists to the present day. It is often the Śrīvidyā which is taken as the standard model of Tantrism, but in the present text it will only be looked at tangentially.[51]

The important Trika ('threefold') based on the non-Saiddhāntika Tantras is so called because of the three goddesses Parā, Parāparā and Aparā named in the *Mālinī*. Abhinavagupta tries to show how these goddesses are themselves emanations of a single, underlying reality of consciousness and he suffuses the text with his idealism partly derived from his initiation into the Krama system, a rigorously idealist system that saw the world only in terms of vibrating consciousness. This text forms the basis of Abhinavagupta's system, and his commentary on the text (*vārtika*), along with the independent work *Tantrāloka* and its summary the *Tantrasāra*, is exegesis of this scripture.[52]

The Tantric Theology of Revelation

While texts of primary revelation, the Tantras, are mostly concerned with cosmology and ritual and not explicitly with philosophical argument, tantric theology, such as the recognition school (Pratyabhijñā), tried to maintain the universality of supreme consciousness[53] and to refute schools such as the Nyāya which maintained a form of dualism in which the body and self can exist without each other. Yet while wishing to maintain the universality and superiority of their doctrines over the vedic schools, and so identifying universality with truth, this identification is not matched at the level of ritual and its textual instantiation. Here, rather than truth being identified with universality, it is identified with particularity; with the particularity of revelation (*viśeṣaśāstra*) in contrast with the general revelation (*samāyaśāstra*) of the Veda and lower scriptures. On the one hand, in doctrine and argument we have the refutation of other schools and the maintaining of the universality of consciousness; on the other, we have the refutation of other schools by the disparaging of universality and the emphasising of the particular, esoteric revelation of the Tantras in a graded hierarchy, revealed through an initiatory structure through a master (*guru*, *ācārya*). For the monistic Śaivas, the higher up the scale the more particular the revelation and the closer to the truth of pure consciousness; the lower down the scale, the more general the revelation and the further from the truth of pure consciousness. This is not so much a contradiction, because the claims operate at different levels, as an attempt to bring together the universal and the particular, which can be seen, above all, in the tantric ideas of the power, vision and levels of awakening located within the body.

If we can speak of a tantric theology of revelation, then we might say that it is characterised by a belief in a hierarchy of revealed truths and that this hierarchy is liturgically expressed in a hierarchy of initiation. Thus for Abhinavagupta, Śaiva Siddhānta initiation revealed in the dualist Tantras is the expression of, and gives access to, the cosmic level from which its revelation originates (namely Sadāśiva). By contrast, Trika initiation revealed in the non-dualist Tantras is an expression of and gives access to a higher revelation from the supreme Śiva or even from the Goddess (Kālasaṃkarṣiṇī). In all cases we see that the tantric traditions generally regarded their scriptures as transcending those of the vedic tradition. One should, perhaps, speak of tantric theologies of revelation in so far as monistic traditions such as Abhinavagupta's 'recognition' school (Pratyabhijñā) must ultimately undermine the very notion of revelation as coming from a source distinct from the self, whereas theistic or dualist theologies, such as the Śaiva Siddhānta and Pāñcarātra, maintain a stronger notion of revelation because it is truly the divine word expressed to beings who are ontologically distinct from its source. But while this issue of dualism and non-dualism is important, there are general features of tantric revelation and its interpretation that distinguish it from the Veda and vedic schools of interpretation, particularly the Mīmāṃsā, although there is some overlap between Pratyabhijñā epistemology and Mīmāṃsā. We can express this first in terms of a rejection of Mīmāṃsaka doctrines, and second in a particular understanding of language that draws heavily on the Grammarian school.

The tantric theology rejects the Mīmāṃsaka proposition that scripture is without authorship. The Tantras are composed and revealed by a transcendent theistic reality for the sake of suffering souls.[54] They give an account of the path to liberation and an account of how the world came to be as it is. Rāmakaṇṭha, the Śaiva Siddhānta commentator on the *Kiraṇa-tantra*, says that a teaching (*śāstra*) is authoritative 'only because it is the creation of the Lord, not because it is unauthored [as the Mīmāṃsakas assert in the case of the Veda] since that is impossible.'[55] The *Kiraṇa-tantra* is taught by the Lord, Hara (a name for Śiva), to Garuḍa and records their conversation, Garuḍa having received the requisite initiation to hear the scripture, which is only opened to the initiated.[56] In his commentary on the *Sārdhatriśatikālottara*, Rāmakaṇṭha says that Āgamas are revealed by Sadāśiva to the Vidyeśvaras and thence to the sages, becoming more and more abridged in their descent due to the limited span of human life, their limited energy, limited intellect, limited wealth and possessing greed and delusion.[57] The *Mataṇgaparameśvara-tantra* describes the transmission of the treatise from the mouth of Parameśvara as a subtle sound to the lineage of the various masters. Sadāśiva announces it in 10 million verses, Ananta condenses it in a 100,000 verses to the sage Śrīkaṇṭha, who recites its 3,500 verses to the sage Mataṅga.[58] Again, the *Sārdhatriśat ikālottarāgama* declares that it is a condensed version in 35 verses of a version of 100,000 verses revealed by Śiva to his son Kārtikeya, not a small book Rāmakaṇṭha dryly observes (*na hy alpagrantham*), which itself was a condensation of the *Vātulāgama* of 10 million verses![59] In its opening verses the *Mālinī* describes its descent to the world from the mouth of the supreme Lord, who communicates the text to the Goddess Umā, saying that he himself had obtained it from the Supreme Self Aghora. Kumāra, who heard the exposition, told the text to the sages (*ṛṣi*), who in turn conveyed it to humanity.[60] The *Jayākhya-saṃhitā* of the Pāñcarātra was originally taught, it says, by the Lord (Bhagavat) to the sage Nārada, but in the current age, due to the absence of dharma, must be rendered in a shorter and simplified form.[61] This is a standard pattern in the Tantras: they perceive themselves to be smaller, simpler versions of texts which are lost or which are too long and complex to be understood by modern humans and so a more limited version is required. As the text descends we might say that it becomes more diluted. Unlike the Mīmāṃsaka position, meaning lies in the intention of the author, namely a transcendent theistic reality, to communicate a message to those with the qualification to hear it.

Extending this idea we might even say that as the voice of Śiva is expressed in the texts of revelation, in the Tantras, it is also expressed in the cosmos itself. As in the texts there is an inherence of word (*śabda*) and denotation or meaning (*artha*), so in the hierarchical cosmos there is an inherence of sound with cosmic structure. The course of cosmic unfolding involves a relation between language, the signifier (*vācaka*), and that to which it points, the signified (*vācya*). According to the monistic Śaivas, this relation is one of inherence; word and meaning are united whose meaning explodes upon consciousness (*sphoṭa*).[62]

Behind this more philosophical formulation is the idea of divine sound, that the absolute power is primarily manifested as sound (*nāda*, *śabda*). This cosmic sound manifests and resonates in all the levels of the cosmos, through supreme and subtle to gross levels where it is expressed as mantra. The Siddhānta text the *Sārdhatriśatikālottarāgama* says that this sound or *nāda* is the supreme seed within all beings[63] whose form, says the commentator Rāmakaṇṭha, is an inner sound which (and he here quotes an unidentified text) moves up through the body to the mouth and takes on the quality of formulated sound (*varṇatva*) as a word (*śabda*). Without *nāda* sentence could not be heard nor words denote; it is the basis of conversation (*saṃjalpa*). Thus even transactional speech has its root in the hierarchical cosmos pervaded by the power of the Lord as sound. This cosmic sound emanates from Śakti and from it the 'drop' (*bindu*) which generates the lower universe.[64]

Revelation and Doctrine

Before we move to express the ways in which scripture is internalised within the practitioner's body, we need finally to make some remarks about the metaphysical content of the tantric revelation. Abhinavagupta and others in the Pratyabhijñā tradition were metaphysical non-dualists, believing that what is revealed through scriptures is a supreme reality of consciousness only and that all appearance is but a form of consciousness. Subjects and objects adhere within this substratum of consciousness, and liberation is the recognition (*pratyabhijñā*) of one's identity with that. The limited indexicality of the practitioner fills out to the cosmic indexicality of Śiva; 'I' (*aham*) becomes 'I-ness' (*ahanta*). The universe, says Abhinavagupta's student Kṣemarāja, is identical with consciousness, which, although appearing to be distinct from consciousness, in reality is not, as the reflection of a city in a mirror appears to be distinct from it, yet in reality is not.[65] This monistic idealism (to which we will return in Chapter 7) is what is revealed in scripture. The true revelation, on this view, is not simply the text but the power of consciousness behind it. As with all monistic systems, it is difficult to maintain consistently a pure monism in language which implicitly contains a distinction between subject and object; inevitably the Śaiva monists needed to lapse into a language of emanation and manifestation. The universe, along with the scriptures of the different traditions, is the emanation of a consciousness which at the highest level is pure and unsullied, but which becomes more and more differentiated into subject and object. This is a 'descent' or manifestation of consciousness as lower cosmic levels. All other traditions are partial revelations from Śiva, fragments (*khaṇḍakhaṇḍa*) extracted from the one revelation (*āgama*) but which cause people to wander in the world deluded (*mohita*).[66] Thus Kṣemarāja places different scriptures and their teachings at different levels of this hierarchy. The Buddhists and Mīmāṃsakas are only at the level of the higher mind (*buddhi*), while the Pāñcarātra is at the level of unmanifest nature (*prakṛti*), the Vedāntins at the level of Īśvara in the 'pure course' of creation, and so on, with only the Śaiva teachings of pure consciousness, the Trika, at the top in maintaining the doctrine that consciousness is transcendent (*viśvottirṇa*) and immanent (*viśvātmaka*) in manifestation.[67] The scriptures of the respective schools are thus linked to those levels in a graded hierarchy. The scriptures of the Siddhānta are lower than those of the non-Saiddhāntika traditions (in their view) because they teach dualism, that the self is distinct from the Lord and the manifest and unmanifest universe. In contrast, the scriptures of the Trika, particularly the *Mālinīvijayottara-tantra*, emanate from the highest cosmic level for the non-dualists.

If we are to maintain, as the non-dualist Śaivas did, that the actual text before the reader is a physical manifestation or pale reflection of a pure work, then it follows that the 'work' as the revelation proper is identical with consciousness. For the Śaiva monist the true revelation is that all is consciousness. While recognising that the scriptures of the Siddhānta were dualist, texts of non-Saiddhāntika tradition and texts that were close to the Saiddhāntikas became subject to rigorous interpretation through the lens of this monistic metaphysics by the Kashmiri non-dualists. The Śaiva texts that occupied the middle ground between the Siddhānta and the more extreme Śaiva and Kaula texts, namely the *Netra-tantra* and *Svacchanda-tantra*, came under the scrutiny of Kṣemarāja, who wrote commentaries on both texts, claiming them for the monists. This raises interesting questions about the relation of doctrine to these revealed texts and the historical influences at work in them.

Alexis Sanderson has argued that most of the Tantras are in fact dualistic in their orientation. This is clearly and explicitly so with the Tantras of the Śaiva Siddhānta, but is also the case with most texts of the non-Saiddhāntika tradition. Indeed, he argues that the root text of the Trika tradition, the *Mālinīvijayottara* itself is actually dualist; Abhinavagupta projecting on to it his monism derived from Krama sources and from his own lineage in the 'recognition' or Pratyabhijñā school.[68] References to non-dualism in the text are to ritual, namely that in worship one should adopt the highest non-dualism (*paramādvaita*), which means that one should not perform external worship without internal awareness.[69] Furthermore, the 'non-dualism' of the practitioner identifying himself with the deity in ritual procedure is common to all Tantras, including explicitly dualist texts. We shall see in the following section how such identification is the internalisation of the text and does not necessarily reflect a metaphysical non-dualism. Indeed, as Sanderson observes, texts that are primarily concerned with ritual are implicitly dualistic. He writes:

> Certainly dualism is more natural to the Tantras considered in their primary character as a system of rites and meditations. Nondualism, I suggest, connotes, just as it does in orthodox Hindu thinking about the Vedic revelation, an undermining or subordination of the ritualism that inspired these systems. It is a metaview of a complex of practices that suggests their ultimate superfluity and therefore is hardly likely to have been the basic theoretical attitude of those who elaborated the mainstream tradition.[70]

This is surely right. It does indeed make sense that elaborate ritual systems that imply a structure, and the notion of a goal to be achieved that is implicitly or explicitly separate from oneself, are not metaphysical non-dualists. As Sanderson observes, a non-dualist metaphysics undermines a ritual structure that implies within it distinction and separation in the ritual process. One could perhaps argue that soteriological ritual, as in the Śaiva Siddhānta, implies dualism or pluralism in the sense that this procedure is thought to transport the self through the cosmos to its freedom. When the ritual process is aligned with cosmological unfolding and contraction, there is clearly the implication that this cosmos creates a distance between self and cosmic origin, or between self and its freedom from entanglement in the cosmogonic process. Ritual in the Śaiva revelation implies a structured path to the goal of liberation. For the metaphysical dualists there is no problem with this, but for the non-dualists there is, in the sense that the self's identity with consciousness undermines any notion of separation between self and goal.

That the Tantras are mainly dualist in their metaphysics is furthermore attested by the strong influence of Sāṃkhya. The Sāṃkhya tradition maintains a strict dualism between self and matter or nature and describes the unfolding of matter in terms of categories, the *tattvas*, which are fundamental to the tantric texts. We cannot understand the Tantras without reference to the Sāṃkhya system. Indeed, the Śaiva Siddhānta could be said to be almost purely samkhyan in its metaphysics, with the addition of a transcendent theistic reality. In Sāṃkhya the self is entangled, or appears to be entangled, in nature and the goal of practice is to free the self from such entanglement and to experience its isolation (*kaivalya*) both from nature and from other selves.[71] This is not dissimilar to the Saiddhāntika view that at liberation the self becomes distinct from nature, from power (*śakti*), and realises itself to be a Śiva, equal to Śiva but ontologically distinct and distinct from other selves. For the Śaiva Siddhānta the tantric revelation is intended to show bound souls the way to this freedom and knowledge out of entanglement in matter. Through the initiation and the ritual procedure revealed, along with the grace of Śiva, the self can cleanse itself of the substance of impurity and, in a way not dissimilar to Jainism, for whom karma is a substance, through this purification rise through the hierarchy of the cosmos to its liberation. For the monist, of course, this way of speaking is ultimately simply a *façon de parler*, for in truth liberation is the recognition of identity with consciousness, a truth revealed in scripture and understood in one's own experience (*svānubhava*).

The tantric revelation is primarily concerned with ritual closely linked to cosmology. Sometimes the metaphysics of the texts are explicitly dualistic, as in the Śaivāgamas of the Siddhānta, and sometimes the metaphysics are not, in which case the texts are open to monistic interpretations by the Śaiva idealists. This lack of a developed concern with philosophy and argument in the Tantras suggests that doctrine is subordinate to the practical concerns of ritual and, in some cases, yoga and meditation. It is not to the epistemological discourse in Indian thinking that we should look to make sense of these texts but rather to the cosmological discourse of Sāṃkhya and its implied yogic dimensions along with ritual procedures whose origins lie in Brahmanical, vedic ritualism. The

Mīmāṃsakas maintained that the most important thing about the Veda was the injunction to act, to perform ritually. We might say that in a parallel way the most important thing about the Tantras is their injunctive force, that they impel their adherents to ritual action as being more important than philosophical speculation, and that this ritual action is the internalisation of the text, the internalisation of tradition, and the forming of the self in text-specific ways. It is to the details of this process that we must now turn.

FOUR

Tantric Civilisation

TANTRIC texts and ideas became increasingly influential from the earlier centuries of the common era through to their expansion in the tenth, eleventh and twelfth centuries, and, although these traditions became attenuated largely due to Muslim polities in South Asia, their impact was nevertheless felt into the nineteenth century and into later modernity. We might even speak of 'tantric civilisation' flowering during the medieval period before the rise of the hegemony of the Delhi Sultanate and continuing after this in the South and in Nepal. While the concept of civilisation arose with the development of historical consciousness in the West,[1] it is nevertheless a term that can be meaningfully applied elsewhere, and we might take it simply as shorthand for the operation of macro-cultural forces. While the focus of this book is on the micro- rather than the macro-level of culture, in looking at texts and their expression in practice we nevertheless need to pay attention to the broader historical contexts in which these texts and practices have arisen and to propose ways that the micro-structure of the internalisation of tantric revelation articulates with broader social and political forces in so far as the body, or more specifically its divinisation, is the root metaphor of tantric civilisation.

We can take 'civilisation' to be a broader concept than 'society' in that a civilisation might contain a number of social systems and unlike a social system is not teleological: a civilisation is not functional in the way that a society is in directly maintaining the specificity of power relations such as a particular kinship system and family dynamics. But perhaps, unlike 'culture', a civilisation entails a polity or structural politics that articulates with culture and social structure and is geographically located over a particular spatial area. There are Sanskrit analogues for the term 'civilisation' such as *Āryāvarta* in the older literature, the homeland of the Aryans, an area to the north of the Vindhya mountains, which is contrasted to the land of 'barbarians' (*mleccha*) outside of this. *Āryāvarta* is the land of ritual action (*karmabhūmi*) where liberation is possible and where dharma is maintained.[2] There are also terms for refinement, politeness and sophistication implied by 'civilisation', such as *sabhya*, 'being at court' or refined and courteous, and *suśīla*, 'cultured'. Although there is no direct translation of 'tantric civilisation', it nevertheless conveys the important idea that the tantric traditions had historical depth, a textual semantic density, and ideas expressed in art and in polity. Not only are the Tantras and their traditions concerned with individual practice leading to the personal goals of power and/or liberation, they are concerned with broader culture and political developments, particularly the building of temples and, closely related to this, the legitimising of kings.

Tantric civilisation arose within what Sheldon Pollock has called the 'Sanskrit cosmopolis',[3] a transcultural formation focused on Sanskrit as a written, literary language of culture articulated in 'literature' (*kāvya*) and in the 'praise poem' (*praśasti*) found especially in inscriptions that issued from the courts of kings.[4] Imperial formations bought into this culture – the just king is one who promotes correct language (*sādhuśabda*)[5] – which helped serve to legitimise their authority although cannot be reduced to this function. But while on the one hand we have the development of a Sanskrit cosmopolis throughout South and Southeast Asia during the early centuries of the common era, on the other hand we have the rise of vernacular languages as the chosen medium for expressing identity and ethnicity from around 1000 to 1500 CE.[6] These consciously defined themselves in relation to the Sanskritic model; Pollock has illustrated this in some detail in relation to Kannada, as has Freeman with the development of Malayalam literature.[7] It is against this general cultural-linguistic background that we need to understand the rise of the Tantras, particularly the fact that they were written in Sanskrit at a time when regional vernaculars were developing. In many texts this Sanskrit is not polished and highly literate, a peculiarity characterised as 'divine' (*aiśa*), which suggests that these texts' authors and redactors were not completely at home in this milieu but nevertheless thought it imperative to locate these texts and traditions within the wider, 'high' literary culture of the Sanskrit cosmopolis; we see the success of this strategy in writers such as Abhinavagupta who were not only tāntrikas but aesthetes, deeply immersed in literary culture. While the great edifice of Sanskrit literature and traditions cannot be reduced to a means of articulating and legitimising political authority in medieval India, this literature nevertheless did express and legitimate an ideology of kingship that sees polity as the expression of divine power along with the expression of that power in the construction of temples. The Tantras play into this structure. Although the legitimising of kings is not their main, overt concern, they came to be used in this way. The tantric texts are part of the Sanskrit cosmopolis and as such must also be seen in the context of literature that expresses values encapsulated in the 'goals of life' (*puruṣārtha*) on the one hand, and the rise of the vernaculars on the other. Indeed, Tantrism did have an impact on vernacular devotionalism (*bhakti*), especially in its erotic, Vaiṣṇava forms, and tantric civilisation is evident at popular, village level where tantric deities, especially ferocious goddesses and guardians, become important for the life of the community. The cultural, religious and political history of India in the medieval period cannot be understood without Tantra. David White is surely correct in maintaining that 'Tantra has been the predominant religious paradigm, for over a millennium, of the great majority of the inhabitants of the Indian subcontinent. It has been the background against which Indian religious civilisation has evolved.'[8] The root metaphor of this civilisation is arguably the body, or more specifically the divinisation of the body which is its entextualisation.

The Divinisation of the Body as Root Metaphor

The body needs to be understood in terms of both representation and lived experience. As representation, on the one hand, it provides the model for the hierarchical universe and the ways of mapping the self, and, on the other, it is the means of experiencing a world structured by text and tradition. In both representation and in experience the central theme of tantric civilisation is the body's divinisation. This divinisation of the body is a way in which the body can be said to become the text and which operates at a number of levels. At the level of individual practice, the body of the practitioner becomes divine through ritual construction in text-specific ways (as I demonstrate with particular examples). In the political realm the body of the king becomes divine through ritual construction which parallels the divinisation of the deity in the temple. The temple as the analogue of the palace is the body of the deity. Indeed, as the god is to the temple, which itself reflects deity and cosmos, so the king is to the body politic and palace. At a popular, often low-caste, level the body becomes divine in possession (*āveśa*). Indeed, Rich Freeman has put forward an argument to say that possession is the common theme that unifies the tantric body, linked to language, especially performative utterance.[9] But certainly in English the term 'possession' has negative connotations and we might argue that, rather, divinisation is a more accurate term to describe a process that occurs at a number of cultural levels where its function also differs. For the practitioner seeking liberation the divinisation of the body is a necessary ritual step in the existential realisation of that truth; for the king the divinisation of the body is political empowerment by the deity and the legitimisation of his regime – divinisation enlivens the temple and its deities; and for the low-caste divinisation is possession which can be an empowerment and the bestowing of voice for someone otherwise voiceless, although it can also simply mean illness.

These processes of divinisation are made somewhat complex by the tension between 'institutionalised Tantra' and 'transgressive Tantra' (which roughly map on to Samuel's priestly and shamanic forms). The latter, much of the material contained in the Bhairava and Tantras of the Southern transmission, has emphasised those scriptures that transcend the orthodox revelation of the Veda whose practices transgress orthodox dharma, particularly in the emphasis on eroticism in worship and the violence of its deities. But this violence and eroticism quickly become incorporated within institutionalised Tantra, particularly where political power is concerned. Indeed, Tantrism becomes orthodox through official patronage as much as through Brahmanical incorporation. Through institutionalisation, sacred violence and eroticism become cultural tropes articulated in text and art, and contained in high tantric ritual. Of particular importance here is the temple. Many Tantras, notably the Śaiva Siddhānta Tantras and Upāgamas, contain long sections on temple building, the installation of icons in temples, and temple worship. There are also texts specifically devoted to tantric temple architecture, such as the *Mayamata*,[10] the *Dīptāgama*[11] and *Śilpaprakāśa*,[12] and some Tantras such as the *Ajitāgama* and *Rauravottarāgama* have significant sections given over to temple architecture and the installation of icons. These texts described different designs for temples and prescribe the deities to be installed, such as what deities are to be placed on the temple façades (*diṅ mūrti*).[13]

The current section therefore proposes to broaden the parameters of the discussion to examine the relevance of the body as the internalisation of text in terms of polity, temple art and popular religion, specifically possession. I intend to pursue two interrelated lines of argument to show that when tantric rites are injected into the pre-existent structure of kingship, the king becomes the analogue of the tantric Brahman, and to show that this needs to be understood in terms of the model in tantric revelation of the internalisation of the text. The divinisation of the body is applied to the king. We must conclude from this the primacy of the body as an index of tradition-specific subjectivity and the primacy of revelation and its internalisation in any understanding of tantric civilisation. Clearly there are macro-cultural forces at work, such as economic constraints, trade and caste, in the creation of what Inden has called 'imperial formation' in the medieval period,[14] but important here is that sovereignty is mediated through revelation, through the structure of internalisation and entextualisation. The internalisation of revelation, the body becoming deified through the mediation of text and tradition, is the primary tantric model at the base of tantric civilisation, which can be demonstrated in the three realms of polity, temple sculpture and possession.

Tantric Polity

Kingship in the medieval period was formed by historical contingency and justified by textual tradition. From the early medieval period to the rise of the Delhi Sultanate, the history of India is characterised in political terms by the development of feudal kingdoms and of the increasing awareness of regional identity with the rise of important regional centres focused on temples and the development of region-specific styles of art and architecture. After the collapse of the Gupta empire and generally from the mid-eighth century, kingdoms such as those of the Rāṣṭrakūṭas in the Deccan, an early form of the Rajputs called the Gurjura-Pratīhāras of Mālava-Rajasthan, and the Pālas of Bengal, were engaged in bitter rivalry; kings and princes pursued policies of military adventurism and an ideology of warfare developed, which became, in Davidson's phrase, 'a facet of the erotic play of king, who was understood as the manifestation of a divinity'.[15] The king, as divine, was the male consort of the land represented by the Goddess.[16] Tribal and clan power developed during this period, with Brahmans being given land in return for legitimising the new rulers and instigating a process of Sanskritisation whereby local customs and deities became integrated into the overarching, Brahmanical paradigm.

One example is the Candella clan of the Gond tribe, which built the famous temples of Khajuraho. They wielded considerable power and influence and could, for example, reinstate to his throne their nominal Pratīhāra overlord, Mahīpāla (*c.* 900).[17] In the Deccan the most important dynasties to develop were the Chalukya and the Cola empire (*c.* 870–1280 CE), which replaced the Pallavas, although it was the Pallavas who exported the cult of the divine king to Southeast Asia in the kingdom of Fu-nan, which fell to the Khmers. Indeed, Indic kingdoms continued to develop in Southeast Asia with the Indonesian empire of the Śailendras, of Orissan origin, establishing settlements as far as Bali and Java. A Cambodian inscription dated to 1072 CE (Śāka era 974) refers to the introduction of Tantras into the Khmer kingdom during the reign of Jayavarman II, of particular importance being the continuation of texts of the left current, eliminated from India, in Cambodia and Java. We know of these from the Cambodian Sdok kak Thom inscription.[18] With the Colas we see the development of Tamil culture and the growth of the extraordinary temple cities of Thanjavur (the Cola capital), Cidambaram, Darasuram and Gangaikondacolapuram, whose Śaiva temples demonstrate not only an impressive imperial power but a thriving, Brahmanical, Āgamic culture. By contrast in Kashmir tantric culture faded from around 1320 to 1819 CE, during which time Kashmir was under almost constant Muslim rule and the majority of the population turned to Islam.[19]

These medieval kingdoms shared an ideology of divine kingship: that the king was a deity or manifestation of a deity. As Davidson observes, the corollary to this was 'the feudalisation of divinity, wherein the gods became perceived as warlords and the rulers of the earth'.[20] The king is not merely a 'secular' ruler but a divine king, a god incarnate, as expressed in the very term *deva*, which can mean both deity and king. As Hocart has argued, the king became the high point of the social structure identified with the sun, with the rest of society below. Officialdom is equated with lesser gods of the sky, and the queen is identified with the earth. The commoners beneath this also formed part of this total structure.[21] What Inden calls a 'world ordering rationality' becomes integral to Hindu kingship, so 'that the divinity of that kingship can be seen as an issue of "reason" and "will" in the formation and re-formation of political societies in ancient India.'[22] Kingship gave order to the world, and a world without a king (*arājaka*) was in chaos.[23] We must also remember that the medieval Hindu kingdom was not like a European kingdom. Rather, as Burton Stein has shown, it was segmentary in character, comprising a number of embedded socio-political structures that formed a pyramid. This hierarchy meant that the village was embedded within the locality, the locality within the supralocality, and that within the kingdom. Within this structure, lesser kings paid ritual obeisance to higher, more powerful ones.[24] Tantric notions of kingship are therefore easily injected into this already existing institution.

Although the idea of divine kingship has been criticised, especially in a postcolonial context, we do need to maintain this notion in order to understand kingship and its legitimisation in the tantric context.

According to dharma literature the functions of the king are the protection of the people, the maintaining of social order through the maintenance of caste boundaries, and the administration of justice. The king is also the patron of ritual, who assumes the classical, vedic role of the patron of the sacrifice (*yajamana*).[25] In Manu's terms the king is the protector of caste (*varṇa*) and dharmic stages of life (*āśrama*).[26] But the new tantric conception of kingship saw the king as a deity warrior whose power is derived from the violent and erotic warrior goddesses worshipped as the retinue of a deity such as Bhairava, located at a particular level of revelation. The power of the king was linked to the power of the Goddess or goddesses and this power endowed at coronation or through tantric initiations by specialist priests. Indeed, through consecration and initiation these kings sought legitimacy from the textual traditions and sought to derive power through their identification with deities and use of their mantras.[27] There are certainly continuities with more ancient conceptions of kingship – even in the *Laws of Manu* the king is regarded as embodying fragments of the gods[28] – but with the medieval period a new sense of divinity and an aggressive, power-hungry lordship came into play that sought legitimacy from theology. The erotic violence of the Goddess is contained within the king and controlled through a political structure that is scripturally and ritually legitimated. This legitimacy and new concept of kingship were achieved in the first instance through texts of secondary revelation, the 'ancient texts' or Purāṇas formally concerned with the five topics of cosmogony (*sarga*), the regeneration of the cosmos (*pratisarga*), the genealogy of populations (*vaṃśa*), the great epochs of Manu (*manvantara*), and the genealogy of kings (*vaṃśānucarita*).[29] An important text that exemplifies this, studied by Inden, is the *Viṣṇudharmottara-purāṇa*. Inden shows how this text expressed Pāñcarātra or tantric Vaiṣṇava theology. While the text is not a Tantra, rather locating itself at the apex of a 'scale of texts' within the Puranic, orthodox tradition,[30] it nevertheless embodies the theology of tantric Vaiṣṇavism. In contrast to the Purāṇas, few tantric texts show explicit concern for the nature of kingship – although texts such as the *Netra-tantra* may well be from courtly circles – yet the ideal of kingship is directly influenced by them in the medieval period, as Davidson[31] and White[32] have shown. The focus of the Tantras, as we have seen, is on daily and occasional rituals, the formation of mantras, cosmology, the installation of icons, and temple building. But the influence of a tantric ideology of power is deeply embedded in medieval ideas of kingship, and the Purāṇas themselves are influenced by Tantrism,[33] although it is also true that orthodox Brahmans maintained a distance between themselves and dangerous or defiling tantric mantras.

The impact of Tantrism on kingship extends from India through to Southeast Asia. At the heart of the tantric idea of kingship is the ritual diagram, the *maṇḍala*, where the deity and his consort are surrounded by a retinue of deities who are themselves emanations or belonging within the same sphere, clan or lineage. The classical model is thus the lord of the clan Kuleśvara and his consort Kuleśvarī, surrounded by goddesses such as the eight mothers (see pp. 154–7). The king is the analogue of Kuleśvara and his queen, from whom he derives power through sex, the analogue of Kuleśvarī. Power flows from her to the king to the deities of the clan and so to the wider community.[34] White has convincingly argued that underlying this structure are the goddesses of clans and land, and the formation of alliances between ruling families is important in this understanding. At one level the king is identified with the high god Viṣṇu or Śiva and so transcends particular political alliances within the kingdom, while the tutelary goddesses represent connections to land and powerful ruling families, who 'ratified and energised the pragmatic religious life of the kingdom as a whole'.[35] This mandalic model of kingship can be seen in Nepal, as Tofflin has shown, where three gods are important for royalty and from them the king derives his power: the sovereign god Viṣṇu; the master of ascetics and of Nepal, Paśupati; and the secret tantric goddess, Taleju. Indeed, among the Newars of Nepal the power of the Goddess lies in royalty.[36] The most important tantric rite connected with kingship is the king's consecration or anointing (*abhiṣeka*) and Davidson has shown the connection between royal consecration and tantric initiation.[37] The *Jayākhya-saṃhitā* interestingly links the anointing (*abhiṣeka*) of four classes of initiate with four kinds of political actor. Thus the procedures for the *samayin*, *putraka*, *sādhaka* and *ācārya* (see pp. 133–4) are to be modelled on the procedures for anointing a military general (*senapati*), a prime minister (*mahāmantrin*), a prince (*yuvarāja*) and a king (*rāja*).[38] Here we have an explicit identification of the procedure of anointing with political institution, with the king analogous to the master (*ācārya*); as the master embodies the divinity disclosed by the text, so does the king disclose the divinity. There is documentary evidence that kings were consecrated with tantric mantras, at Viyajanagara,[39] for example, and an early king of Nepal, a practice which continued into modernity.[40] These tantric rites of anointing at coronation using tantric mantras fitted easily into an ideology of divine kingship and simply injected a further layer of textual empowerment into the pre-existing puranic scheme. The transgressive violence and eroticism of tantric deities become tapped and controlled by the institution of kingship. That this layer of further empowerment was regarded with suspicion by the orthodox in the case of Kashmir is clear from a number of sources (such as Jayanthabhaṭṭa's play, *Āgamaḍambara*, which we have cited (pp. 51–2)), but it is also the case that kingship was supported by wholly orthodox Brahmans using Purāṇas as their core texts, as Inden has shown, but whose theology was tantric, as in the case of the Pāñcarātra *Viṣṇudharmottara*.

Some passages in tantric texts deal directly with kingship. The *Netra-tantra* states that the tantric teacher (*ācārya*) needs to worship the eight mothers for the protection of king and kingdom. He should construct a 'lotus' diagram for appeasement, prosperity, good luck, protection of women and sons, and for the protection of the king and intimidation of other rival kings. The teacher should use mantras for the well-being of the king, for his protection from illness, his happy sleep and good digestion.[41] The *Īśānaśivagurudeva-paddhati* contains some material on kingship and it undoubtedly assumes that its teachings are for royalty as well as for initiated Śaivas. We see this in the chapter on battles and in the extensive sections on temple building and temple architecture. Only kings, with their armies, go to war and, while others build temples too, it is kings who build large, prestigious temples that glorify the deity and thereby themselves.

In the chapter on protection in a battle, the text presents five birds connected with the five actions of Śiva (see p. 57) and with different mantric syllables. These birds are furthermore related to five stages in the king's life, namely childhood, youth, kingship, old age and death, which in turn are related to five activities of enjoyment, sacrifice, marching to war, ruling, retirement or the cessation of action, and dying.[42] Through studying the omens of birds we can determine the positive or negative outcome of a battle for a particular person, who should prepare accordingly by, for example, wearing armour for good bodily protection (*suguptadeha*) or dividing his wealth if the augury is pessimistic.[43]

Through consecration the king becomes the analogue of the tantric Brahman. As the divinisation of the body is described in the texts, so the king's body is divinised in consecration, and as the body of the practitioner becomes an index of a tradition-specific subjectivity, so the king's becomes an index of the wider social body. In a way not dissimilar to medieval Europe,[44] the king's body points to the health of the society as a whole. In one sense the king is the ideal householder who can fulfil the goals of *dharma* in the projection of the people, *artha*, the pursuance of wealth and political success, and *kāma*, the pursuance of pleasure, especially sexual pleasure with courtesans; in another sense he is like the Brahman in mediating transcendent power and, indeed, himself becoming divinised. The king absorbs the violent and erotic power of the divine and transforms it into political strategies of expansion and consolidation. This becoming divinised is a formal empowerment through the king's ritual anointing in which power descends upon him. The body of the king becomes a divine body, as the body of the practitioner becomes divine through initiation (and every day following that). As the practitioner's, the king's body becomes entextualised through tradition-specific mantras.

The Tantric Temple

While the primary and most important forms of tantric deities are always as mantras rather than as plastic representations, there is nevertheless significant overlap between tantric and puranic texts in the areas of temple-building and iconography. As the body of the king becomes divinised in the rite of anointing, so the temple deity becomes enlivened through the appropriate rites (as in standard temple Hinduism). The divine body of the king in the palace recapitulates the divine body of the deity in the temple and there is a parallelism between the temple and the palace, as Tofflin has shown existed in Nepal to recent times.[45] Temples are an important concern in tantric literature, and texts of the Śaiva Siddhānta contain much material on the construction of temples, installation of deities, and temple rites. The *Rauravottarāgama* describes different kinds of temple styles, octagonal (*drāviḍa*), circular (*vesara*) and square (*nāgara*), along with the deities to be installed.[46] The text describes the installation of the main deity, the Śiva *liṅga* on its pedestal (*pīṭha*), the installation of the Goddess and her marriage to Śiva, and the installation of the guardians of the doors (*dvārapāla*),[47] descriptions which, with some variation, are found in other Tantras as well. Temple tantrism continues into present times in temples of Tamil Nadu and, especially, Kerala where 'tantric Hinduism' is normative, some Nambudiri families using the fifteenth-century *Tantrasamuccaya* as their base text.[48] Even the more extreme cults of goddesses, the Yoginīs, were expressed in temples during the early medieval period, as White has shown.[49] In line with orthodox, puranic tradition, such temples can be seen as the body of the deity, and indeed when discussing the temple the distinction between the tantric and non-tantric becomes blurred. The great Śaiva temple at Cidambaram, for example, a centre of orthodox power and learning, performed temple rites according to Śaiva Siddhānta texts, yet there were also non-dualist theologians such as Maheśvarānanda writing against dualist interpretations of scripture within the institution of that temple.[50]

Along with guardians and protectors, temple façades of the medieval period are famous for their erotic sculpture, which is the focus of wide interest and often associated with 'Tantrism' and 'tantric art', especially in the West, because it seems to disrupt the Western disjunction between 'religion' and 'sexuality'. Indeed, the presence of erotic sculpture associated with Tantrism has reinforced the idea of later tantric culture that *bhukti* is *mukti*, pleasure is liberation, and, in the *Kulārṇava-tantra*, *bhoga* is *yoga*, pleasure is the method.[51] But to begin to understand these images we must look to their context and the systems of value operative at the time of their composition.

Tantra and Erotic Sculpture

Both the terms *mukti* and *bhukti* point to values within the history of Indian civilisation that are in tension. Pleasure, particularly sexual pleasure or *kāma*, has a long history as one of the four legitimate goals of life (*puruṣārtha*) along with *dharma*, prosperity (*artha*) and liberation (*mokṣa*). While one of the key texts of tradition, the *Bhagavad-gītā*, is virtually silent on the subject of *kāma*, as Killingley observes,[52] it is nevertheless treated systematically and deeply in other literatures, most notably the kāmaśāstra, of which the most famous text is the *Kāmasūtra*. This literature rejoices in sexual pleasure and, though it may seem mechanistic in relation to Sanskrit erotic poetry and even sexist to contemporary Western sensibilities, demonstrates the importance and legitimacy that sexual desire was perceived to have in classical Indian civilisation before the rise of Islam and the advent of puritanical colonialism. Liberation, by contrast, was traditionally a transcendent (*viśvottīrṇa*) state achieved by world renouncers through asceticism and celibacy; the reversal of the flow of the body outwards towards the objects of desire. Sanskrit literature is replete with sages falling from their austerities due to being seduced by beautiful women, usually sent by gods such as Indra fearing the power created by their abstinence and austerity,[53] demonstrating the tension between cultural values and the difficulty in transcending worldly concerns. Dumont highlighted two realms of value, that of the householder and the renouncer.[54] While we might dispute who precisely is a householder and whether the Brahman is closer to the renouncer than to Dumont's 'man-in-the-world', the distinction does nevertheless point to an aporia in Indian civilisation. Part of the ideology of tantric traditions, particularly the more philosophical accounts, is that liberation and the world-affirming value of desire are not incompatible, but desire can be used to transcend desire. It is precisely here that the difference between desire in wider Indian civilisation and tantric traditions can be seen. For the kāmaśāstra pleasure, the result of desire (the term *kāma* can mean both 'pleasure' and 'desire'), is an end in itself. Sexual pleasure has no goal in this context other than its own fulfilment. In contrast to the ideal and value of dharma, where having children is a purpose with a high priority, the purpose of *kāma* is not children but pleasure for its own sake. In this sense *kāma* is barren and indeed transgressive of dharma. Pleasure rather than progeniture is the goal.

Although much is often made of desire in Tantrism, in the kāmaśāstric sense, it is distinct from its tantric use, although the boundaries between tantric and non-tantric *kāma* have sometimes been blurred even within the tradition itself. As White has shown (as we will see in Chapter 7) in early tantric traditions of the extreme left, sexual desire was used to produce sexual fluids, power substances, that were to be offered to the deities of the *maṇḍala*.[55] We also find in these extreme texts the advocation of consuming bodily waste products, and one thinks here particularly of extreme Buddhist Tantras such as the *Caṇḍamahāroṣana-tantra* where waste products are to be consumed as the diet 'eaten by all the Buddhas' without 'even slight disgust'.[56] All bodily products are thought to contain power potentially through their transgressive use in a ritual context.[57] Only in later tantric traditions does *kāma* come to be regarded as itself a means of transformation to the condition of the deity. Thus we have a shift from the appeasement of ferocious and erotic deities with the 'sacrifice' of sexual substances to the practice of sexual union in a ritual context as the transformation of desire such that the experience of coition is thought to reflect or recapitulate the bliss of Śiva and Śakti. We also have the use of sex to produce sexual fluids, which are then contracted back into the male partner in an often elaborate rite, the *vajrolī mudrā*.[58] In both of these senses *kāma* is different from the *kāma* of the kāmaśāstra. In the tantric traditions of the left *kāma* is not an end in itself but a means to an end; desire used to transcend itself as a thorn can be removed by a thorn, or perfection attained by those things that would normally lead one to fall from the path, in the image of the *Kulārṇava-tantra*.[59] And the strong links between eroticism and death place sexual desire in Tantrism even further from the kāmaśāstras. In

Shulman's words, Tantrism presents a 'barren eroticism'.[60] Indeed, the extreme antinomian practices of the left cannot be seen in terms of pleasure; as Hardy points out, there are other occasions where promiscuity could take place on festival occasions such as holi.[61]

Conceptually the distinction between *kāma* in the Tantras and *kāma* in erotic science is clear in the former being teleological (its goal being power and/or liberation) and the latter being an end in itself, but some blurring of the boundary does occur. A notable feature of the magnificent temples of medieval India is the erotic scenes sculpted on the temple walls known to gawking tourists and giggling schoolchildren. These have often been taken as paradigmatic of 'tantric art', but, given that 'tantric eroticism' is of a distinct kind, do these sculptures have any relation to tantric civilisation and, if so, what could it be? This is a difficult question, to which a number of responses have been made, such as that they are protective against demonic powers, that they reflect what goes on in the heavens, or that they are depictions of tantric ritual activity.

Erotic sculpture on medieval and later temples is a common feature, still seen on temples in the South, though little remains in the North, largely due to temples being destroyed. One interesting and plausible theory put forward by Fred Hardy, first expressed to him by people in a temple's environs, is that the sculptures are intended to keep demons away from the pure sanctuary, acting as mirrors to reflect the demons' obscenity back on themselves.[62] Given that the universe was peopled with supernatural powers, both auspicious and inauspicious, and the temple was considered to be a pure abode of the deity, this is a highly plausible thesis. Indeed, the façades of temples contain the pantheons of deities that form the outer wall (*āvaraṇa*) of the main deity's power, namely the guardians of the directions and the guardians of the doors. Erotic sculpture fits well into this context of magical protection. However, this is not attested in any texts and at least one text, the *Śilpa-prakāśa*, links such sculptures with the kāmaśāstra (see below). Moreover, many of these sculptures have very great elegance and beauty, and one would perhaps expect the grotesque to function in this way rather than the beautiful. White, on the other hand, has argued that there is indeed a connection between Tantrism and the coital couples (*maithunas*) of erotic temple sculpture, pointing out that there are ruins of Yoginī temples scattered across the central Indian region where Kaula practices were performed in the royal courts. With special reference to the Bheraghat Yoginī temple in Orissa, White argues that the *maithunas* on the sides of early temples in all likelihood depict tantric rituals because they appear to follow a sequence.[63] Such depictions only lasted for a comparatively short duration (White thinks no more than two hundred years), after which time the *maithuna* motif becomes decontextualised from its ritual origin. In other words, we might say that erotic depictions shift from representations of tantric sexuality, which therefore point to the transcendence of sex as action for its own sake, to depictions of sex more in keeping with kāmaśāstra. Either way, whether these representations are linked to trangressive tantric practice or to kāmaśāstra, this points against their being linked to 'fertility cults' other than in a very broad and general way.[64]

This is clearly the case by the time of the composition of the *Śilpa-prakāśa*, a text of temple architecture composed by a tantric practitioner, judging by his name, Rāmacandra Kulācāra, between the ninth and twelfth centuries in Orissa.[65] This text describes the building of a temple as parts of the deity's body, the deity being the foundational god Mahāpuruṣa. What is of note is that the text clearly links the temple with the idea of desire and with the science of erotics, the kāmaśāstra. Desire (*kāma*) is the root of the universe, says the text, from which all things are born, and through desire all is reabsorbed into primordial matter (*mūlabhūta*). 'Without Śiva and Śakti creation would be mere illusion. Without the action of desire (*kāmakriyā*) there would be no life, birth and death.'[66] This is to place desire as the most important goal of life, and so is in accord with a strong theme in Sanskrit literature. Moreover the text links *maithuna* couples with the kāmaśāstra, saying that there should not be representations of sexual union (*saṃghama*) but only depictions of love play as there are many types of love play in the kāmaśāstra.[67] Of course, the truth of temple sculpture goes against this recommendation as there are innumerable examples of fully coital representations on temple walls, including scenes involving multiple actors. The 'orgy' scenes on the sides of Khajuraho or Konarak are against the norms of dharma but not at variance with kāmaśāstra, and, indeed, there are occasions of 'orgiastic' worship contained in some texts.[68] But what is significant is that maithuna couples are here directly linked to the kāmaśāstra, an important shift in relocating eroticism to a context of aesthetics. With the erotic carvings on temple walls, eroticism is stripped of its violence and link with death that we find in early tantric appeasement and taboo breaking. The depiction of the body on temple walls is a representation of the body in an idealised eroticism that is grounded in text; an eroticism which rejoices in the body yet which points beyond itself to a divine transcendence. The body's representation here is divinised and textualised in a way that goes beyond transgression or protection. Indeed such representation points to the sexualised body as a manifestation of the deity, as other deities on temple façades are manifestations: the temple is the body of the deity and is not devoid of sexuality.

Possession

As the divinisation of the body occurs at the level of the individual practitioner, in the body of the king, and, in an extended sense, with the temple, so the same topos occurs in possession and exorcism and even in popular devotion (*bhakti*). Indeed, if anything is characteristic of popular religion in India it is possession. It would be possible to read the history of religion in South Asia in terms of possession as the central paradigm of a person being entered by a deity which becomes reinterpreted at more 'refined' cultural levels. We see this with the term *samāveśa,* whose primary designation is, like *āveśa*, 'possession', coming from the root *viś*, 'to enter', but which comes to mean 'immersion' in non-dual consciousness for the Śaiva theologian Abhinavagupta.[69] The whole idea of the self becoming *brahman*, the very term *vipra*, 'shaker', as a term for a Brahman and ritualised divinisation through initiation and consecration (*abhiṣeka*) might be seen as pointing to this foundational, recurring topos. Indeed, Rich Freeman's thesis is that institutionalized possession is a central paradigm of worship which is anciently attested from Tamil Caṅkam literature of the early centuries of the common era.[70] Clearly possession is a fundamental trope in the history of Indian religions, but I wish to propose that a more basic metaphor is not possession per se but rather the body becoming divine through entextualisation, through the identification of the self with the 'text' both oral and written.

Possession has a 'good' aspect when the deity enters a performer and so gives a blessing (*darśana*) to the assembled community or makes a prophesy, or a 'bad' aspect when possession is uninvited and manifested as illness, especially illness in children, about which much of the literature is taken up. Smallpox, for example, was thought to be due to the hot goddess euphemistically called Śītalā, 'the cool one', or Mariamman in the South. Possession can be seen as the divinisation of the body, which is also its entextualisation. In becoming the host for the deity or supernatural being external to the self, the body becomes constructed in tradition and text-specific ways. While the process and symptoms of possession might be common – even across cultures – it is the specificity that is important and that gives the possession legitimacy for a particular community.[71]

A fine example of this is the public, costumed, ritual possession of the *teyyam* dancers of Kerala, described by Rich Freeman. These rites continue to the present day, and Freeman has provided an excellent ethnography of the tradition, showing its historical and textual depth. These local deities of northern Kerala, each with her own particular costume and make-up, are danced at annual festivals by professional dancers who incarnate them. These traditions have been preserved mainly through oral narratives, and the goddesses they embody were linked to royal lineages. Indeed, the *teyyams* are often apotheosised warrior chiefs and the traditions had royal patronage. These rites embody complex caste and gender relationships; the performers are of a lower caste than the hosts for whom they perform, and the dancers are exclusively male while the deities are generally female. The actual performance follows a ritual sequence in which the castes performing the rites each have their own make-up rooms; the rites, which take place over several days, become more elaborate and complex, with a more simple phase (*tōrram*) being followed by a more elaborate one (*veḷḷāṭṭam*) and so into the fully costumed *teyyam*. I refer the reader to Freeman's important work on this, which he links to a general theory of possession in South Asia and to its linguistic mediation. But what I wish to emphasise here is that the *teyyam* dancers follow a text; they enact the narrative of the particular deity and perform the *teyyam* songs such that the body becomes the text. Freeman notes that the most significant aspect of the rite is the ritual transformation of the practitioner into the deity. He describes the process as follows:

> each dancer comes individually before the opened shrine in which the priests have been performing *pūja* to receive from them a folded banana leaf containing sandalwood paste and a ritual vessel of water (*kiṇḍi*). The dancer uses these to sprinkle himself and daub the paste over specified parts of his body in a prescribed fashion, starting with his head and ending at his feet. This sandalwood paste comes from the deity and being co-substantial with it, helps to transubstantiate the body of the dancer into that of the god. The places the paste is daubed are additionally said to correlate with the significant nodes and portals of the body according to the physiological conceptions of *tantra*, through which the performer absorbs, and is purified by, the divine energy. Some compared this explicitly with the ritualized bodily purification, the *deha-śuddhi* rites of tantric priests.[72]

The divinisation process culminates in the dancer gazing into a mirror when the thought arises 'this is not my form – this is the actual form of the goddess that I am seeing.'[73] Here Freeman shows how the everyday subject of first-person predicates becomes subsumed by the first-person predicate of the deity, who is a being within a cultural narrative, within a text. The dancer becomes the deity: to use Urban's technical terminology, the indexical-I becomes the 'I of discourse' in the text (see pp. 178–80) and the body of the dancer becomes entextualised. The process we have identified as characteristic of tantric traditions, namely the divinisation of the body as entextualisation, is clearly visible here where the *teyyam* dancer is directly linked to tantric conceptions of centres of corporeal power or *cakra*s, and the purification of the body is directly linked to text and tradition.

While this is an example of 'good' possession, tantric texts and tantric-influenced texts are also concerned with 'bad' possession, with illness such as smallpox, madness or trance (*unmāda*) and epilepsy (*apasmara*) caused by malevolent beings who need to be appeased or acknowledged in some way. Some tantric texts bear witness to traditions of possession and exorcism. Three early texts in particular stand out which seem to bear witness to three distinct, though arguably interrelated, traditions, namely the *Netra-tantra*, the *Kumāra-tantra*, and the *Īśānaśivagurudeva-paddhati*. Other texts also bear witness to possession and exorcism, such at the fifteenth- or sixteenth-century Kerala text the *Tantrasāra-saṃgraha* by Nārāyaṇa, concerned with health more generally through mantra and toxicology. There are also connections between the material on possession in these texts and broader concerns of Ayurveda, especially the 'science of (exorcising) demons' (*bhūtavidyā*). The precise relationship and intertextuality of all this material is a desideratum. Before this is done the following comments can be only of a general nature as pertaining to our theme.[74]

The popular Śaiva cults of the Kashmir valley in the medieval period, those of the Lord Netra and Svacchandabhairava, both forms of Śiva each with their own Tantra (see p. 59), contain material on magical protection, rites for a desired goal (*kāmya*) such as the destruction of enemies or seduction, and possession and exorcism. The *Netra-tantra* presents us with a fascinating taxonomy of beings which need to be appeased to deflect possession, which include categories such as 'mothers' (*mātṛkās*) and 'demon-grabbers' (*bhūtagraha*). These innumerable beings are classified by the *Netra* according to their desire; thus there are those wanting meat offerings (*balikāma*), those desiring to harm and kill (*hantukāma*) and those wanting sexual pleasure (*bhoktukāma*).[75] These beings are part of the hierarchical cosmos and each group forms a clan or family (*kula*) of a higher deity. By appeasing the higher deity the lower are thereby appeased. Thus the class of beings called *vināyakas* are themselves removed by worshipping their lord, Vighneśa (namely Gaṇeśa) by offering him sweetmeats and plenty of alcohol.[76] If someone is possessed by one of the innumerable 'mothers' who wish to harm a person, then the practitioner needs to perform worship to their source, namely the seven 'great mothers' (*mahāmātṛ*), Brahmī, Maheśvarī and so on, from whose wombs they originated (see pp. 155–6).[77] Once these higher beings are appeased with offerings of rice, flowers, and four kinds of meat from domestic and wild, aquatic and flying animals, then so are the lower manifestations.[78]

The *Netra-tantra* presents a tradition of possession and exorcism which, while having significant overlap with other Śaiva systems, is nevertheless distinct. The *Kumāra-tantra,* which Filliozat thinks originated in the north and spread to Tibet and Southeast Asia, contains material on possession by a number of different beings; the text is particularly important for the anti-demonic rituals it contains to appease the possessors of children, who give them sickness and fever. The text presents details of these ritual procedures, which comprise making offerings (*bali*), ablutions, fumigation, mantra repetition and pious works.[79] The text details the different kinds of being that possess children, such as the mothers (*mātṛ*), Nandanā, Pūtanā, Kaṭapūtaṇa and so on,[80] who are made calm (*śānti*) by various offerings. For example, Kaṭapūtanā, who has seized a small child with a fever, is appeased by making a clay effigy and offering perfumed betel, good white rice, white flowers, five standards (*dhvajāḥ*), five lamps, and five pulse cakes (*vaṭakāḥ*) in the direction of the north-east, bathing the child with blessed water (*śāntyudakam*), offering garlands consecrated to Śiva, a snake skin, incense and so on, along with the appropriate mantra.[81]

There is some overlap between the concerns of the *Kumāra-tantra* and the southern text of the Śaiva Siddhānta, the *Īśānaśivagurudeva-paddhati*, with one chapter focused on the Śaiva exorcist deity Khaḍgarāvaṇa considerably overlapping. Here we find possession by twelve mothers (*mātṛkā*) or 'grabbers' (*grahī*) who are within the sphere of Khaḍgarāvaṇa, 'Rāvaṇa with the sword', who is described in the ISG as having three heads each with three eyes and with ten arms holding a skull-topped staff, a trident, a sword, drum, a shield, a skull bowl, with the fear-not and boon-giving gestures.[82] The mothers within his sphere take away children but can be exorcised according to the same processes as found in the northern text.[83] It would seem then, that the Rāvaṇa cult existed in the South and indeed the *Kumāra-tantra* does have a Tamil version.[84] We are, however, in a different world with the *Īśānaśivagurudeva-paddhati*; it contains a distinct typology of eighteen kinds of supernatural beings,[85] the same typology occurring in the Kerala text the *Tantrasāra-saṃgraha*.[86] In a way not dissimilar to the *Netra-tantra*, Īśānaśivagurudeva groups these beings into those wanting to harm (*hantukāma*) and those wanting sexual pleasure (*ratikāma*), who are respectively fierce (*agneya*) and gentle (*saumya*). These innumerable beings, who inhabit remote places such as rivers, gardens, mountains, lakes, empty places, Buddhist stūpas, (deserted?) temples and cremation grounds, possess vulnerable people with a low social standing or who are in a liminal condition such as children, people on their own at night, people whose wealth has been lost, those intoxicated with love, and those who wish to die. The text goes on to list various women vulnerable to possession, such as those who have bathed after menstruation, those who are naked, filled with passion, intoxicated, pregnant or prostitutes.[87] The world is populated by these supernatural beings, particularly Yoginīs who take theriomorphic forms; one should never show anger towards them.[88] Possession is also related to caste: there are demons who possess Brahmans (*brahmarākṣasa*), warriors (*kṣatriyarākṣasa*) and commoners (*vaiśya*).[89] The *Tantrasāra-saṃgraha* presents similar concerns, although here interfaces much more explicitly with Ayurveda. Indeed, the text is particularly interesting in locating the origins of 'trance' or 'madness' (*unmāda*) in both naturalistic and supernatural causes, due to the anger of a deity of guru certainly, but also due to unwholesome food, or emotional upset such as grief, fear, and desire for joy, and born from an inbalance in the three humours (*tridoṣajāḥ*) known to Ayurveda.[90]

One interesting feature of this material is that the *Īśānaśivagurudeva-paddhati* does not maintain a distinction between the possessing being (the *bhūta* or whatever) and the possessed person. For example, the text describes the 'angry possessor' (*heḍraga grahī*) as one who kneels or whose face is on the ground, grimacing, with clenched fists, and one afflicted by an 'ash' as being (*bhasmagrahī*) is ill-mannered, trembling and babbling with her/his eyes crossed.[91] This is a description of the possessed person but the text does not make any distinction clear, so in afflicting the possessed with 'remedies' the exorcist or mantrin is afflicting the possessing being. Having described these beings, the text goes on to prescribe how to banish them with varying degrees of harshness; if medicine and offerings (*bali*) have not freed the possessed, then the medicine (*citkitsā*) may be force.[92] Thus, the exorcist or master of mantras, the *mantrin*, should release the ghosts by repeating mantras, but if this does not work he needs to resort to firmer ritual methods. Thus the opening of chapter 43 describes the following ritual procedures.

> 1–2. Repeating [the mantra] 'Heart, the sound of the Lord etc...' [while offering] pulse and jaggery, [the mantrin] visualising himself as Rudra, should hold down and beat [the possessed person], on account of which the demons free him in a moment. [Repeating the mantra] 'at the end of the heart...]' and so on and preparing this pulse, the demon frees one who eats it. A man who repeats [this mantra] *namo bhagavate* etc. should free the demons, ghosts and so on. 3. Having repeated [the mantra] 'savour, the sound of the moon of the heart' etc. seven times, [the mantrin] should fasten the top-knot of the possessed [to a tree] [then] the possessor will in time return once more in the citadel of fire and wind. 4–5. Writing on the possessed with ash and fixing him with mantra repeated a hundred and eight times, [the mantrin] should thrown water on his face. Repeating mantras and binding him to a pillar with a rope muttered over with mantras, [the mantrin] should fix [the demon]. 6. [Then] making a substitute body with rice flower (*priṣṭapratikṛtim*), he should invoke the demon into it, bringing it to life, [the mantrin] should destroy it with a knife. 7. [Then the mantrin] should cut the esoteric centres of the body (*marman*) with a trident and make blood flow if he has not [yet] freed the possessed from the possessor. 8. He should then offer the cut image anointed with black mustard into the fire pit, [then] abandoning the thousand [pieces in the fire] the burned demon flees.[93]

Here we have the mantrin identifying himself with Rudra, empoying mantras given in the text, writing mantras upon the possessed person, and even inscribing him with a trident to make blood flow from the secret centres (*marman*) known to Ayurveda. With these procedures the demons leave and return to their abode in fire or wind. Other procedures involve piercing the ersatz body (*puttali* or *piṣṭapratikṛti*) with sharp sticks.[94] Or the mantrin should 'write the demon' (*likhed graham* – the name) on the floor with charcoal and then, as before, pierce the body's centres (*marman*) with sticks of the neem tree. Either the 'crushing demon' dies or, having been released, he leaves immediately.[95] There is an ambiguity in this verse about who dies, especially as the demon is identified with the possessed person in the text. If these procedures fail, then the mantrin should make offerings (*bali*) such as grain and blood-water (*raktatoya*) to appease the demons.[96] The offering of 'blood-water' strongly supports the view that this text is from Kerala, where, even to this day, a thick substance of substitute blood, 'blood-water' (*guruti*) is offered to deities.[97] This substance is to be used to purify and protect the house; thus the mantrin should scatter offerings (*bali*) in all directions for the pacification (*śānti*) of all the bhūtas and to ensure liberation for the possessed and possessors alike.[98] We can read 'liberation' (*mokṣa*) as being brought back into the fold of textually sanctioned, Brahmanical control. The supernatural beings succumb to the power of scripture sanctioned by tradition, so the possessed succumb to tradition through its inscription on their bodies.

Possession thus happens to people generally of low social standing, such as women and low castes, or those who are in liminal conditions such as emotional distress. The text is an excellent example of the ways in which the body is entextualised. We have a detailed account of how the possessed body is constructed through ritual procedures and an account of the colonisation of the body by tantric, Brahmanical orthodoxy represented by the mantrin. The interiority of the first person is subsumed by a more powerful first person, and the 'I' comes to refer not to the everyday self but to a greater self defined within the parameters of the tradition. The body is colonised by textually defined supernatural beings, it is then recolonised by the Brahmanical tradition, tamed, controlled, and brought back into conformity through being entextualised in ways legitimised by a tantric, Brahmanical orthodoxy. Indeed the ritual procedures are familiar to us from other contexts, especially divinisation in the *dehaśuddhi* or *bhūtaśuddhi*. This inscription of the text on to the body is at times literal, with the subtle centres of the possessed being inscribed with Śiva's trident. The ritual procedures are tradition-specific – as we see from overlap with the *Kumāra-tantra* – showing how the body becomes the vessel for supernatural beings, in a way not dissimilar to the divinisation of the body in the tantric ritual process of the *bhūtaśuddhi*, but this process is controllable and unwanted entry by lower categories of supernatural agents can equally be affected through ritual means. The entextualisation of the body is the control of the body and arguably the community's self-policing of its boundaries, as well as giving expression to those otherwise excluded from mainstream channels of expression.

So far we have seen how divinisation functions as a theme at different levels of tantric civilisation outside of the individual practitioner. The king becomes divinised through tantric *abhiṣeka*; the representation of erotic bodies on temples walls are divinised; and the body in possession becomes divinised in the sense that an external power occupies it. Kingship, the temple and possession share this common theme of transformation through empowerment, and this empowerment is determined in text- and tradition-specific ways. One last area that needs be mentioned here is devotion. Devotion or bhakti as a particular form of interiority is not central to tantric discourse and practice generally, but it is undoubtedly present as is attested by devotional hymns to deities and the supplication of practitioners to their gods for the purposes of power and/or liberation. Moreover tantric themes have affected the wider devotional culture of medieval India in profound ways. There is not time to examine these now, but suffice it to suggest that erotic *bhakti*, such as that articulated in the *Bhāgavata-purāṇa* and the Gaudiya Vaiṣṇava tradition more widely, is pervaded by tantric ideas, not only seen in the centrality of tantric Vaiṣṇava theology in the form of the Pāñcarātra, but seen in the erotic devotion (*madhura/śṛṇgara bhakti*) of the late medieval Caitanya sect and the Gosvamins. Here devotion to Kṛṣṇa is akin to the devotion of lovers, and as the deity enters the practitioner through formal ritual structure in tantric daily ritual or in possession, so the deity is invited to enter into the devotee. The types of devotion articulated by rūpa Gosvamin in his *Bhaktirasamṛta sindhu*[99] are ways in which the body becomes entextualised. Indeed, this kind of devotionalism becomes explicitly fused with a left-hand ritual practice in the Vaiṣṇava Sahajiya sect.[100] The reverse is also true, that bhakti becomes influential and important in tantric traditions, especially the Pāñcarātra and Śaiva Siddhānta in the South, but also in monistic Śaivism.

We see from these examples that the body as structuring topos is closely connected to tantric revelation and the body's divinisation is closely linked to the text and the ritual construction of the body based on textual models. The body is central as a foundational metaphor in the history of tantric civilisation. More could be said about interface between Tantrism, especially possession, and *bhakti*, but the examples given here are sufficient to show that divinisation is a theme common to this culture that has lasted for a millennium. We must now leave these more general considerations and return to the particularity of text and tradition in order to show how text and body interrelate, and to show in the context of practice the specificity of the claim of the body as text.

PART II

The Body as Text

FIVE

The Pāñcarātra

ALTHOUGH there are considerable difficulties, we can perhaps claim that our textual sources demonstrate three general levels at which the tantric traditions operated. First, there is the level of the individual practitioner, performing rites outside of the public gaze, who has undergone a possibly secret initiation in order to gain, primarily, supernatural power and final liberation. Second, there is what we might call temple tantra, which in the past supported royal claims to identification with tantric deities and is concerned with the installation of icons in temples, the performance of formal, temple worship, and rites of passage including funeral rites. This temple tantra still exists in South India in the Śaiva Siddhānta tradition, in South Indian Śrī Vaiṣṇavism, and in Kerala where it is normative, temple Hinduism. Lastly we have popular religion, which is primarily concerned with the appeasing of ferocious deities, possession and exorcism. All of these layers of tantric practice involve the entextualisation of the body, and common ritual processes can be identified.

Although the vedic body forms the backdrop of tantric developments, the tantric traditions extend, modify and reject much of the vedic discourse about the body. While there are ideas in the tantric tradition that reflect the vedic, such as the theme that the body recapitulates the structure of the cosmos, some ideas and practices are prototypically tantric, such as the divinisation of the body and tantric mantras. The tantric traditions are aware of Brahmanical purity laws as articulated in the dharmaśāstra and either accept and appropriate these laws at some level of practice or consciously transgress them in particular rites as being irrelevant to power and salvation.

In this chapter I will begin to show in some textual detail, with reference to the Pāñcarātra, the tantric Vaiṣṇava tradition, how the body becomes inscribed by the text through which the practitioner internalises the tradition. The emanationist, hierarchical cosmology is reflected and enacted in the body in text-specific ways. Through an examination of this detailed example, we will be able to appreciate tantric ritual and soteriology in general, for to attain liberation is, broadly speaking, to trace a route back through the cosmos to its source, which is to trace a route through the body. This tracing a route through the body is the inscribing of tradition on to the body. While there are undoubtedly continuities from Brahmanical orthodoxy and orthopraxy, the specificity of the tantric traditions and their mutual differentiation lies in the way the body becomes the text. Understanding the entextualisation of the body allows us to see the commonality of process at work within tantrism and also the differentiation and particularity of tradition.

We begin our account with a description of an emanationist cosmology that is recapitulated in the body through ritual (both external and internal). The cosmos is mapped on to the body, not in an invariant way, but in different ways for different purposes in different texts. The entextualisation of the body is tradition- and text-specific, although the process is shared across traditions. This kind of mapping of the cosmos is of central importance for the tantric practitioner as it has soteriological consequences. Through symbolically mapping the cosmos in this way, the practitioner can retrace the emergence of the cosmos back to its source, the transcendent source of all phenomena. Historically much of this cosmology is derived from Sāṃkhya philosophy. Like Sāṃkhya the earliest texts and traditions are predominantly dualistic, or present a qualified dualism. There are no early texts that present an uncompromising monistic doctrine, as Sanderson has argued. Among the earliest texts are those of the Pāñcarātra, which intend to maintain some distinction between the transcendent Lord and his creation and creatures, even though by 'creation' we mean that the Lord acts upon already pre-existent matter and upon beginningless souls. Although these texts are tantric and centrally concerned with ritual, they are also pervaded with devotionalism (*bhakti*). Indeed, *bhakti* could be said to be an important dimension in the Pāñcarātra textual corpus, as Oberhammer has shown with regard to a devotional creation narrative forming the 'frame story' (*Rahmenerzählung*) to the ritual description of the *Paramasaṃhitā*. Indeed, as Oberhammer describes, one can connect this text with the Viśiṣṭādvaita tradition, with its central emphasis on grace, whereby the individual entrusts himself to the highest God knowing that he cannot contribute to his own salvation.[1] But while there may be a strong theistic metaphysics in these texts, they are concerned with the ritual construction of the body as divine in order to approach this deity and share the common ritual concerns of other Tantras. Let us take our first example from Pāñcarātra cosmology and ritual.

Emanationist Cosmology

Accounts of cosmology in the texts are emanationist, which means that lower levels of the cosmos are thought to emerge or emanate from the higher due to the action of the will of a transcendent being. These cosmologies are generally structured with different levels embedded within each other, such that, to use Isayeva's insightful remark in respect of the *Māṇḍukya Upaniṣad*, 'each higher level completely absorbs and incorporates all the ones below it'.[2] Let us illustrate this with a concrete example.

One of the most important texts of the tantric Vaiṣṇava revelation is the *Jayākhya-saṃhitā*, one of the Pāñcarātra's 'three gems', whose first chapters present an emanationist cosmology.[3] The *Jayākhya* contains one of the earliest and most elaborate representations of cosmology and its interface with the daily ritual sequence of the practitioner. The text must be dated prior to the Kashmir Śaiva author Utpalācārya (925–975 CE), who quotes it.[4] First, we have pure creation (*śuddha-sarga*), in which the transcendent Lord, the

Supreme Vāsudeva, manifests in different forms that have different cosmological functions. Below this we have intermediate creation, in which limiting constraints begin to operate on individual souls, followed by impure creation where souls are bound by the cosmic principles.[5] In chapter four of the *Jayākhya*, the sage Nārada asks the Lord (Bhagavat) to tell him about the pure creation and the Lord answers that the supreme absolute (*brahman*) is identical to the personal being of Vāsudeva, from whom emanate lower forms. Let the text speak for itself:

> [The ultimate reality] is non-distinct from Vāsudeva and other manifestations. Having a hundred-fold radiance of fire, sun and moon, Vāsudeva is the Lord, the truth of that [absolute], the supreme Lord. Agitating his own radiance through his own energy (*tejas*), the Lord whose form is light manifests the god Acyuta, like lightening, O Brahman. [Then] that Acyuta of firm radiance spreads his own form, dependent on Vāsudeva as a wisp of cloud (depends) on the summer heat. Then shaking himself he [in turn] produced the god Satya, whose body is shining, as the ocean [produces] a bubble. He is called the light made of consciousness who produces himself by means of himself [as the god] called Puruṣa who is great, an unending stream of light. That supreme Lord is [in turn] the support of all the [lower] gods, their inner controller, as the sky [is the support] of the stars. As a fire with its fuel sends forth a mass of sparks, O twice-born one, so the Supreme Lord, who is yet desireless, [sends forth manifestation].[6]

Here Vāsudeva (i.e. Kṛṣṇa, the son of Vāsudeva) emanates the forms of Acyuta, Satya and Puruṣa,[7] deities we are familiar with from the related Vaikhānasa tradition. The Pāñcarātra knows these as *vyūhas*[8] emanations, who in other Pāñcarātra literature possess the names of Vāsudeva's brother Saṃkarṣaṇa, his son Pradyumna and his grandson Aniruddha.[9] While in their essence these gods are non-distinct from Vāsudeva, each is an aspect of the supreme being with a cosmological function in the manifestation of lower worlds.[10] Vāsudeva has six pure qualities (*guṇa*), namely knowledge (*jñāna*), majesty (*aiśvarya*), power (*śakti*), strength (*bala*), energy (*vīrya*) and splendour (*tejas*), from which the *vyūha*s are made.

In other Pāñcarātra texts, after the pure creation comes a middle layer or 'mixed creation' containing the categories of lower material energy, the Māyā Śakti, along with the cosmic self of Puruṣa. In the

Jayākhya, this Puruṣa is not the *vyūha* but a lower manifestation conceptualised as the basis for all empirical beings in the lower order of creation. It is a 'beehive' (*kośa madhukṛta*) from which all individual souls (*jīva*) emanate, contaminated by the dust of beginningless karmic traces (like the scent of pollen[11]), and to which they return during the periodic destruction or reabsorption of the lower creation.[12] The universe in which they are born and which they inhabit is made up from Māyā Śakti, who generates the lower orders. In the *Lakṣmī-tantra* she is identified with the Goddess Mahā Lakṣmī as the power (*śakti*) of Puruṣa, herself divided into the three goddesses, Mahā Śrī, Mahā Kālī and Mahā Vidyā, as manifestations of the three cosmic qualities or *guṇa*s. Mahā Śrī is identified with a body made of qualities (*gauṇamaya vapus*) and the other two with a body of time (*kālamaya vapus*). This complex scheme is the result of the incorporation of an earlier system of twenty-four categories (*tattva*) in the Sāṃkhya tradition into the Pāñcarātra and an identification of abstract, cosmic principles with deities.

From Māyā emanates Prakṛti, the foundation of material creation, from whom emanates the 'great one' (*mahat*) (see below). From this is generated the 'I-maker' (*ahaṃkāra*) and thence the mind (*manas*) for dealing with worldly transaction, the five senses, five capacities for acting, the subtle elements (sound, touch, form, taste and smell) and the five material elements (space, air, fire, water and earth).[13] The individual soul is covered, as it were, by these emanations of Śakti and thereby entrapped. Thus liberation comes to be envisaged as the separation of the soul from this material entrapment through the grace of God.

What is significant about the Sāṃkhya categories is that they both represent stages in the development or unfolding of the cosmos and are also categories for the analysis of the person. There is both a cosmic and an individual function to the *tattva*s; a cosmic dimension which would seem to have been present from the very beginning of thinking in this way.[14] It is clear that there are difficulties in making the *tattva*s as an analysis of the person correspond to an analysis of cosmical unfolding. The first emergent principle from foundational matter (*prakṛti*) is the great one (*mahat*), which is usually identified with *buddhi*,[15] often translated as 'intelligence' but perhaps better rendered as 'higher mind' as its function is not only one of discrimination but it also has a cosmological function beyond the individual.[16] This might be reflected in its alternative name, 'the great one' (*mahat*). In the Sāṃkhya system of philosophy and in the Tantras, the *buddhi* contains within it the constraints that become operative at the lower levels. These constraints are called the *bhāva*s, which we might render as 'dispositions', and the *pratyayas*, we might render as 'motivations' or 'foundational conceptions', the dispositions being the cause of the foundational concepts.[17] The dispositions are listed as 'moral duty' (*dharma*), knowledge (*jñāna*), dispassion (*vairāgya*) and majesty (*aiśvarya*), along with their opposites, *adharma*, *ajñāna* and so on. The foundational conceptions are perfection (*siddhi*), contentment (*tuṣṭi*), powerlessness (*aśakti*) and error (*viparyaya*). All are contained within the *buddhi* and are themselves governed by the famous qualities (*guṇa*s) of lightness (*sattva*), passion (*rajas*) and dark inertia (*tamas*), which come into operation from within the material foundation (*prakṛti*).[18] Thus there is a complex causal sequence that constrains or limits a being to what it is. The qualities within the material foundation of the lower universe generate the dispositions within the *buddhi*, which in turn give rise to the foundational conceptions that govern a person.

From the *buddhi* the 'I-maker' (*ahaṃkāra*) is produced. This, under the sway of the *guṇas*, generates three forms which govern the lower evolutes, namely rajasic ahaṃkāra, which generates the worldly mind (*manas*) and the five senses; sattvic ahaṃkāra, which generates the five action capacities (talking, handling, walking, reproducing and eliminating waste); and tamasic ahaṃkāra, which generates the subtle elements (sound, touch, form, taste, and smell). These in turn generate the five material elements (space, air, fire, water and earth).[19]

In absorbing this ancient cosmological structure and complicating it through adding their own levels, the tantric traditions inherit a model of causation called 'transformation' (*pariṇāmavāda*), whereby an effect is a real transformation of its cause,[20] along with Sāṃkhya. In Sāṃkhya there is an eternal distinction between the individual self (*puruṣa*) and the material foundation (*prakṛti*), which the tantric traditions adopt but reinterpret within their own metaphysics. Thus in the Pāñcarātra we see that the puruṣa is reinterpreted to mean not the individual self, as in Sāṃkhya, but a cosmic self that is the basis or foundation of all particular selves, which absorbs those selves back at a dissolution of the cosmos and throws them out again at a creation. Unlike the atheistic Sāṃkhya, the Pāñcarātra claims that all this cosmic process is generated by a transcendent God, the Lord of the universe; while matter is generated out of his female energy, the souls retain some distinction from him even once they are liberated. While there is a sense in which the liberated soul becomes one with the Lord, the texts display a great deal of ambivalence about this and wish to maintain their ontological distinction. As Marion Rastelli observes with regard to the *Jayākhya-saṃhitā*, this is above all a philosophy of 'difference in identity' (*bhedābheda*) in which the self is not identical but a fragment (*aṃśa*) of the Lord.[21] Thus we read in the *Jayākhya* (quoted above) that manifestation is akin to sparks from a fire; the sparks partake of the same substance yet are also distinct. So the *Jayākhya* can say that although the Lord abides in distinctions, he is really one (*eka*).[22]

Clearly the Pāñcarātra is theistic in positing a transcendent Lord as the creator and source of the universe, and the individual, animating principle as a particle of that transcendent being, yet retaining some distinction. Although the Lord is one, this is no monism in which the totality of the transcendent is coextensive with the totality of the universe. In his essence (*svarūpa*) the Lord has no point of comparison (*anaupamya*), omniscient, omnipresent, beyond being (*sat*) and non-being (*asat*), he possesses all qualities yet is bereft of them; standing far away he is yet in the heart, and so on.[23] This apophatic language would not be out of place in Christianity and it conveys the utter transcendence of the theistic reality it proposes. In relation to this the self, constrained by the restrictions that govern the lower order universe, seems insignificant. Yet while the self's being is wholly dependent upon the transcendent theistic reality, Para Vāsudeva, it remains distinct in the face of his utter transcendence.

Having given an account of manifestation, the text then goes on to show how this is mapped on to the body in daily ritual procedures and that the cosmological scheme is not simply presented

Pāñcarātra cosmology

Transcendent Vāsudeva	**Pure Creation**
The vyūhas	↓
Vāsudeva	
Saṃkarṣaṇa/Acyuta	
Pradyumna/Satya	
Aniruddha/Puruṣa	

Further emanations as sub-vyūhas, incarnations (*avatāra*) and temple images (*arca*)

Puruṣa (source of bound souls)	Māyā (source of lower creation)	**Mixed Creation** ↓

The lower *tattvas*	**Impure Creation**

as information, but is used in ritual procedures and is thought to have soteriological effects. That is, the structure of the universe is part of the process of the soul's liberation, as the path to liberation is a path through this cosmological scheme. The 'map' presented in Pāñcarātra cosmology functions to show the practitioner a way through to transcendence.

The Purification of the Body[24]

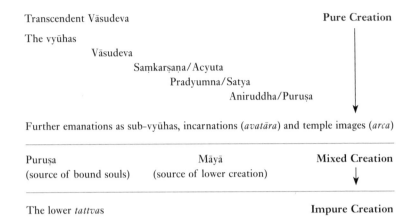

The very structure of the *Jayākhya* reflects the entextualisation of the body. First the text presents an account of the hierarchical cosmos along the lines of the description we have just seen, and second it presents the ritual pattern that the initiated practitioner must follow in his daily practice, broadly comprising, after purificatory ablutions (*snāna*), the purification of the elements within the body (*bhūtaśuddhi* or *dehaśuddhi*), the divinisation of body through imposing mantras upon it (*nyāsa*), internal worship of the deity (*antara/ mānasa-yāga*) performed purely in the imagination, followed by external worship (*bahya-yāga*) with offerings of flowers, incense and so on to the deity.[25] This general ritual structure is found in all tantric traditions. To illustrate the ways in which the body becomes text I will focus on the stages of this ritual process, the purification of the body, the divinisation of the body, mental or inner worship, followed by external worship. In order to explicate the point fully, it is necessary to consider the issue in greater detail.

The origins of the *bhūtaśuddhi* practice are unclear. The *Jayākhya* presents the fullest account of it in the tantric literature, although the purification of the elements is also found in Buddhist Vajrayāna ritual, although some Vajrayāna texts (the Anuttarayoga Tantras) are themselves derived from Śaiva prototypes.[26] The roots of the *bhūtaśuddhi* may, however, be much older. There are arguably two sources: offerings made into the sacrificial fire in vedic ritual, and early cosmological speculation of Sāṃkhya and proto-Sāṃkhya metaphysics. For example, the *Bṛhadāraṇyaka Upaniṣad* describes making offerings of ghee into the sacred fire to the earth, atmosphere and sky,[27] although making offerings to the sequence of elements does not occur. The general idea of the identification of the body with the cosmos is of course ancient, with textual antecedents in the Veda,[28] where, particularly in the Brāhmaṇas, correspondence (*bandhu*) between the sacrifice and the cosmos becomes central to ritual performance and speculation.[29] Second, its origins may arguably be found in early Buddhist meditation exercises (*kṛtsna/kasiṇa*) and the cultivation of the meditative sign (*nimitta*) that leads into meditative absorption (*dhyāna/jhāna*). Indeed, it is possibly here that we find the origins of the visualisation methods that were to become so important in the tantric traditions, both Hindu and Buddhist. These exercises are ten among forty objects of meditation described in Buddhaghosa's *Visuddhimagga*,[30] although they also occur in the Pāli canon itself.[31] The *kasiṇas* comprise the five elements and five colours,[32] focusing upon which leads into the higher levels of meditation. For example, the earth *kasiṇa* is a clay disc, an object that is concentrated upon until the image is internalised within consciousness without external support. In this way the *kasiṇa* is akin to the internally arising sign (*nimitta*), like an afterimage, which leads into *jhāna*.[33] Traces of these practices can perhaps be found in the *bhūtaśuddhi*.

In a Hindu context, the *bhūtaśuddhi*'s earliest occurrences are in the *Jayākhya* and in the Śaiva *Kāmikāgama*.[34] There is a passage in the *Netra-tantra*, a Śaiva text from Kashmir, which mentions the five elements in connection with the pots required for consecration (*abhiṣeka*) of the teacher (*ācārya*) and practitioner (*sādhaka*), although no ritual details are given, the text functioning more as a mnemonic of assumed knowledge on behalf of the reader.[35] In Śaiva Siddhānta a standard source for the *bhūtaśuddhi* is the *Somaśambhu-paddhati* (eleventh century CE), itself based on the *Kāmikāgama* and the *Acintyaviśvasādhākhya*, which, Brunner-Lachaux observes, follows Somaśambhu in places line by line.[36] The *Īśānaśivagurudeva-paddhati* follows Somaśambhu, as does the *Aghoraśivācārya-paddhati* (twelfth century CE). The term *bhūtaśuddhi* also occurs in other treatises of the Śaiva Siddhānta, including a text simply named the *Bhūtaśuddhi*.[37] Later the *bhūtaśuddhi* is found in medical or Ayurvedic practices within the regime of cleansing the body's impurities.[38] To demonstrate a common structure in the *bhūtaśuddhi* rite, and so to demonstrate a common structure of the body being inscribed by tradition, I shall follow the ritual procedure described in the *Jayākhya* and in the next chapter show parallels with the Śaiva material.

The *Bhūtaśuddhi* in the Tantric Revelation

In spite of the professed divergence of the Śaiva and Pāñcarātra systems and the desire of their protagonists to distance their traditions from each other, there is a high degree of overlap, not only in terms of theology, but especially at the level of ritual representation. This similarity of ritual process in our texts points to a ritual substrate common to the theologically distinct Pāñcarātra and Śaiva traditions. Although ritual contents in terms of mantras and deities vary, the sequence of daily and occasional rites cuts across sectarian distinctions and points to an almost independent life of ritual representation in these texts, and to the common structure of entextualising the body, although in tradition-specific ways.

Part of this textually represented ritual substrate are various hierarchical cosmologies which share the common pattern of lower forms emanating from higher, as described in the passage quoted above. A common scheme found in tantric texts is the 'six ways' (*ṣaḍadhvan*), which are parallel ritual courses through the cosmos inscribed on the body.[39] These ways incorporate the cosmological categories (*tattva*) and their division into five realms (*kalā*). In the Śaiva system we have thirty-six *tattvas*, which adds eleven Śaiva ones to the twenty-five Sāṃkhya ones, while the Pāñcarātra assumes only the Sāṃkhya categories, although it has cosmological functions analogous to the higher Śaiva ones, as we have seen. There is a common overall structure here of a pure, mixed and impure creation, although for the monistic Trika Śaivism the broad distinction is between the pure and the impure creations. While these cosmologies are theologically important – as can be seen in Bhojadeva's linking of higher beings to different levels of the cosmos in the *Tattvaprakāśa*[40] – their primary importance is as ritual rather than theological entities; cosmology has a primarily ritual function in these traditions.[41] This can be illustrated particularly well in the *bhūtaśuddhi* sequence where the cosmos is mapped on to the body and dissolved, as the lower levels of the cosmos are dissolved into the higher during the cosmic dissolution (*pralaya*). The terminology here is that of the *tattvas* of Sāṃkhya in which the gross elements (*bhūta*) that comprise the physical world are dissolved into the subtle elements (*tanmātra*) that are their source. The purification of the body through dissolving its constituent elements into their cause would seem to be a characteristically tantric practice.[42]

Within all tantric ritual, visualisation of ritual action and deities is of central importance in daily and occasional rites, and in both the Pāñcarātra and Śaiva Siddhānta to perform a visualisation is to perform a mental action that has soteriological effects. Once initiated, the Śaiva or Vaiṣṇava adept in these cults was expected to perform obligatory daily worship. For the Pāñcarātrin his practice meant following the Pāñcarātra saṃskāras, whereby his body was inscribed with tradition by being branded at initiation (*tapa*) with a hot iron discus (*cakra*), being given a ritual name, reciting mantra, and engagaing in ritual practice (*yāga*).[43] The Pāñcarātrin's daily observances involved five obligatory acts adopted from vedic orthopraxy, characterised by Gupta as the recitation of laudatory verses or *stotras* (*brahmayajña*), daily liturgy (*devayajña*), making offerings to malevolent supernatural beings (*bhūtayajña*), making offerings to the ancestors (*pitṛyajña*) and the feeding of (Vaiṣṇava) guests (*nṛyajña*).[44] The Saiddhāntika similarly follows the orthoprax injunctions of the dharmaśāstra, performing rites at the junctures (*saṃdhyā*) of the day, particularly the *pūjā* at dawn (as do the Pāñcarātrins).[45] The purpose of this daily rite, apart from its being a sign of the devotee's adherence to the cult of his initiation, was to enable him eventually to destroy the limiting factors (*mala*) which constrain his soul (*jīva*) within the cycle of reincarnation (*saṃsāra*) and so to be ready for liberation (*mokṣa*) by receiving the grace of the Lord (Śiva or Viṣṇu) at his death. In this sense the Pāñcarātra and Śaiva Siddhānta are very different from the monistic traditions of non-Saiddhāntika Śaivism, as Sanderson has demonstrated.[46]

The *Jayākhya* describes four classes of adept, the *samayajña*, *putraka*, *sādhaka* and *ācārya*,[47] each having undergone a particular ablution (*abhiṣeka*) as part of his initiation (*dīkṣā*).[48] As other texts, the *Jayākhya* has the male practitioner in mind, although it does allow women initiation, aligning them with śūdras.[49] Chapter 10 of the *Jayākhya* is devoted to the *bhūtaśuddhi* and the spiritual ascent of the soul (*jīva*) ready for the creation of the divinised body.[50] Through symbolically destroying the physical or gross body, the adept can create a pure, divinised body (*divyadeha*) with which to offer worship to the deities of his system. He does this first only in imagination and second in the physical world, for – as in all tantric systems – only a god can worship a god. The textual representation of the *bhūtaśuddhi* is set within a sequence in which the physical or elemental body (*bhautika-śarīra*) is purified and the soul ascends from the heart through the body, and analogously through the cosmos, to the Lord Nārāyaṇa located at the crown of the head. The text presents us with a detailed account of this process, which can be summarised as follows.

Going to a pure, unfrequented, but charming place, the adept offers obeisance to the Lord and pays homage to the lineage of teachers (*gurusantati*), and having received the mental command (*mānasī-ājñā*) from the Lord and lineage of teachers, he is ready to perform mental action (*mānasīṃ nirvahet... kriyām*).[51] The practitioner purifies his hands with the weapon (*astra*) mantra and purifies the place by visualising Viṣṇu, like a thousand suns, vomiting flames from his mouth. The earth then appears as if baked by the fire of mantra.[52] In this process we see the construction of a 'ritual body' in opposition to the 'genetic' or 'biological' body, which, in its non-ritual state, is impure (*malina*), subject to decay, not autonomous (*asvatantra*), and made from blood and semen (*retoraktodbhava*).[53] The non-purified body is the opposite of the Lord's body possessed of the six qualities.[54] This purification of the body entails the construction of the ritual body; a process which had begun with bathing and which continues with the selection of the place and the placing of a blade of sacred grass, flower or leaf in the tuft of hair, with mantra.[55] The symbolic destruction of the body takes place through dissolving the elements of the cosmos within it. As in the final dissolution of the cosmos, when each element or category retracts into its source, so in daily ritual this process is recapitulated within the adept's body. The actual process occurs through linking together sequences of syllables to form mantras associated with the elements, such as the OṂ ŚLĀṂ PṚTHIVYAI HUṂ PHAṬ corresponding to the earth element, which are modified for each element, replacing the seed syllable (*bīja*) ŚLĀṂ with ṢVĀṂ, HYĀṂ and KṢMĀṂ as necessary.[56] Each of the elements is visualised in a certain way, associated with particular symbols, and as pervading a particular part of the body in a hierarchical sequence. Each element is in turn symbolically destroyed in the imagination through being absorbed into its mantra and into the energies (*śakti*) of the powers (*vibhava*) or subtle elements (*tanmātra*) which gave rise to it. For example, the *Jayākhya* describes the purification of the earth element as follows:

> [The practitioner] should visualise a quadrangular, yellow earth, marked with the sign of thunder, connected with the five, sound etc. [i.e. the five subtle elements *śabda*, *sparśa*, *rūpa*, *rasa* and *gandha*] and filled with trees and mountains, adorned with oceans, islands, good rivers and walled towns. He should visualize [that earth] entering his own body from the outside with an inhaled breath, and uttering the mantra he should imagine it as tranquilized, pervading in due order from the knees to the soles of the feet by means of the retained breath, O best of twice born ones. Then, [the earth is] gradually dissolved in its own mantra-form, and this mantra-king [dissolved] in the energy of smell. After that he should emit the energy of smell with the exhaled breath.[57]

This process of inhaling the visualised element that pervades a particular area of the body, dissolving it into its mantra, then into its subtle cause, and exhaling it, is followed with the other elements. The energy of smell having been exhaled into the substratum of water, the water element is then imagined as having the form of a half-moon, marked by a lotus, and containing all aquatic media – the oceans, rivers, the six flavours (*rasa*) – and aquatic beings. Inhaling the image, it pervades the adept's body from the thighs to the knees and is dissolved into its mantra, then into the energy of taste (*rasaśaki*), which he emits with the exhaled breath.[58] The same process occurs with the remaining elements. The triangle of fire containing all fiery and bright things, including beings at higher levels of the cosmos with self-luminous bodies (*svaprakāśa-śarīra*), is inhaled, pervades the body from the navel to where the water element had begun, is dissolved into its mantra, into the energy of form (*rūpaśakti*), and exhaled as before.[59] Similarly the air element is inhaled, pervades from throat to navel and is exhaled as the energy of touch (*sparśaśakti*).[60] This merges into space (*ākāśa*), which, in the same way, is inhaled, pervades to the aperture of the absolute (*brahmarandhra*), dissolves into its mantra, then into the energy of sound (*śabdaśakti*), and is emitted through the aperture at the crown of the head (*brahmarandhra*).[61] All this is accomplished by the power of the mantras of the elements. Having left the body through the *brahmarandhra*, individualised consciousness (*caitanya jīvabhūta*) has transcended the 'cage of the elements' (*bhūtapañjara*) by rising through the stages of space, the stars, lightening, the sun and moon, stages which are themselves found in the Upaniṣads.[62] In this way the soul ascends in imagination up the central channel of the body (*suṣumṇā*) from the heart, through the levels of the cosmos (*pada*), to the Lord at the crown of the head. He is envisaged in his supreme body (*paravigraha*) as a mass of radiance (*tejopuñja*) standing within a circle of light;[63] a standard identification of Nārāyaṇa with the sun. The joy that arises is the supreme energy of Viṣṇu (*parā vaiṣṇavī śakti*)[64] and results in a state of higher consciousness (*samādhi*) that is the ineffable freedom from ideation (*saṅkalpanirmukta avācya*).[65]

He enjoys this state of bliss, but the process of purification is not yet complete. Having transcended the subtle elements along with the gross body, the sādhaka should burn it with the fire arising from his feet, generated by the power of his mantra. All that remains is a pile of ashes that are then washed away to the quarters in his imagination by a flood of milky water arising from his meditation.[66] With the universe of his imagination now filled with the ocean of milk, a lotus emerges out of it containing Nārāyaṇa, whose essence is his mantra, the truth of the six cosmic paths.[67] The sādhaka's body, identified with Nārāyaṇa, is purified, freed from old age and death and has the appearance of pure crystal and the effulgence of a thousand suns and moons.[68] Having purified his body in this way, his soul enters the inner lotus of this subtle body (*puryaṣṭaka*) through the aperture of the absolute from which it had earlier vacated its residence. With a calm awareness (*prasannadhī*) the adept is ready to perform worship of the deity (*yajed devam*);[69] that is, ready to perform the divinisation of the body through imposing mantras upon it, followed by mental sacrifice (*mānasayāga*) and external sacrifice (*bāhyayāga*), described in the following chapters.

The Divinisation of the Body

The divinisation of the body is a crucial juncture in tantric worship, for through this procedure the practitioner identifies himself with the deities of the tradition. With the divinisation of the body through imposing or fixing mantras upon it, we see the formation of a body in ways specific to text and tradition. It is perhaps in the divinisation process that we see the particularity of the entextualisation and the variable indexicality that constitutes subjectivity in these traditions. The mantras and deities imposed on the body are specific to the particular text, and the body is thus formed in a text-specific way. The process of imposing mantras on the body is called *nyāsa*, from the verbal root *ny* plus *as*, to put or cast down,[70] within whose semantic range is to place something in a picture, to paint and depict. The practitioner touches the requisite part of the body and recites the correct mantra. The *Jayākhya* is in no doubt about the importance of this procedure as it makes the practitioner 'equal to the god of gods' (*devadevasama*), fearless, and having power over unexpected death.[71]

The simple plank laid on the ground upon which the practitioner is seated becomes the 'throne' (*āsana*) for the divinity he will become. Beginning with the hands, specific mantras from the pantheon of the *Jayākhya* are imposed on all the fingers. Thus the root mantra (*mūlamantra*) along with the form mantra (*mūrtimantra*) (namely *oṃ kṣīṃ kṣiḥ namaḥ, Nārāyaṇāya viśvātmane hrīṃ svāhā*) should first be fixed on the right thumb followed by the other gods beginning with the forefinger. The *śakti mantras*, comprising the four Vaiṣṇava goddesses Lakṣmī, Kīrti, Jayā and Māyā in their sound form as their mantras, are placed on the fingers. Thus the *Lakṣmī mantra* is placed on the ring finger, the Kīrti on the middle finger, Jayā on the ring finger, and Māyā on the little finger. Next the *aṅga mantras* are imposed on the hands in reverse order from this procedure, the 'heart' (*hṛt*) mantra on the little finger, followed by the 'head' (*śiras*), 'tuft' (*śikhā*), 'armour' (*kavaca*), to the 'weapon' (*astra*) on the thumb and the 'eye' (*netra, locana*) on all the fingertips. This is followed by imposing further sets on mantras on the hands, the *vaktra mantras* comprising the deities Nṛsimhā, the man-lion incarnation of Viṣṇu; Kapila, the founding sage of the Sāṃkhya tradition identified with Viṣṇu; and Varāha, the boar incarnation. The 'marking' or *lāñchana mantras* comprise the objects held by Viṣṇu such as the conch, discus, and club, themselves regarded as deities, and the secondary, *upāṅga mantras* comprise the all important *vyūhas*, the emanations Vāsudeva, Saṅkarṣana, Pradyumna, and Aniruddha along with Satya. All of these are finally sealed with the pervading, seven-syllable mantra that is imposed over them all.[72]

With the hands divinised, the practitioner goes on to place mantras of the same deities throughout the body, on the head, eyes, ears, mouth, shoulders, hands (again), buttocks, heart, back, navel, hips, knees and feet.[73] For example, Lakṣmī and Kīrti are fixed on the right and left shoulders with Jayā on the right hand and Māyā on the left.[74] This stage of the process is completed with the great seven-syllable mantra of Nārāyaṇa being applied to the body from head to foot, covering and protecting it like armour. Indeed, Nārāyaṇa is the inner support of all the mantras, all the deities.[75] Finally the practitioner is fully divinised and identified with Viṣṇu–Nārāyaṇa. He visualises himself as Viṣṇu possessing the six divine qualities (*guṇa*) of the

Pāñcarātra divinity, namely knowledge (*jñāna*), majesty (*aiśvarya*), power (*śakti*), strength (*bala*), energy (*vīrya*) and splendour (*tejas*).[76] His ritual action has ensured the identification of himself, his everyday indexical-I, with the absolute divine subjectivity of his god. His ego (*ahaṃkāra*) is ritually transformed into the absolute subjectivity of Viṣṇu, and thus he can say at the end of the divinisation process 'I am the Lord Viṣṇu, I am Nārāyaṇa, Hari, and I am Vāsudeva, all-pervading, the abode of beings, without taint.'[77] Divinised in this way, the practitioner can proceed to inner worship and finally external worship of his god.

With this ritual sequence we are presented with an excellent example of the way the body becomes the text in tantric traditions. The practitioner imposes deities as mantras upon his body and these mantras and deities are text- and tradition-specific. While the material of the *Jayākhya* is recapitulated to a large extent in the *Lakṣmī-tantra*, the text is unique in its full explication of the ritual process of the identification of the practitioner with the universe and divinity. While the process, as I argue, is common to tantric traditions, the content is always text- and tradition-specific. Thus the initiate into the Pāñcarātra, specifically the *Jayākhya-saṃhitā*, becomes divinised by Pāñcarātra deities through Pāñcarātra mantras.

This divinisation of the body in a ritual sequence furthermore functions to expand the practitioner's subjectivity. Once again we see how indexicality is variable and the subject of first person predicates, the indexical-I of everyday transaction, becomes expanded to the cosmic subjectivity of Viṣṇu. It is this indexical variability that is important in the ritual sequence that is directly linked to the entextualisation of the body. With the Pāñcarātra there is a potential theological problem in that Viṣṇu–Nārāyaṇa is thought to be ontologically distinct from the devotee, and this would generally seem to be the case, but at the level of ritual this theological desire for separation is eroded. We are dealing here with a tradition that might be characterised as having both monistic and theistic or dualistic dimensions, or, as its later theological articulation has it, a theology of 'qualified non-dualism' (*viśiṣṭādvaita*). The Lord is transcendent in himself (and essentially unknowable in his inner essence, as Rāmānuja claims) but is known in the ritual process. The question of the relation between doctrine and ritual in the tantric traditions is complex, but the evidence of the *Jayākhya* and other texts indicates a level of processual invariance between traditions. The pattern of ritual remains constant, but is filled out with text- and tradition-specific content, especially the mantras. The theological distinction between self and transcendent Lord is suspended in the ritual process and the subjectivity of the practitioner becomes coterminous with the subjectivity of the Lord, an identification that is created and enacted in ritual, in the entextualisation of the body. The ritual process continues with inner worship.

Inner Worship

The *Jayākhya* describes a process of visualisation for establishing the supreme Lord within the heart envisaged as a throne (*antara-mānasa-yāga*). During the inner worship, the practitioner visualises the hierarchical cosmos in the forms of deities located within his own body. The account that follows is from the *Jayākhya*, although an almost identical account is found in the *Lakṣmī-tantra*. Rastelli shows how the throne, as visualised in this sequence, also occurs in other Saṃhitās.[78]

We have here a constructed vision of the body in which the hierarchical universe pervades the practitioner's body from the genitals to the heart.[79] First, the power of the earth, the *ādhāra-śakti*, is mapped on to the penis; Rastelli notes that that this power corresponds to the famous Goddess Kuṇḍalinī,[80] although she is not explicitly mentioned in the *Jayākhya*. Above her is the 'fire of time' (*kālāgni*), then the Tortoise (*kūrma*) bearing the insignia of Viṣṇu, the discus and club. Above him is the cosmic snake Ananta, upon which Viṣṇu is represented as lying, in traditional mythology; above him is the Earth goddess and above her at the level of the navel is the ocean of milk. Out from this arises a white lotus which gives rise to sixteen supports of the throne. These comprise the eight dispositions (*bhāva*) of the *buddhi*, the four sacred scriptures or Vedas and the four ages of the world (*yuga*). They support a white lotus, upon which are the sun, moon and fire. Above these, although not explicitly named in this sequence in the *Jayākhya*, is the 'throne of being' (*bhāvāsana*), upon which rests the vehicle of Viṣṇu, the great mythological bird Gāruḍa, and the boar incarnation Varāha. Viṣṇu is invoked in due course upon his mount. Each of these visions is in turn identified with one of the hierarchical categories or *tattva*s of the Sāṇkhya system, with the addition of two more *tattva*s, time (*kāla*) and lordship (*īśvaratva*), making a total of twenty-seven. I shall cite a long passage of the constructed vision in the *Jayākhya* in order to present some flavour of these ritual, visionary texts, and in order that we can demonstrate in concrete terms the entextualisation of the body. The visualisation in the *Jayākhya* is described as follows:

> So having formerly become Viṣṇu [through the purification of the body previously described], the practitioner should then worship Viṣṇu with the mental sacrifice. [1] Imagining [the area] between the penis and the navel filled with four parts, one should visualise the energy whose form is the earth (Ādhāra-śakti), above that the fire of time [Kālāgni], above that Ananta, and then the Earth Goddess [Vasudha Devī]. [2–3b] From the place of the 'bulb' (*kaṇḍa*) to the navel is divided into four parts. Visualising the ocean of milk in the navel and then a lotus arising [out of it], extending as far as a thousand petals and whirling with a thousand rays [of light], having the appearance of a thousand rays, he should fix the throne on its back. [3c–5b] The fourfold [dispositions] dharma, knowledge, detachment, and majesty, descend by means of their own mantras to the four [directions] of Fire [the south east] and so on [south west, north west and north east], fixing those four up to the abode of the Lord Īśāna [the north east]. On the four feet of the throne they are white, with lion faces, but the forms of men in their body and possessing exceeding strength. [5c–7] The parts from the eastern direction up to the northern abode are fixed with the opposites of dharma, knowledge, detachment, and majesty. These are of human form, blazing like the red bandhuka flower. [8–9b] The four [scriptures] the Ṛg-veda and so on have the form of a horse-man, are yellow, and [situated] in between the east and the direction of the Lord [north-east], between the east and the direction of Fire [the south east], between the south-west and Varuṇa [the west], and between the wind [north-west] and Varuṇa [the west]. [9c–10] The group of ages, namely Kṛta and so on, have the form of a bull-man, are black, and are located in the directions between Īśāna [north-east] and Soma [north], between Antaka [another name for Yama, the south] and Agni [south-east], between Yama [south] and the demon [Yakṣasa, the south-west], and between the Moon [the north]

> and the wind [north-west]. [11–12b] They all have four arms; with two they support the throne and with two they make obeisance to the Lord of the universe. [12c–13b]
>
> Above them he should fix first a white lotus [and then] threefold [forms, namely sun moon and fire], way above with those mantras, arising from himself and previously articulated, O Narada. On the back of that he should establish both the King of Birds and the Boar. Having imagined [the area] from the navel to the heart pervaded by five equal sections, he should worship the mantra-throne. [13c–15].[81]

In this complex ritual process the structure of the body is made to correspond to the structure of the cosmos: the body becomes an index of the cosmos, which, as we shall see, is itself conceptualised in terms of the body. But this is a representation always mediated by the text. The cosmos is represented in the text and the cosmos within the body is represented in the text. The enactment of this correspondence in daily ritual therefore makes the body conform to the text. We can understand the text as body more clearly by paying attention to the language of the texts themselves, particularly their indexicality, and through the processes that are involved in their reading.

External Worship

After creating himself as the deity, inscribing the body with the text in visualisation and imposing mantras upon it, the practitioner is ready to perform external worship (*bāhya-yāga*), making offerings to the deity in the physical world. The *Jayākhya* raises the question that the performance of external worship may seem superfluous,[82] and to the question as to why external worship should be performed after the internal the *Lakṣmī-tantra* says that while inner worship removes karmic traces (*vāsanā*) from internal causes, external worship removes karmic traces from external causes.[83] The *Jayākhya* describes the construction of a diagram (*maṇḍala*) in which to house the deity for the purpose of worship. Offerings are gathered together and Nārāyaṇa's presence along with his retinue of deities is invoked through mantra and visualisation and installed in the *maṇḍala*. Incense and food are offered to the deity, along with bell sounds and so on – in other words, a standard *pūjā* for a Hindu deity. Mantra repetition is performed with a rosary (*akṣamālā*),[84] followed by the fire offerings (*homa*) made into the fire-pit (*kuṇḍa*), as would occur in a standard Brahmanical rite.[85] Some concluding rites round off the ceremony and the practitioner is enjoined not to forget the Lord.

The ritual procedure for the initiate presented in the *Jayākhya-saṃhitā* follows a standard pattern that in some sense shows the conservative nature of tantric tradition in following a textually prescribed ritual procedure and also shows the continuities with standard, Brahmanical practice in the early medieval period. The composers of the *Jayākhya* and the practitioners who followed the text were not radicals trying to disrupt the Brahmanical system, but practitioners upholding the traditional values of their community through participating in the rites. The tantric Pāñcarātrin saw his tradition as complementing and completing the vedic, and the deity and practice of his cult as ensuring salvation. Through entextualising the body in ritual he is making himself conform to the tradition and attempting to undergo a transformation in text-specific ways. We will look at further examples of this from the Śaiva tradition before going on to present an analysis of some of this material showing how the indexical-I becomes identified with the I implied in the texts.

SIX

Śaiva Siddhānta

In the texts of the Śaiva Siddhānta, the central tantric Śaiva tradition which provides the normative rites, cosmology and theological categories, we find a similar process occurring as that in the Pāñcarātra. The Śaiva texts prescribe not only ritual procedures along with their theological justification but behaviour for a whole way of life. The texts lay down details of how tradition is internalised and how the narrative of a life is to be made to conform to it through a ritual pattern occurring over a lifetime, through control of the general bodily habitus, and through developing tradition-specified codes of conduct.

The ritual manuals *Somaśambhu-paddhati* and *Īśānaśivagurudeva-paddhati* (which quotes the former), are separated from the *Jayākhya* by at least a couple of centuries, and their origins are in different parts of the subcontinent: the *Jayākhya* is probably from the Kashmir region,[1] Somaśambhu (second half of the eleventh century CE) was the abbot of a monastery at Golaka (*golakī-maṭha*) in South India, probably in Tamil Nadu or the Telugu region, himself in a lineage of compilers of ritual manuals;[2] and the *Īśānaśivagurudeva-paddhati*, which postdates Somaśambhu, is probably from Kerala.[3] Considering the regional, temporal and cultic diversity of these texts, it is therefore very striking that such common process occurs at the level of ritual representation as, while there is a line of development from Somaśambhu to Īśānaśivagurudeva, there is no such direct historical link with the JS. While we need to raise the question as to whether a repeated ritual sequence that shares a structural process with another text is the *same*, there is clear textual evidence that the texts follow a sequence of purification of place and body, divinisation of the body, inner worship followed by external worship. We are arguably looking in the medieval tantric traditions at a shared pattern of ritual behaviour, which may be accompanied by different cosmological terms and a different understanding of precisely what is occurring. The monist theologian Abhinavagupta, for example, claims in his commentary on the *Parātrīśikā* that the ritual sequence in the text should be understood as occurring within consciousness itself,[4] thereby critiquing the Śaiva Siddhānta view that ritual itself is efficacious in liberation, and raising the question as to whether a ritual sequence that appears similar or identical at a surface level is nevertheless quite different because of the different metaphysics underlying it. While this is a valid point, I would simply wish to claim that at a descriptive phenomenological level there are shared ritual terminologies and processes that suggest that in terms of ritual action there is a constant pattern across traditions even though there may be a divergent theological superstructure. Indeed, more than this, Hélène Brunner has convincingly argued that three Tantras seem to share a common ritual inheritance with regard to daily Śaiva ritual, namely the *Svacchanda-tantra*, the *Mṛgendra-tantra* and the *Kāmikāgama*. The *Svacchanda* is purportedly non-dualist and from the north, while the *Mṛgendra* and *Kāmika* are from the south and dualistic, yet they all participate in a common ritual heritage which is later described by Somaśambhu and those who base their own manuals on his. Indeed, Brunner observes that the three Tantras form the base of modern Śaiva ritual in the south, as can be witnessed in the Śaiva temples of Tamil Nadu.[5]

To illustrate the ritual process let us begin, as we did with the Pāñcarātra, with cosmology in the Śaiva Siddhānta, or how the cosmos is mapped on to the body in the ritual process, which is a mapping of the self and placing of the self in a cosmological context. While the Pāñcarātra used the Sāṃkhya categories, the Śaiva Siddhānta developed this much more, adding eleven Śaiva categories or *tattvas* to the twenty-five Sāṃkhya ones. The pattern of supreme, mixed and impure creation that we find in some Pāñcarātra texts we also find in the Śaiva Siddhānta. Following the pattern of the previous chapter, we will begin with the cosmological account in a Śaiva Siddhānta as presented in Bhojadeva's *Tattvaprakāśa* and Bhaṭṭa Rāmakaṇṭha's commentary on the *Kiraṇa-tantra*. We will then be in a position to move on to an account of ritual, showing how the body becomes populated with the cosmic hierarchy; in the terminology I have developed here, how the body becomes entextualised and the cosmos mapped on to the self.

Śaiva Siddhānta Doctrine

Doctrinally the Śaiva Siddhānta is 'dualistic' in maintaining an ontological distinction between self and transcendent Lord, though it might more accurately be called pluralistic in maintaining not only this distinction, but a distinction between self, Lord and universe which itself comprises innumerable particularities (although these particularities stem from a common substrate).[6] Bhojadeva (*c.* 1000–1050)[7] in his *Illumination of the Categories* (*Tattvaprakāśa*) sums up the doctrine in his opening verses, that in the Śaiva scriptures (*śaivāgama*) the principal topic is the triad of Lord (*pati*), bound soul or beast (*paśu*), and universe or bond (*pāśa*).[8] The soul is likened to a cow tethered by a rope, to be freed from its tether by the Lord. This bond has five components, which the commentator Śrī Kumāradeva, citing a scripture, lists as pollution (*mala*), action (*karma*), illusion-power (*māyā*), the universe, that arises from that illusion (*māyotthamakhilam jagat*) and the power of concealing (*tirodhānakarī śaktiḥ*).[9] The innumerable souls, although in reality distinct, are bound within the universe from which they may be freed (*mukta*) by Śiva's grace (*prasāda*). Once freed they realise themselves to be Śivas or to be like or equal to Śiva (*śivatulya*, *śivasamāya*), but they remain ontologically distinct. Only Śiva has always been free (*anādimukta*).[10]

The general cosmological function of the five components of *pāśa* is to bind souls into the cycle of transmigration through the innumerable worlds of the cosmos. Bhojadeva – as Śaiva Siddhānta texts generally – classifies kinds of souls according to their degree of entrapment by these bonds, namely (and I follow Goodall's reading here[11]) those who are separated from fetters because of knowledge or consciousness (*vijñāna-kevala*), but still entrapped by impurity (*mala*); those who are separated from fetters due to the cosmic dissolution (*pralaya-kevala*); those who are entrapped by both impurity and action (*karma*); and those who are not separated from all bonds and possess the power of limited action (*sakala*), entrapped by all three – pollution, action and illusion-power (*māyā*).[12] The first two of these categories are also known by the names *vijñānākala* or *vijñānakevalin* and *pralayākala* or *pralayākevalin*.[13] The degree of entrapment is their degree of impurity. Rāmakaṇṭha in his commentary says that the term *paśu* only refers to those souls (*ātman*) who are subject to impurity (*samala*). Of these, he says, there are two types, those who have the force called *kalā* and those who do not. Those who possess the power of *kalā* are in turn of two types, those with subtle bodies (*sūkṣma-deha*) and those with gross bodies (*sthūla-deha*). Those without *kalā* are also of two types, those without *kalā* because of knowledge or higher awareness, the vijñānākevalins, and those without it because of cosmic dissolution, the pralayākevalins.[14] The term *kalā* in the sense here is rendered by Goodall as 'power of limited action', although it is also used on a broader cosmological canvas to refer to levels of the hierarchical cosmos within which the *tattva*s operate (see below).[15] This power of limited agency shows that the sakala souls have the power of action and can accumulate new karma through their action in the lower worlds, while the vijñāna and prayala souls, on this account, are devoid of the power of agency and only reap the fruits of their actions.

The consciousness-only souls are further subdivided by Bhoja into those whose impurity is completely finished (*samāptakaluṣa*) and those for whom it is not (*asamāptakaluṣa*). Out of the former Śiva makes eight 'Lords of Wisdom' (*vidyeśa* or, more commonly, *vidyeśvara*) and out of the latter a countless number of mantras.[16] There are a couple of problems here in that if the eight Lords are free, then in some sense they are not entrapped by the power of impurity, yet in order for them to act they need to be embodied, although their bodies are pure and not made of *māyā*, unlike the pralayakevalins which are held in the worlds of *māyā*.[17] These eight Lords are highly significant in cosmological terms, for through them Śiva creates or impels the lower levels of creation. In his commentary, Aghoraśiva names them as Ananta, Sūkṣma, Śivottama, Ekanetra, Ekarudra, Trimūrti, Śrīkaṇṭha and Śikhaṇḍin, who are qualified to perform the five actions in the lower worlds (of creation, maintenance, destruction, concealing and revealing).[18] Among them Ananta is the most important as Śiva's agent or regent. Like the rest of the Vidyeśvaras, says the *Kiraṇa-tantra*, his body is pure (*śuddhadeha*), he is omniscient (*sarvajñā*) and he reveals all the scriptures.[19] In his commentary Rāmakaṇṭha says that the vidyeśvaras teach all the Śaiva Siddhānta scriptures. Ananta has a body simply because he has the cosmological function of the creation of lower worlds, or more specifically the stimulation of *māyā* to evolve. His body is therefore 'pure' in not being made of *māyā* but being made from a pure origin (*śuddhayonimaya*) which is not due to the results of past action (*akarmaja*).[20] While these eight Lords express Śiva's will, they do not appear to have agency themselves but only the agency of Śiva; they are free of *kalā*, the power of limited agency in the lower worlds.

Bhoja divides the dissolution-only beings in a similar fashion to the Vidyeśvaras, into those whose pollution and karma have matured and so enter liberation and those whose pollution and karma have not matured and who exist as subtle bodies.[21] Presumably the sense here is that these two kinds refer to beings who, because of their karma, have become pralayakevalins and who will either, in the course of time, leave that state and go into final liberation from there or return to the lower worlds, being born in wombs due to the impulse of karma, although Aghoraśiva observes that those whose *mala* has matured enter liberation through the door of the descent of power (*śaktipāta*).[22] Indeed, he quotes a text that says that liberated pralayakevalins become Lords of worlds (*bhuvaneśāḥ*). The souls with limited agency (*sakala*), who have all three impurities, inhabit the lower worlds of creation, although they too include divine beings. Among them, says Bhoja, Śiva makes a hundred and eighteen Lords of mantra (*mantreśa*), linked to the power of limited agency, higher powers which animate mantras as sound formulas in this world.[23]

The cosmological function and consistency of accounts of these levels of beings are not always clear in our sources; there is some variation between, for example, the dualist Śaiva Siddhānta account exemplified by Bhoja and the monistic 'Kashmiri' Śaiva doctrine seven experients, exemplified by Kṣemarāja,[24] whose origin is the *Mālinīvijayottara-tantra*. But the point that is important for our purposes is that this hierarchy of souls, graded in accordance with their degree of pollution, their subtlety, and power as agents of Śiva, is tied into a system of ritual. The souls whose pollution has matured (*paripākamala*), says Bhoja, Śiva joins to the highest category or level of the cosmos (*śiva-tattva*) through the descent of power (*śaktipāta*) at initiation (*dīkṣā*) when he takes on the form of a teacher or master (*ācārya*).[25] Aghoraśiva quotes a text that says that, on account of a strong descent of power (*tivraśaktipāta*) through the master, the lost soul (*saṃsārin*) is not reborn again but becomes filled and pervaded with the condition of being Śiva (*śivatva*).[26] This condition of being Śiva, Śiva-ness or equality with Śiva (*śivatulya, śivasamāya*) is the purpose of the bound soul's existence; without being joined to the structures of the Śaiva Siddhānta tradition through the grace of Śiva, they remain wandering through the manifold universe according to the fruits of their actions. Indeed, if the universe has a purpose, for texts such as the *Mṛgendrāgama* and *Kiraṇa-tantra* it is to give souls experience in order that in due course they may achieve liberation; the purpose of the universe is to free bound souls[27] which allows them to burn up the fruits of their action and to be receptive to Śiva's grace. Because souls have no beginning in this system, in the act of creation and in the act of concealing himself Śiva is allowing souls the opportunity to be liberated and free, just as he is himself. Śiva unites these remaining bound souls with experience (*bhogabhukti*) appropriate to their actions,[28] and so they wander until liberated through the ripening of their bonds, through the Śaiva Siddhānta ritual structure, and ultimately through Śiva's grace. The suffering of souls is a kind of medicine that in the end procures their desired goal of liberation.[29] The souls thus have bodies made of *māyā* in the lower creation in order to experience worlds. Without a body a world cannot be experienced and liberation cannot be attained; only through the body is the experience of a world undergone and only through a body is liberation reached.[30] In one sense the universe is simply Śiva's sport and dance, yet in another sense it is a manifestation of his grace to allow beginningless souls to gain freedom.

The *Tattva* Hierarchy

For the Śaiva Siddhānta the structure of the universe is linked to the degree or level of concealment of Śiva. The universe unfolds in increasing degrees of coagulation, from subtle to gross, which increasingly entrap the soul, who becomes lost within it and subject to suffering due to pollution, karma and illusion-power. As with other Hindu systems, the Śaiva cosmos is created, or rather manifested from a quiescent state, and destroyed or reabsorbed over and over again over vast periods of time. Through his energy or Śakti, the Goddess, Śiva acts upon pure substance in potential called the 'great power of illusion' (*mahāmāyā*) or 'the drop' (*bindu*), which then develops the 'pure' levels of the cosmos. From *bindu* then emerges the material substrate of the lower universe, the power of illusion or *māyā*, from which emerge the elements that comprise the lower or impure universe. *Bindu* and *māyā* are the material causes (*upādāna*) of the worlds.[31] After a period of time the universe is reabsorbed back to the level of *māyā*, and in a great dissolution back to the level of *bindu*. After a period of sleep the process begins over again.[32] I have rendered *māyā* as 'illusion-power', which, although somewhat dissatisfactory, conveys the idea of *māyā* as a lower emanation of Śakti, a power that conceals Śiva and entraps lower souls through the operation of the 'coverings' (*kañcuka*) that include limited agency and time.[33] For the Śaiva Siddhānta *māyā* is a substance (*vasturūpa*), the eternal (*nitya*) root (*mūla*) of the universe, says Bhoja.[34] As substance it is not in itself illusory or unreal, but is rather the cause and context of the soul's illusion that it is entrapped in the lower worlds. Indeed, the *Kiraṇa-tantra* calls *māyā* a 'seductress' (*mohinī*) because through her the soul has experience (*bhoga*) of external objects (*viṣaya*),[35] although we must not forget that *māyā* is not a conscious being for the Siddhānta, but a form or force that is insentient (*jaḍa*).[36] The Śaiva Siddhānta presents a realist ontology in that the cosmos is a real substance that entraps the soul.

bindu/mahāmāyā
↓
māyā
↓
prakṛti

A number of terminologies are used to describe this process of unfolding. Perhaps the most important is the system of the categories or *tattva*s. The Śaivas add eleven to the twenty-five Sāṃkhya ones (see figure). This is most important because it is an attempt to explain in detail the unfolding universe and the soul's entrapment within it, and is also integral to Śaiva soteriology and the ritual system. The cosmos unfolds in order that souls can experience the results of their actions, and so *tattva* hierarchy describes that entrapment. Yet through understanding this entrapment and, above all, through the ritual reabsorption of the *tattva*s, the soul can become free. The *tattva*s are therefore the cause of both bondage and liberation in one sense, although the ultimate cause is Śiva's grace.

Prakṛti becomes a lower manifestation or reflection of *māyā*, which itself is a lower manifestation of *bindu*. *Bindu* is identified with the first, the *Śiva-tattva* from which emerge the other pure *tattva*s, namely *Śakti-tattva*, *Sadāśiva* or *Sādākhya-tattva*, *Īśvara-tattva* and *Śuddhavidyā-tattva*. *Māyā*, itself classed as a *tattva*, produces those in 'mixed' creation, and the *prakṛti tattva* produces the lower categories as described in Sāṃkhya.[37] While thirty-six is a standard number in the texts, there is some variation of content. The *Mataṅgaparameśvarāgama*, an upāgama of the *Parameśvarāgama*, lists the twenty-five Sāṃkhya *tattva*s replacing matter (*prakṛti*) with the 'unmanifest' (*avyakta*) and 'quality' (*guṇa*), and in the pure creation listing dissolution (*laya*), joyous experience (*bhoga*), governance (*adhikāra*), pure knowledge (*vidyā*), and *māyā*.[38] Other texts have some variation on the thirty-six and the *Mṛgendrāgama* lists thirty-nine.[39]

The *tattva*s are not in themselves sentient but are categories that comprise the bodies and coverings of souls, and are also levels

The thirty-six categories or *tattva*s of Śaivism

PURE CREATION

1. Śiva
2. Śakti
3. Sadāśiva
4. Īśvara
5. Śuddha Vidyā

IMPURE CREATION

6. **Māyā**

five coverings or kañcukas

7. Kalā – particularity of authorship
8. Vidyā – limited knowledge
9. Rāga – passion/ attachment
10. Kāla – limited time
11. Niyati – spacial constraint
12. Puruṣa – limited self

---

13. **Prakṛti** – matter/ nature
14. Buddhi – higher mind
15. Ahaṃkāra – ego
16. Manas – mind

organs of cognition	*organs of action*	*subtle elements*	*gross elements*
17. Hearing	22. Speech	27. Sound	32. Space
18. Touching	23. Handling	28. Touch	33. Air
19. Seeing	24. Locomotion	29. Form	34. Fire
20. Tasting	25. Excretion	30. Taste	35. Water
21. Smelling	26. Generation	31. Smell	36. Earth

---

of experience for those souls. Thus the *Śiva-tattva* is not to be confused with Śiva, the transcendent efficient cause of creation. There are, therefore, a number of English renderings of the term *tattva* whose semantic field incorporates the notions of 'reality', 'essence', 'principle' and 'category'. While interpreting the *tattva*s in a non-dualist way as emanations of consciousness, the non-dualist

Śaivas nevertheless adopt the Siddhānta system. Their readings of the *tattva* hierarchy are illuminating. For the non-dualist theologian Abhinavagupta, *tattva* designates a constituent of a level of reality (*vastu, prameya*), a principle underlying reality or a level of it (for example, in the sense of earth being an appearance of an underlying principle of hardness), and a category of perception (*padārtha*).[40] These are furthermore integrated into a system of correspondences with other hierarchical cosmological schemes, all of which become important in ritual procedures.

The Six Paths

The cosmological schemes are collectively known as the 'six paths' (*ṣaḍadhvan*); they are found or mentioned in most texts.[41] The term designates different paths of emanation and reabsorption of the cosmos that the soul takes on its symbolic journey in ritual back to and beyond the source of the cosmos. These paths are named *varṇa* (phonemes), *mantra*, *pada* (words), *kalā* (cosmic regions), *tattva*, and *bhuvana* (worlds). Both the Śaiva Siddhānta and the non-Saiddhāntika systems maintain the doctrine of the six paths. For the monistic Śaivas these are manifestations of consciousness paired in a hierarchical sequence, *kalā* with *varṇa*, *tattva* with *mantra*, and *bhuvana* with *pada*, whereas for the realist Śaiva Siddhānta, as Brunner-Lachaux observes, they are traced in matter (*māyā* and *bindu*) and must be understood as parallel to each other and not in a hierarchical sequence.[42]

Path of Sound (*vācaka*)	Path of Objects (*vācya*)
varṇa (phoneme)	*kalā* (power)
mantra	*tattva*
pada I (word)	*bhuvana* (world)

There is no space to describe them in detail (for which see the work of Brunner and Padoux),[43] but the idea can illustrated with a brief account of the path of the worlds, the *bhuvana adhvan*.

The path of the worlds (*bhuvana*) is particularly interesting as it clearly illustrates the idea that the body contains within it the cosmos and that the ritual dissolution of the cosmos in the body is a dissolution of all possible realms of experience into which a soul could be born. The Siddhānta texts formally contain 224 worlds, so many in each *kalā*, although there are many more, this number being notional. Indeed, the listing of worlds that beings inhabit is an important and interesting feature of some Tantras, which allows us to understand the vast cosmological imagination of the composers of these texts and enables us to see how later developments of tradition or new traditions did not abandon the old but built up further worlds upon the old. For example, in the *nivṝtti kalā* the *Rauravāgama* contains 108 worlds, beginning with the lowest of Kālāgni,[44] which are recapitulated with some variation in other Āgamas and in the *Somaśambhu-paddahti*.[45]

The non-Saiddhāntika Tantras of the north follow the same structure and list many of the same worlds. For example, the non-Saiddhāntika *Mālinīvijayottara-tantra* lists among the various worlds in the *nivṛtti-kalā* six types of beings in the community of beings (*bhūtagrāma*) who inhabit the material world, namely those of the vegetable kingdom (*sthāvara*), insects and other crawling things (*sarpjāti*), the birds (*pakṣajāti*), wild (*mṛga*) and domestic (*pāśava*) animals, and the human world (*mānuṣabhuvana*).[46] Indeed, the *Mālinī* may have been a dualist text like those of the Siddhānta.[47]

While the basic pattern is fairly simple in the sense that the scheme represents the two dimensions of the hierarchical universe, time and space, word and object, with all the paths parallel to each other and each path arranged in a graded sequence from supreme to subtle to gross, the details of the paths are nevertheless quite complex and each path is pervaded by the others.[48]

Although there is no doubt an explanatory dimension to the six paths, the function of this whole complex structure lies primarily in ritual. It is only in the ritual context that the scheme comes to life and becomes embodied. As the universe is populated with multiple worlds, levels and beings, so the practitioner's body is populated with worlds, levels and beings, themselves derived from the textual sources of the tradition. The destruction of the six paths within the body enacted in daily ritual leads to the soul's liberation at death or the soul becoming a Vijñānakevalin until its final liberation at a great dissolution.[49] The body is the meeting point or mediation between the universal and the particular, in that it enacts the particularity of revelation, of text, and at the same time enacts the proclaimed universality of the cosmic structure revealed in the texts. The entextualisation of the body makes the body particular to text and tradition, but this is also understood as the universalisation of the body through locating the universe of beings within it.

The Ritual Process: Initiation

Initiation conducts the soul to perfection from the human condition (*puṃsbhāva*) in which the soul is located at the level of the *puruṣa-tattva*,[50] by purifying the six paths within the body. This purification overcodes the vedic body with the tantric cosmology; indeed some texts claim that Śaiva initiation eradicates caste. The *Rauravāgama*, for example, lists a number of Śaiva groups and seems to say that simply following and adopting the ways of the Śaiva are sufficient and that this constitutes initiation. In constructing the body through the Śaiva rites (*śivasaṃskāra*) and following the Śaiva path one thereby deconstructs the vedic body, and the Brahman and outcaste can both become Śivas. Adopting the bodily habitus of the Śaiva ensures liberation:

> From combining ashes and *rudrākṣa* beads and from binding [the body] by the ritual process of Śiva, wearing the topknot and sacred thread, one is said to be initiated. A living being should devote himself to pure śaiva [path] in this Tantra. By giving himself over to the śāstra he is said to be initiated into the śāstra. Wearing matted hair or shaved, the teacher of Śiva makes entrance before the immovable icon (*liṅga*). They say he is a living Maheśvara. Entering the condition of the Maheśvara he abides possessing the mark [of the Śaiva]. Brahman or outcaste, with good qualities or bad, combining ash and rudrākṣa beads, without doubt [he becomes] a Śiva. After becoming a Śaiva in this way he should act as a Śaiva.[51]

While the *Rauravāgama* is unusual in not seeming to advocate here a formal initiation, acting like a Śaiva generally means not only wearing a chignon or shaved head and bearing the marks of a Śaiva, but having undergone formal initiation and consecration. Most

Śaiva texts follow almost the same ritual sequence as we found in the *Jayākhya-saṃhitā*. Generally absent from the Saiddhāntika and more closely aligned vedic traditions is the sexualised ritual of the non-Saiddhāntika traditions, although it is not wholly absent; sexual imagery is clearly present in visualisation and worship of the Śiva *liṅga*, the phallic representation of Śiva embedded in its pedestal throne (*pīṭha*) or vulva (*yoni*).[52] For a good account of the Śaiva Siddhānta ritual structure I refer the reader to the clear description by Davis and, especially for more detailed treatment, to Hélène Brunner-Lachaux's edition and translation of the *Somaśambhu-paddhati*. This is a milestone in the study of the tantic traditions, a major work of scholarship; its notes highlighting intertextuality and useful diagrams of how the cosmos is mapped on to the body have become a fundamental resource for the study of Tantrism.[53] It is to Brunner-Lachaux's edition and commentary that I largely turn in the following, abbreviated account, in order to demonstrate the Śaiva entextualisation of the body. Śaiva ritual – as with all tantric ritual – is classified as daily rites (*nitya-karman*), occasional rites (*naimittika-karman*) and rites for a desired goal (*kāmya-karman*). This classification provides all that is necessary for somebody to live the life of a Śaiva Siddhāntin and to form their life in accordance with the tradition.

The Śaiva Siddhāntin is constructed through the rites, with the texts of tradition being mapped on to the body. The occasional rites refer especially to initiation (*dīkṣā*) and funeral rites (*antyeṣṭi*) which reflect the former. Most important for the Śaiva Siddhāntin is initiation, for through this he is given access to the tradition, its texts and rites, and guaranteed eventual liberation.

Initiation presupposes the master. The master of the tradition, called the *ācārya*, *guru* or *deśika*, is crucial in the transference of power to the disciple and in teaching the rites and mantras. The master has knowledge of Śiva and the traditions, and mediates between the practitioner and transcendent goal.[54] This is not a comment on the inner awareness of the master; rather, the master is socially defined as having himself undergone a particular kind of consecration (the *ācāryābhiṣeka*) that is itself indicative of his degree of traditional knowledge and ability to install icons, consecrate temples and perform initiations. It is less the intellectual and moral qualities of the master that are important (although these are desirable, along with no bodily impurities) and more the ability and authority (*adhikāra*) to perform the correct rites at the correct time; the ability to act as a channel for the transmission of tradition. This ability is a formal, socially acknowledged qualification that functions independently of the inner qualities or personality of the teacher. Indeed, during the rites of initiation the master becomes Śiva. It is Śiva who initiates the disciple through the master. The most important quality that the disciple (*śiṣya*) should possess is the quality of devotion to the master (*gurubhakti*), which is thereby devotion to Śiva.[55]

The Tantras contain many kinds of initiation, and there is variability in the texts from formal acceptance by the master with minimal rites to more elaborate ritual procedures. In some texts, those of the Śaiva Siddhānta among them, initiation is formalised with no anticipation of the disciple's inner condition; in others the disciple is required to display signs of possession by the deities of the *maṇḍala*, such as trembling which reflects important differences within tantric traditions. Somaśambhu, basing his account on Śaiva revelation, describes three initiations – the general (*samaya*), particular (*viśeṣa*) and liberating (*nirvāṇa*) – although Brunner-Lachaux shows how the particular is assimilated into the general and how the distinction into three initiations is later.[56] The general initiation (*samaya-dīkṣā*) provides entry into the tradition, while the liberating liberation (*nirvāṇa-dīkṣā*) ensures final liberation at death. The structure of initiation follows the pattern of types of disciple as we have seen in the Pāñcarātra. Thus one who has undergone the *samaya-dīkṣā* is called a *samayin* and one who has undergone the *nirvāṇa-dīkṣā* is a *putraka*, a son of Śiva. There can be one or two further stages in the development of the disciple, should he become a teacher (*ācārya*) through the rite of consecration (*ācāryābhiṣeka*),[57] which means he then has the authority to initiate disciples. Alternatively there is formal recognition for someone to become a seeker of power and pleasure in higher worlds, a *sādhaka*, through that consecration (*sādhakābhiṣeka*).[58]

The distinction between the *ācārya* and *sādhaka* reflects an important distinction between seekers after liberation (*mumukṣu*) and seekers after power and pleasure in higher worlds (*bubhukṣu*). The latter, says Brunner-Lachaux, desire liberation ultimately, but also desire supernormal power (*siddhi*) in this and future lives.[59] It is, of course, legitimate to explain the distinction in terms of personal preference – and this is what the tradition does, as reflected in the desiderative terms, 'those who desire' liberation or power – but we could also be witnessing here an echo or remnant of an earlier *sādhaka* tradition that has become assimilated into the Śaiva Siddhānta system. The *ācārya sādhaka* distinction reflects the earlier distinction between the path of mantras, which is considered to be a path of power, and the higher path (*atimārga*) classified as having only liberation as its goal.[60] It also reflects a distinction found in the *Mṛgendrāgama* between the 'elemental' (*bhautika*) and 'unorthodox' (*naṣṭhika*) *sādhaka*, the former being attached to lower goals such as riches (*bhūti*), power, and obtaining an agreeable woman (*satpatnīparigraha*), the latter to liberation.[61] Indeed, the term 'elemental' (*bhautika*) retains the ambiguity of the English rendering, suggesting both the basic elements (earth and so on) and a class of supernatural beings who possess people (*bhūta*s) and from whom followers of cremation-ground Tantrism sought controlled possession in order to gain power, especially the power of flight.

In the initiation procedures we see how the initiate is formed through the tradition being mapped on to his body and how the narrative of his life is made to conform to the narrative of tradition to the extent of his receiving a new name, and his inner life, including his dreams, becoming interpreted within the boundaries of tradition. The actual ritual sequence of the communal initiation involves preliminary rites that include the formation of a circle diagram (*maṇḍala*) into which the deities of the Śaiva pantheon are installed, homage to the guardians of the portals to the *maṇḍala*, and preparation and performance of the fire ritual (*homa*). The communal initiation proceeds with the master identifying himself with Śiva, placing Śiva and his throne in the body of the disciple, and placing the hand of Śiva (*śivahasta*) on his head, thereby conveying initiation to him.[62] The *viśeṣa-dīkṣā* completes the task of constructing the disciple as a *samayin*, the characteristic feature of which is the guru transporting the soul (*ātman*) of the disciple to the womb of the

Goddess of Speech (Vāgīśvarī), who has been installed in the fire.[63] He is then born from her. While symbolically he is clearly a 'son of Śiva', as Śiva in the form of Vāgīśvara is her consort, he is not technically termed a *putraka* until after the next level of initiation, the *nirvāṇa-dīkṣā*.

The *nirvāṇa-dīkṣā* is the most important rite in the Śaiva Siddhānta, which grants access to eventual liberation. Once having undergone this rite there is no turning back. The ritual itself takes two days, as described by Somaśambhu; the first day comprises preliminary rites (*adhivāsana*), followed on the second day by the initiation (*dīkṣā*) itself.[64] The *adhivāsana* rites are performed in a sacrificial pavilion (*maṇḍapa*), the same as for the preliminary initiation. It is here that we begin to see the explicit entextualisation of the disciple's body. The main feature of this rite is that the master installs in the body of the disciple the totality of the cosmos contained in all the levels, and the entextualised body is then itself transferred to the substitute of a cord that extends his whole length. In his visualisation the master enters the central channel of the disciple's body through the aperture at the crown of the head. Having gone down to the heart, the master then leaves the body by the same route in his imagination, taking the disciple's soul with him along with the constitutents of the universe. He brings the soul and constitutents of the universe into his own heart through the aperture at his own crown, and finally emits them from there, establishing the disciple's soul and cosmos on the cord. This cord (*pāśa*), which represents the universe that binds his soul also represents the hidden channel (*nāḍī*) that pervades the vertical axis of the body. All the levels of reality need to be purified, which means detaching them from the soul. In theory any of the six ways can function to purify the soul in this way, but Somaśambhu gives the purification by the way of the *kalā*s. The five *kalā*s are established by the master in the body and transferred on to the cord through *nyāsa*; their purification is the purification of all the other paths as well. As Brunner-Lachaux remarks, the rite is very long because the master must extract each of the *kalā*s from the disciple's body to place on the cord and must extract the disciple's very soul, to be placed in the cord also. In this way, Brunner-Lachaux remarks, 'the cord thus prepared is the image of the disciple, with his *ātman* imprisoned by bonds (hence the name *pāśasūtra*, "cord of bonds").'[65] The disciple spends the night in the pavilion, and the *dīkṣā* proper commences the next day after the master has interpreted his dreams. If the dreams are inauspicious, the effects are redressed by expiatory rites (*prāyaścitta*).

The second day of the rites comprises a repetition of the first initiations, after which the cord is suspended from the topknot of the disciple and each *kalā* is purified in turn, beginning with *nivṛtti*, so enacting the reabsorption of the cosmos. This involves the master imaging all the different worlds that the disciple could be born into, within that realm. The master visualises the sexual union of Śiva and Śakti in the forms of Vāgīśvara and Vāgīśvarī and places the soul of the disciple into the womb of Vāgīśvarī. Somaśambhu's text reads as follows:

> 93. He [the master] should declare to the Vidhi [Brahman] that which is to be done by your grace. 'O Brahman, I will initiate this mumukṣu according to [your] authority'. 94. Then he should invoke the red Goddess Vāgīśvarī with the heart [mantra], who is the cause of the sixfold way in the form of will, knowledge and action. 95. He should worship and satisfy the Goddess and afterwards [he should worship and satisfy] Vāgīśvara in the same way, the cause of agitation in all wombs. 96. [Then] in the hollow of the heart, with the weapon [mantra] beginning with the seed syllable and ending with HUṂ PHAṬ, he should knock his [the disciple's] heart and should enter it, knowing the rule. 97. The consciousness of the disciple in the heart is like a spark. [The master] should then separate it with the Jyeṣṭhā [mantra so that the soul is] joined by bonds to the place of nivṛtti: oṃ hāṃ haṃ hāṃ haḥ huṃphaṭ. With [the mantra] oṃ hāṃ haṃ hāṃ svāhā, he pulls [the soul] up with the hook gesture when he breathes in and mentally grasping it with the *ātmamantra*, he can then unite it to his own soul. Oṃ hāṃ haṃ hāṃ ātmane namaḥ [homage to the self]. 98. Visualising the sexual union of the parents, he breathes out and takes the consciousness [of the disciple] from Brahman through the successive stages of the Lords of the kalās to the place of Śiva.[66] 99. Having offered the rite of impregnation, [the master] should cast [the soul] into the womb of Vāgīśvarī and simultaneously into all wombs, with the arising gesture associated with the Goddess Vāmā. [The accompanying mantra is] oṃ hāṃ haṃ hāṃ ātmane namaḥ. 100. With the same mantra he offers worship and nourishes [the self] five times. With the heart [mantra] he should form a body for him [the disciple]

> in all wombs. 101. He should not perform the rite of producing a male because [it may be] the body of a woman and so on, and [he should not perform] the ritual of parting the hair according to the sacred rite because the body may be blind and so on. 102. With the śiras [mantra the guru] brings about birth of all the embodied ones simultaneously. Then again with the śikhā [mantra] he should visualise their appropriate rank (*adhikāra*). 103. With the *kavaca* mantra he should visualise their experience which is the erroneous identification of the self with its objects, and with the weapon mantra [he should visualise] the dissolution. 104. With the Śiva [mantra] he performs the purification of the currents, with the heart [mantra] the purification of the *tattva*s, and for each [of the rites] from the rite of conception, he should offer five oblations in due order.[67]

In this way the master extracts the soul from the disciple, places it in himself, transports it to the realm of Śiva and then into the womb of the Goddess Vāgīśvarī, who is located in the sacred fire. This visualisation is accompanied by the appropriate section of the cord being cast into the flames. In entering Vāgīśvarī's womb, the disciple's soul is entering all wombs, and being born from her represents the end of all other births in that realm. This birth is accompanied by three rites, which completely consume all remaining karma appropriate to that level, namely the rites of *adhikāra* ('rank', 'authority'), *bhoga* ('enjoyment', 'experience') and *laya* ('dissolution'), which we are familiar with from the *Jayākhya-saṃhitā* (see pp. 108–19). The master provokes the soul's birth, its correct place in the cosmic order, its experiences, and its erroneous identification with sense objects, through visualisation, through ritual gesture and, especially, through uttering the appropriate mantra. The following rites eradicate all trace of the soul in the realm of *nivṛtti*, detaching all exhausted *karma*, parts of *māyā*, and partially the power of *mala*. The master cuts the appropriate section of the cord representing *nivṛtti* and burns it in the fire. He then retrieves the soul of the disciple from the fire and places it in the next, higher section of the cord. The process of purification occurs over again for the remaining four *kalā*s. With the burning of the last *kalā*, *śāntyatītā*, the soul is purified and replaced in the disciple's body.

The passage from Somaśambhu's text, quoted above, is striking in a number of ways. It is rich in references, indicating the semantic density of ritual action. The rite is a construction of the self, or rather the construction of a new self, whose bonds of action, illusion and pollution – at least at the level of *nivṛtti-kalā* – are destroyed, so that all that remains are the fruits of action that the disciple needs to work out in his present life as one initiated (and so ensured of liberation in due course). The term used for this construction is *saṃskāra*, 'put together', the same term used in the vedic ritual construction of the rites of passage. There is an implicit identification of the rites of passage with the ritual procedures in the *nirvāṇa-dīkṣā*.[687] The model for the tantric rite is provided by the vedic saṃskāras, although the process is speeded up and condensed into two days. Although a 'construction', initiation is in fact the elimination of most of the bonds that keep a being bound in the cycle of birth and death. The *Kiraṇa-tantra* asks a pertinent question of Śiva: if all bonds are removed by initiation, then how can the body remain? The Lord answers that as a potter's wheel still turns even after the making of a pot is completed, so too the body remains. The seeds of action of many existences (*sañcita-karma*) are burned by the mantras at initiation and the acquiring of future action (*āgamin*) is also blocked, but that which sustains the body in the present life (*prārabhda-karma*) has to be exhausted through experience.[69] The exhausting of karma is also a journey through the levels of the cosmos. The womb of Vāgīśvarī, which represents all wombs at the respective levels to be purified, signifies the myriad births through which a soul must pass or would otherwise pass were it not for initiation. The journey along the cord is a journey through the cosmos and through the body.

The Ritual Process: Daily Rites

Having undergone the *nirvāṇa-dīkṣā*, although in one sense superfluous because the disciple is guaranteed liberation, he must nevertheless pursue a rigorous regime of daily rites (*nitya karman*). These use up his remaining karma so that at death he will go to liberation with Śiva's grace. Many texts give details of the procedures and generally follow a pattern of purification through various kinds of bath (water, ashes, mantras), the purification of the body and its revitalisation, followed by inner and outer ritual.[70] Some texts, such as the *Rauravāgama*, do not give full ritual details for they assume the reader's knowledge of other sources (although the *Rauravāgama* does give details for visualising Sadāśiva).[71] It is important within the tradition that pollution is a substance that is erased through action rather than cognition. Yet while this is the general standpoint, there are passages in Siddhānta texts that stress cognition within the *buddhi* as having liberating force,[72] although such statements do not necessarily contradict the position in that even thought is a mental action, but generally after initiation it is ritual that destroys pollution with Śiva's grace.

The *Rauravāgama* says that there are two kinds of daily ritual, either performed for oneself (*ātmārthapūja*) or for the sake of others (*parārthapūja*) in public rites before the icon of Śiva (*liṅga*) in the temple.[73] In both we see the text mapped on to the body. The general pattern of daily rites is to purify oneself or one's body and ritual environment before going on to worship through visualisation followed by physical offerings. The *Rauravāgama* lists purification of the self/ body (*ātmaśuddhi*), purification of the place (*sthānaśuddhi*), purification of ritual implements and substances (*dravyaśuddhi*), purification of the Śiva *liṅga*, and mantra. One should praise the Lord of the heart (Sadāśiva) with the mind first, followed by external oblations.[74] In the daily rite described in the *Somaśambhu-paddhati* we have, as in the *Jayākhya-saṃhitā*, morning ablutions, evacuation of bodily impurities (listed in the Śaiva texts[75]), bathing rites,[76] followed by the sequence we are now familiar with, of purification of the body, creating a divine body through mantra, mental worship and external worship. The text gives precise details on purification, more detailed than the *Jayākhya*, and again closely akin to the vedic *smṛti* texts on correct behaviour.[77] There are precise details about ablutions, excretions, and activities such as cleaning the teeth. We are a long way from any idea of spontaneous expression and bodily abandon: the *Somaśambhu*, as with the *Jayākhya*, presents a picture of establishing a regime for the strict control of the body and restriction of the senses.

The preliminary rites in the *Somaśambhu* involve mantra repetition and empowering the body even before the *bhūtaśuddhi* proper. The 'pilgrimage sites' or 'crossing points' (*tīrtha*) are established on the hands, in a process familiar from the *Jayākhya*. Thus the ancestors (*pitṛ*) are established on the index finger, the deity Prajāpati on the little finger, Brahman on the thumb and the other gods at the ends of the fingers.[78] Offerings of purified water are made to Śiva, to the gods, and to the ancestors within one's family lineage (*gotra*) from father to paternal grandfather up to the father of the father of the paternal grandfather. Offerings are made to the equivalent temporal distance on one's mother's side.[79] This in itself is interesting in showing how the practitioner sees himself within a continuity of generations and wholly integrated through the daily ritual sequence into his family, which is in turn a part of the cosmic order. The narrative of the practitioner's life, its daily routines and mundane activity, from the very beginning forms part of the narrative of his family lineage, which itself is a part of the cosmical hierarchy, with Śiva at the top. There is a flow of power through the cosmos, through one's ancestors, to oneself.

The *Īśānaśivagurudeva-paddhati* and *Somaśambhu-paddhati* use the term *dehaśuddhi*, along with *bhūtaśuddhi*, for the purification of the body and Īśānaśivagurudeva follows the account given by Somaśambhu. As in the *Jayākhya*, self-purification (*ātmaśodhana*) occurs through the purification of the elements (*bhūtaśuddhi*), which is the first in a series of purifications in the Śaiva system, along with a purification of the place, of ritual material, of mantras and of the *liṅga*, the 'phallic' image of Śiva used in worship. For the *bhūtaśuddhi*, the *Somaśambhu* prescribes facing north with a self whose passions are subdued (*vinītātman*).[80] The practitioner – and here we have the explicit description of new elements entering the process – visualises two hollow tubes from the big toes of both feet running up the legs and joining a central channel, which then goes to the crown of the head. Along this central channel that traverses the body's vertical axis are cosmological blockages or 'knots' (*granthi*) at the heart, throat, palate, between the eyes and in the aperture of the absolute (*brahmarandhra*) at the crown of the head, which prevent the soul from rising to its freedom through the crown of the head to the *dvādaśānta*. These blockages need to be broken (*granthiprabheda*) through the rising power of the self along the body's subtle channel, a process which occurs in the imagination or inner vision in the context of the initiate's daily ritual. The soul (*jīva*), shining 'like a star in the cave of the heart' (*tārakākāraṃ jīvaṃ hṛdayasampuṭam*), travels up the central channel, imagined in the form of a drop (*bindu*), to Śiva at or outside the crown of the head.[81] (There are two *dvādaśānta*s or 'end of twelve fingers'. Sometimes this is identified with the *brahmarandhra*, the length of three times four fingers' width from the centre of the eyebrows, and sometimes it is twelve fingers above the *brahmarandhra*.) Through uttering seed syllables (*bīja*) the self is dissolved (*līna*) in Śiva; then one must perform the purification of the subtle body (*sūkṣma-deha-śuddhi*) by mapping the categories of the cosmos, or *tattva*s, on to it and reabsorbing them, each into its cause in inverse order of their manifestation, up to their origin, the cosmic substance known as the 'drop' or *bindu* (also known as *mahāmāyā*).

The *Īśānaśivagurudeva* is in complete concord with this account in describing the breaking of the 'knots' at the heart, throat, palate, between the eyes, and on the head, and visualizing Śiva at the crown of the head, twelve fingers' length above the point of the meeting of the eyebrows (*dvādaśānta*).[82] The adept should meditate upon the cutting of the 'dark and filthy' knots, which are pierced with the exhaling of the breath, to allow energy to flow in the esoteric channels (*nāḍī*).[83] He should imagine his soul, identified with the mantra HAṂSA, in the pure lotus of the heart. By the force of the air (*vāyu*) in the central channel he should lead the soul up to Śiva, located in the *dvādaśānta* at the crown of the head, seated in the centre of a lotus.[84] The adept then meditates upon his own body as an inverted tree whose roots are in his head, pervaded by the thirty-six categories that make up the cosmos (*tattva*), dissolved in imagination, each into its cause.[85] The sequences in the *Somaśambhu* and *Īśānaśivagurudeva* are in some ways more complex than those in the *Jayākhya*. Only then does the text begin an account of the *bhūtaśuddhi*, and we are back on territory familiar from the *Jayākhya*. This suggests that an elaboration and complexification of the rite has occurred in which a stripped-down version of the *bhūtaśuddhi* has been embedded in a complex sequence of visualisation.

While the map of the subtle body has become more complex with the Śaiva Siddhānta, with additional Śaiva cosmological overlays, much in the accounts of the *bhūtaśuddhi* in the *Somaśambhu* and *Īśānaśivagurudeva* is recognisable from the *Jayākhya*, and the general process of the upward movement of the self from bondage to liberation remains the same. To illustrate the high degree of consistency with the *Jayākhya* let us consider a passage about the first stage in the process of purifying the earth element. The *Īśānaśivagurudeva* reads:

> The image of the earth (*bhūmaṇḍala*), which is a yellow square, marked with the sign of thunder (*vajra*), whose quality is smell, with the Sadya mantra, and the sense-organ of smell, which is associated with the limitative energy of cessation (*nivṛtti-kalā*) and with the divine, four-faced one (Brahmā). Through the seed-syllable HLĀṂ, [the body] is then pervaded with the filling and holding breaths, from the head to the soles of the feet. There will be purification from repeating it [i.e. the seed-syllable] five times and he should [then] meditate upon it as entered into the air [i.e he exhales the earth element into the air element].[86]

As in the *Jayākhya*, the earth diagram is a golden square marked by the 'sign of thunder' (*vajra*) and associated with the sense of smell, but unlike the *Jayākhya* it is associated with the *tattva*s, with one of the five cosmic regions (*kalā*) called *nivṛtti*, and pervades the entire body, rather than from feet to knees. But this pattern is not wholly consistent within the Śaiva Siddhānta; the *Vāmadeva-paddhati* follows the *Jayākhya* model with the earth pervading from feet to knees. The other elements follow the same general pattern, using the same symbols (the crescent moon for water, a red triangle for fire marked with *svastikas*, air as a hexagonal form marked by six drops (*bindu*), and space as symbolised by a round crystal). As in the *Jayākhya*, the adept burns the body in imagination and then floods it with the water arising from his meditation in order to create a pure, divine body for worship. The text follows the same pattern as the *Somaśambhu*, on which it heavily relies.

A general picture therefore emerges of the *bhūtaśuddhi* as a shared ritual substrate that becomes identified with particular Śaiva cosmologies. On the one hand the actual visualisation represented in the texts has become minimised, from the *Jayākhya*'s elaborate visions of each element to Somaśambhu and Īśānaśivagurudeva's rather formal representation. On the other hand, more elaborate cosmological overlays have occurred. Indeed, the system of the *bhūtaśuddhi* has become identified with an independent system of the five 'knots' along the central channel of a subtle anatomy, and the five elements have become associated with the five faces of the aspect of Śiva called Sadāśiva.[87] We can therefore see strong continuity of ritual representation, although with later structural elaboration.

Following the symbolic destruction of the physical, elemental body in the imagination, the adept then creates a pure body made of mantras through imposing them in sequence upon himself, the *sakalīkaraṇa* sequence with the *aṅga* mantras on the hands, in the way that we have seen in the *Jayākhya*. The *Somaśambhu* then describes a rite purifying the place of ritual (*sthānaśuddhi*), although in other sources this follows the stage of mental worship. But let us take up the account of mental worship and the construction of the throne of the deity in the imagination. This throne is virtually identical in its formation with the lions identified with the constituents of the *buddhi* and so on in the *Jayākhya*, although there are nevertheless textual variations.[88]

Having established the throne, the practitioner then visualises the deity (*deva*) Sadāśiva upon it. His body is made of 'knowledge' (*vidyāśarīra*) and is without taint like a pure crystal. He has three eyes on each of his five faces (Sadyojāta, Vāmadeva, Aghora, Tat-Puruṣa and Īśāna), each of which is associated with a particular colour, mantra and cosmic function (creation, maintenance, destruction, concealment and grace). He has ten arms and holds a lance, a trident and so on. Furthermore, the vertical axis of the body is identified in the practitioner's imagination with the levels of the cosmos, the thirty-six *tattva*s, thus the throne corresponds to all of the *tattva*s up to Śuddha Vidyā, and Sadāśiva to the *tattva*s up to Śakti (see Appendix).[89] As in the JS, external worship follows internal worship or making offerings to Sadāśiva in the imagination,[90] followed by the fire ritual, which Somaśambhu presents in great detail.[91] Other rites dealt with in the texts are occasional ritual such as festivals and rites for a desired end.[92]

The Ritual Process: Behaviour

The entextualisation of the body can be seen not only in the specific, daily and occasional rites prescribed for the Śaiva but also in daily comportment. The tradition is internalised by the initiate adopting Śaiva observance, dietary restriction and communal behaviour (*sāmānyācāra*). In the section on comportment (*caryapāda*), the *Mṛgendrāgama* tells us that Śaivas fall into the categories of master (*deśika*), mantra specialist or sādhaka, *putraka* and *samayin* (see above p. 133), some of whom might follow a specific observance (*vrata*) and some who do not. The term 'observance' or 'vow' (*vrata*) indicates a specific kind of asceticism in varying degrees of intensity taken on for varying periods of time, often for a specific purpose. The *Mṛgendra* defines an observer of *vrata* as someone who has given up meat, women and honey (possibly fermented beverage), who sleeps on the ground and is solitary, carrying a pot for water. He must avoid young women, garlands and similar things.[93] These are standard prescriptions for the ascetic, and those who follow such asceticism should indicate their Śaiva affiliation through wearing matted locks in a chignon or going with shaved head and making the body white with ashes, although śūdras women, the sick and the lame cannot wear the matted locks (*jaṭa*).[94] Those who wear matted locks are themselves divided into the two groups previously mentioned, the *bhautika*, whose observance is limited for a specific period of time and the highest or *naṣṭhiika*, namely gurus, putrakas and sādhakas, whose observance is throughout life. Some Śaivas, says the text, are without observance (*avrata*), which seems to indicate that they are householders, although, as Brunner observes, no Śaiva is completely without *vrata* throughout life. Indeed, all Śaivas must perform ritual obligations daily at the junctions of the day and at junctures of the year marked by the moon (*parvan*), namely rites on the eighth and fourteenth days of the month, at the solstices and equinoxes.[95]

Apart from ritual obligations Śaivas must follow a mode of conduct generally in consonance with vedic orthopraxy. The *Mṛgendra* presents the requirements of the master in terms that would find a place in the most orthodox of contexts, and the disciple too should study, listen to the scriptures, abandoning pride, jealousy, hypocrisy and frivolous activity. He must also behave in specific, deferential ways before the master.[96] Even the sādhaka, by definition interested in obtaining pleasure and power, should behave in appropriate ways, not menacing anyone, begging for food, mentally reciting his mantra, and keeping silence.[97] If he sins voluntarily or involuntarily, such as interacting with a woman, or commits a great sin (*mahāpātaka*) such as killing a Brahman, drinking alcohol or having sex with the master' wife, he must do a penance of reciting eleven mantras ten thousand times.[98] Indeed, the sādhaka in the *Mṛgendra* does not appear to be so different from any Śaiva ascetic and makes the contrast with the transgressive ascetics of the non-Saiddhāntika traditions even more striking.

The texts of the Śaiva Siddhānta provide us with detailed examples of the way in which the body is inscribed by the revealed text, from ritual performance to ethical behaviour and general bodily comportment. We have in these texts a description of the hierarchical cosmos presented in various schemes and terminologies which articulate with sequences of ritual action. Of particular importance are the purification and divinisation of the body, in which we see the textual representation of the cosmos mapped on to the body and a cosmological temporality of vast periods of the manifestation and contraction of the cosmos, enacted in the micro-temporality of daily ritual time. We have so far shown this structure to be in place in Pāñcarātra texts and in the ritual manuals of the Śaiva Siddhānta, traditions which of course maintain distinct identities in terms of deities and mantras and at a philosophical level wish to distance themselves from each other. I wish, finally, to take one last example from the monistic tantric traditions of Kashmir.

SEVEN

Ecstatic Tantra

THE non-Saiddhāntika traditions, often referred to as 'Kashmir Śaivism', assume the Śaiva Siddhānta as their theological and ritual background. While, as we have seen, they draw on the more extreme anti-*vaidika* and antinomian revelation of the Tantras of the right and left currents, the tradition known as the Trika and its philosophical articulation in the Pratyabhijñā became established within the mainstream of medieval Kashmiri society. While probably always the activity of an elite minority because of the esoteric complexity and time-consuming nature of the practices involved, it nevertheless became extremely influential on the literatures and practices of all later tantric traditions. The non-Saiddhāntika traditions assume the revelation of the Śaiva Siddhānta and assume its cosmological and ritual schemes, adding layers of complexity to this already complex system and reading the tradition through the lens of a monistic metaphysics. As a consequence, their account of cosmology, while often being terminologically identical (especially in respect of the *tattva* hierarchy), differs from the Śaiva Siddhānta in being understood as the manifestation of consciousness itself rather than an unconscious, material substrate (*bindu* or *mahāmāyā*). I refer to this range of traditions, especially the Trika, as 'ecstatic tantra' because of the emphasis of its key thinker, Abhinavagupta, on the spontaneous expansion of consciousness as the ground of being, the source of revelation, and the source of a liberating, existential cognition. Abhinavagupta's tradition is 'ecstatic' in its emphasis on consciousness as a thematic trope and in its belief that individual consciousness can blissfully transcend itself to realise its true nature as boundless and objectless.

The non-Saiddhāntika material presents us with formidable problems of interpretation, not least because of the extent and complexity of the texts and their interrelation. Rather than attempt an impossible survey or systematic exposition,[1] I shall rather develop the argument about the mapping of experience within the body in terms of the textual tradition within the non-Saiddhāntika religions by demonstrating this in four related areas: first, the filling out of subjectivity with the absolute subjectivity of pure consciousness, especially in the works of Abhinavagupta and Kṣemarāja; second, the mapping of the pantheons of deities on to the body; third, the locating of centres of power within the body, the systems of *cakra*s; and, fourth, a concern with sexual experience in the context of ritual. I shall confine my remarks to specific texts of the tradition, namely key texts of Abhinavagupta and Kṣemarāja and an anonymous hymn, the 'Hymn to the Circle of Deities Located in the Body' (*dehasthadevatācakra-stotra*).

Absolute Subjectivity and Indexicality

The first-person pronoun that in the nominative case (namely *aham*) refers to the subject of predicates, the 'I', is used in the non-dualist tradition of Kashmir to refer to the supreme subject of consciousness, Śiva or Bhairava himself, inseparable from his energy (*śakti*) and containing within it the totality of manifestation. Abhinavagupta introduces the notion in his introductory verses to his commentary on his grand-teacher Utpaladeva's text, the *Īśvarapratyabhijñā*, where he says that *aham* appears at first from the complete unmanifest condition of the absolute.[2] In his *Tantrāloka* Abhinavagupta defines this 'I' as 'reflexive awareness of the omnipresent in the non-duality of Śiva and Śakti, that is to say the supreme and cosmic emission within which all is contained';[3] the definition by Utpala, cited in

Jayaratha's commentary, is that the 'tranquillity in itself of the light of consciousness is called the condition of the "I"' (*prakāśasyātma-viśrāntir ahaṃbhāvo hi kīrtitaḥ*).[4] This 'I' contains within itself the totality of manifestation, as indicated by the very word *aham* in so far as it contains the first phoneme of the Sanskrit alphabet *a*, which symbolises the initial emergence of creation from the unmanifest state, and ends with *m*, regarded as the 'drop' or 'dot', the *bindu* (*ṃ*) to which all creation returns. Abhinavagupta continues in the *Tantrāloka*:

> The flowing forth [of the cosmos] whose nature is energy begins with the incomparable (*a*) and ends with *ha*. Condensing the whole universe, it is then reabsorbed in the supreme. This entire universe abides within energy and she in the highest absolute. This is truly an enveloping by the omnipresent one. In this way, the enveloping of energy [is described] in the revelation of the *Trīśikā*. The universe shines there within consciousness and on account of consciousness. These three factors combine and unite in pairs to form the one, supreme form of Bhairava, whose nature is the 'I'.[5]

The cosmos emerges from the 'I' and returns to it, although this separation and return can never be outside of that consciousness. The three elements of the word *aham* combine to form the totality of the cosmos. The cosmos is within the absolute subject, as the word *aham* contains the first and last letters and, by implication, all between them from *a* to *ha*. The three combinations of *a* and *ha*, *ha* and *m*, and *m* and *a* create a continuous flow of sound, with *aham* becoming *maha*, the former being the expansion of the cosmos, the latter being its contraction: both expansion from *a* and contraction into *anusvara*, the *ṃ* or *bindu*, are mediated through the energy of *ha*.[6] The word *aham* is therefore treated as a mantra; indeed it is regarded as the force of all other mantras and the power that animates all living beings.[7] According to the commentator Jayaratha, this *aham* is unitary consciousness, the supreme beyond everything, the place where all rests, the light of knowledge, knower, and object of knowledge. The 'I' is Śiva, who is both father and mother of the universe, who abides as the universal agent (*kartā viśvatra saṃsthitaḥ*), and who penetrates the universe as phonic resonance (*nāda*). Thus *a* represents the father and initial movement of the cosmos as the first phoneme, *ha* is the mother and in her subtle form the Sanskrit aspirate or *visarga* represented by two dots (transliterated as *ḥ*), and this emission and manifestation finally retrieve the condition of the incomparable (*anuttara*) with the *anusvara* (*ṃ*) or *bindu*.[8]

The passage from the *Tantrāloka* quoted above refers to a text of the Trika śāstra, the *Parātrīśikā*, a series of short verses from the *Rudrayāmala*, one of the Bhairava Tantras of the southern current. In his commentary, Abhinavagupta repeats his point about the absolute subject being the source of all appearance and the goal of practice, whose 'highest meaning is uninterrupted continuity' (*avicchinnatāparamārtham*) in the cosmos and which is delight (*camatkṛti*).[9] This 'I' is absolute subjectivity, 'I-ness' (*ahanta*), pure consciousness (*saṃvit*, *caitanya*, *cit*) without an object, and the ground of being (*āśraya*), containing within it the entire spectrum of manifest universes. This consciousness is purely reflexive (*vimarśa*).[10] Indeed, it is the true experient and ultimately real subject of first-person predicates beyond the illusory conventionality of the everyday 'I', of everyday deixis. Abhinavagupta is aware that this use of the first-person pronoun is far beyond ordinary reference as it implies the undermining of any subject–object distinction. In that state of absolute I-ness, he says, there are no distinctions as are indicated by terms such as 'this' (*idam*), 'thus' (*evam*), 'here' (*atra*) or 'now' (*idānīm*);[11] that is, purely conventional indexicality has no meaning, for this ultimate state transcends conventional language. Indeed, the identification of the practitioner, of the 'indexical-I' that refers to 'me' as a particular, located person, with this absolute 'I' revealed in the texts is the highest goal of the entire, elaborate system.

What is revealed in the Trika śāstra is that the true reference of the first-person pronoun is not the indexical subject of everyday language, but rather the transcendent subject as the source of all phenomena. Indeed, to speak of a subject, an 'I', in this way is to use the term such that it does not imply a distinction between subject and object. While this is a counter-intuitive use of the first-person pronoun, it is nevertheless at the heart of Abhinavagupta's thinking. The absolute 'I' is yet mediated by a number of levels or realms within which the identification of the self with the implied self of the texts also occurs. Thus the supreme I is mediated through the elaborate cosmology and levels in which there is variable identification of the self with its objects of perception. For example, in the pure course of the pure *tattva*s each level is characterised by a different emphasis of the 'I/it' (*aham/idam*) distinction. Sadāśiva, the thirty-fourth *tattva* and the highest level of the cosmos that is clearly manifested, contains the seeds of subject–object differentiation but nevertheless is dominated by a sense of subjectivity or I-ness (*ahantā*) over objectivity (*idantā*); their differentiation is as yet indistinct (*asphuṭa*) and Sadāśiva is aware of the identity of subject and object as characterised by the sentence 'I am that' (*aham idam*).[12] As the cosmos unfolds at lower levels, the subject–object distinction becomes more pronounced and the greater is the sense of separation between them.[13]

In his commentary on the *Parātrīśikā* Abhinavagupta, drawing on the Saiddhāntika ontology, declares that everything in the universe consists in the triad (*trikarūpa*) of 'man' (*nara*), Śakti and Śiva. These three modes, ultimately united in consciousness, he relates to the three goddesses of the Trika – Parā, Parāparā and Aparā – and to forms of language and address. Thus something that appears as 'this' (*idam*) when addressed becomes enveloped by the I-consciousness of the subject (*ahambhāva*). When addressed as 'you', the other becomes a form of Śakti, and in this way the subject assimilates the autonomy of this other 'I' into the delight of his own sense of 'I' (*ahaṃbhāvacamatkāra*) and so both become one in the act of addressing. This is the feature of the Goddess Parāparā, whose nature is identity in difference.[14] In this freedom of delight the supreme Śakti, Parā, is operating through the first person. At this point Abhinavagupta introduces a quotation from the *Bhagavad-gītā* (15.18) that 'I', referring to Kṛṣṇa, am the highest self who transcends the perishable and imperishable. Similarly, the first-person verb 'I am' indicates a transcendence of the perishable and imperishable, not the limited 'I' but the real 'I', which is the self-luminous Śiva. In contrast, however, when the autonomy of the I is subdued by the separateness of the other ('this one'), then the Goddess Aparā predominates.[15] That is, the triad of goddesses is present in language transactions and in the processes of ordinary linguistic identification of the agent of speech with the objects of speech. The reader of Abhinavagupta's commentary is invited to expand the sense of 'I' and to fill out the empty signifier with the text- and tradition-specific content of a transcendent subjectivity. The aim of the Trika is to open awareness to a sense of a pure subject, deeper than the triadic relationship of ordinary speech, a process that occurs not simply through the analysis of linguistic situations but through ritual and practice. There is the explicit entextualisation of the body in daily ritual practice, as we have seen with the Pāñcarātra and Śaiva Siddhānta, but here with the Trika we have overlays upon this ritual structure that claims that awareness needs to expand beyond its boundaries to experience itself as identical with absolute subjectivity. The indexical-I becomes identified with the I of the text, which in this case is understood as limitless, through an expanding of reference such that the 'I' is no longer bounded or limited by location markers such as 'here' or 'now'. This expanded sense of I is a further step in the entextualisation of the body in so far as the body becomes filled with the awareness that it is coterminous with the cosmos. As the 'I' of Śiva fills manifestation, so the indexical-I fills the body and breaks its boundaries, becoming identical with the I of Śiva. Becoming identical with supreme I-ness is also to realise that the body is as boundless as the cosmos.

Of particular note in the non-Saiddhāntika scheme is the use of terminology derived from the grammarian school of philosophy, particularly that of Bhartṛhari. Abhinavagupta's faithful student Kṣemarāja tells us that when Śiva opens his eyes the cosmos is manifested as an appearance of him, and furthermore this manifestation is identified with levels of sound or speech (*vāc*). The cosmos is divine speech and the entire circle of powers that comprises the cosmos can be understood as Śiva's voice. This divine speech that makes up appearance forms a graded hierarchy from the pure to the impure (as we have seen in the example from the Pāñcarātra), from the highest level of Śiva to the level of the individual experient. Kṣemarāja expresses this concisely when he writes:

> Now the power of speech (*vākśakti*), who is the Goddess Supreme (*parā*), comprises awareness of complete subjectivity. Her form is the eternally enunciated great mantra, without desire due to [being one with] the light of consciousness, she is pregnant with the complete

> circle of powers (*śakticakra*) whose form [comprises the letters] from *a* to *kṣa*. She therefore manifests the levels of [limited] subjectivity through the gradual stages of [sound, namely] the 'the seeing' (*paśyantī*), 'the middle' (*madhyama*) and so on. Not manifesting her true nature as the Supreme state, she illuminates mental activity, new every moment, and displays to the experient [bound by] illusion, particular objects which had not been hitherto manifest. She also reveals the perfect (*avikalpa*) level covered by that [mental activity] although it is [really] pure.[16]

Here we see how the embodied individual experient is the consequence of the contraction of supreme consciousness, and how the limited sense of I, the indexical-I, is a result of the contraction of the supreme 'I' (*pūrṇāham*), the unlimited textual-I or the 'I of discourse' in the text, through the power or goddess of speech.[17] The goddess gives birth, as it were, to the cosmos as the circle of powers, which is envisaged as the letters of the Sanskrit alphabet.[18] This unfolding of sound develops as a graded hierarchy, mapped on to the four levels of language that the Kashmiri non-dualists take from the grammarian Bhartṛhari, namely *paśyantī, madhyamā* and *vaikharī*,[19] adding a supreme level (*parā*) beyond *paśyantī*.[20] Subjectivity appears to be particular and limited due to the action of Śakti, but also due to her power she reveals the pure state of consciousness, which only appears to be covered over by the impurity of apparently external mental activity.

This process of the cosmos opening out and closing in is continuous and occurring at each moment, reflected in the mantra *aham*. There is, as it were, a process of systole and diastole, opening and contracting. When pure consciousness contracts as Śakti, the limited embodied experient results, and when consciousness opens out to itself again, limitation is eradicated. As Kṣemarāja says, 'the power of consciousness (*citi*), which is contracted to the object of consciousness, (becomes particularised) consciousness, descending from the level of uncontracted consciousness.'[21] Particular consciousness is the contraction (*saṃkoca*) of Śiva, of pure I-ness, while appearance (*ābhāsa*) is the manifestation of Śakti, a process which is also described as the universe opening out (*unmiṣati*) in appearance and continuation, space and time, subject–object distinction, and as closing in (*nimṣiati*) with the turning back of appearances.[22] Thus the opening out or manifestation of the cosmos as a graded hierarchy of levels from the pure to the impure is a closing in of pure consciousness in so far as this manifestation conceals pure consciousness. Conversely, the contraction or closing in of appearance is the opening out of pure consciousness. To the degree that the universe is manifested, the pure consciousness or I-ness of Śiva is concealed, while to the degree that the universe is contracted, pure consciousness is revealed. The journey through the cosmos to the goal is a journey through less particularised forms of perception to the universal consciousness of Śiva. This is envisaged as a journey through the body and a journey through different stages of awakening.[23] Furthermore the body provides the map for this journey, both as a representation of the cosmic hierarchy through which the soul ascends and as the means or vehicle for experiencing that journey.

In the last verse of his *Pratyabhijñāhṛdaya*, Kṣemarāja says that upon realising absolute subjectivity, the supreme I-ness, one attains power over the group of deities that animate the body and the cosmos, the group of deities identified with the alphabet or circle of power (*śakticakra*). He writes:

> Then due to entry into complete I-ness, whose nature is the energy of the great mantra whose essence is the joy of the light of consciousness, there is the attaining of Lordship over the circle of the deities of consciousness, who are innate and produce the creation and destruction of everything. All this is Śiva.[24]

Upon attaining liberation, understood as the identification of the indexical-I with the absolute subjectivity of revelation, the practitioner attains power over the circle of deities who animate the cosmos and body and who are themselves manifestations of pure subjectivity. On attaining liberation, the yogi realises that the indexical-I has expanded to the absolute I-ness of Śiva and everything is therefore an extension of his own body,[25] as the universe iteself is an extension of pure I-ness. The deities of consciousness are the forces or instrumental causes that bring about the manifestation and destruction of the cosmos. They allow for experience and the interaction of self and world, and allow for the destruction of limited experience in liberation. As the deities of consciousness are expansions of pure consciousness itself, so upon the recognition (*pratyabhijñā*) of the identity of self and absolute, the deities of conciousness are recognised as expansions of one's own consciousness.

The Circle of Deities in the Body

The body is animated by deities who are nothing other than emanations of consciousness itself. In a text that has probably been wrongly attributed to Abhinavagupta by Pandey and Silburn,[26] these deities are described as goddesses of the sense faculties offering their objects or spheres of operation to the absolute, Śiva in union with Śakti in the forms of Ānandabhairava and Ānandabharivī. The 'Hymn to the Circle of Deities Located in the Body' (*dehasthadev atācakrastotra*)[27] describes the deities of the Krama system, one of the Kaula traditions, which were absorbed within the Trika.[28] This anonymous text presents us with a pantheon of deities lying at the esoteric heart of Abhinavagupta's system. What is significant about the text is that it occurs within a liturgical setting, as part of a daily ritual of visualisation and identification of the self with Śiva. In the text we have the identification of a lotus containing a pantheon of deities who represent the totality of the cosmos identified with the body. The text describes how Ānandabhairava and Ānandabhairavī are located in the calyx of a lotus, identified with the heart. They are in sexual union, which symbolises the non-differentiation of consciousness from the world, and are regarded as the essence of a person. They are the essence of experience (*anubhavasāra*) both in the sense of ordinary, unawakened experience that oppresses, as Silburn observes,[29] and in the sense of the liberating experience of recognising the self as consciousness. In this sense, experience or *anubhava* refers to the telos, the goal of practice, the awakening to the recognition of one's identity with both transcendence and immanence.

The text would be recited by the practitioner to identify the deities of his pantheon with himself. The hymn is thus a text of visualisation set within a ritual context. The practitioner, says the text, 'should visualise the splendour which is the basis of everything, a deep bliss of awakened consciousness, one's own tranquillity, without filth, pure, without taint and all-pervading.'[30] There is a central deity, a Lord of the clan (Kuleśvara), along with his consort (Kuleśvarī), surrounded by a harem of goddesses, located in the heart. He is seated upon a throne of jewels, anointed with musk, sandalwood and nutmeg, with various foods being offered to him such as milk, sweetmeats and fruit, all entirely constructed within the mind. Having given the liturgical visualisation, the text presents the hymn that locates the circle of deities in the heart which are also identified with the whole body and with the cosmos. I cite the entire text here:

> 1. Oṃ Homage to Gaṇeśa. Oṃ holy! I praise Gaṇapati whose body is the inhaled breath, who is worshipped at the beginning of a hundred philosophical systems, who delights in the bestowal of desired wishes. 2. I praise Vaṭuka, known as the inhaled breath who removes people's pain; his feet are worshipped by the lineage of Perfected Ones, the hordes of yoginīs, and the best heroes. 3. I always praise the pure, true master whose nature is attentiveness. By the power of his thought he reveals the universe as a path of Śiva for his devotees. 4. I praise Ānandabhairava, who is made of consciousness, whom the goddesses of the senses constantly worship in the lotus of the heart with the pleasures of their own sense-objects. 5. I praise Ānandabhairavī, whose nature is awareness, who continually performs the play of creation, manifestation and tasting of the universe. 6. I constantly bow to Brahmāṇī, whose nature is higher mind, situated on the petal of the Lord of gods [i.e. Indra in the east], who worships Bhairava with flowers of certainty. 7. I always praise Mother Śāṃbhavī, whose nature is the ego. Seated on the petal of fire [i.e. Agni in the south-east]; she performs worship to Bhairava with flowers of pride. 8. I always praise Kumārī, situated on the southern petal, whose essence is the mind, who gives offerings to Bhairava with flowers of discrimination. 9. I constantly bow down to Vaiṣṇavī, seated on the south-west petal, the power of whose nature is that which is heard, who makes offerings to Bhairava with flowers of sound. 10. I honour Vārāhī, who possesses the sense of touch. Seated on the western petal, she satisfies Bhairava with flowers of touch which captivate the heart. 11. I praise Indrāṇī, whose body is sight, whose body is seated on the north-west petal, who worships Bhairava with the most beautiful and best of colours. 12. I bow to Cāmundā, called the sense of taste, dwelling on the petal of Kubera [i.e. north]; she constantly worships Bhairava with offerings of the varied six flavours. 13. I always bow down to Mahālakṣmī, known as the

> sense of smell, who, seated on the petal of the Lord [Śiva in the north-east], praises Bhairava with varied fragrances. 14. I praise constantly the Lord of the body, who gives perfection known as the self, united with the thirty-six categories; he is worshipped as the Lord of the six systems of philosophy. 15. In this manner I praise the circle of deities innate within the body, an elevated assembly continually present, the end of everything, vibrant, and the essence of experience. Thus the sacred hymn to the circle of deities in the body is fully completed.[31]

These are the eight mothers of the Kaula tradition, sometimes listed as seven, namely Brahmāṇī, Śāmbhavī, Kumārī, Vaiṣṇavī, Vārāhī, Indrāṇī, Cāmuṇḍā, and Mahālakṣmī. They are also found, with some variation, in the Purāṇic texts, particularly the *Devīmahātmya*, as forms of Durgā,[32] and in the *Agni-purāṇa*, where they are framed by Tumburu/Vīrabhadra and Vināyaka.[33] In one of the earliest tantric references they are listed in the *Netra-tantra*, where they are the entourage of Kuleśvara.[34] The *Tantrāloka* refers to them in the context of the secret ritual focused on Kuleśvara and Kuleśvarī, where each is in sexual union with a form of Bhairava.[35] In the *Īśānaśivagurudeva-paddhati* we find seven mothers in the context of the worship of attendant deities to Śiva, each with her particular visualised form, colour, mount and so on.[36]

In the *stotra*, quoted above, we see that the body becomes the text upon which the deities of the tradition – the goddesses of the senses – are inscribed. The body is inhabited by the circle of deities; this pantheon animates the body, which becomes the *maṇḍala* wherein they reside. One of the terms for the pantheon of goddesses here represented is 'clan' or *kula*, a term which itself is rich in meaning, as we will see, but one of whose meanings according to a scripture cited by Jayaratha is, indeed, 'body'.[37] These goddesses are identified not only with the body but with different levels of the hierarchical cosmos, thereby creating a homology between body and cosmos. While there is no narrative dimension to this text, set in a broader context of its liturgy this sacralisation of the body entails a temporal and so narrative identification of the practitioner with the cosmos, constructed through text and ritual. We might even say that the story of the body becomes the story of the cosmos, which is the story of the unfolding of the essence of experience. The hymn is an excellent illustration of the entextualisation of the body in a ritual context and how the metaphysical speculation about pure subjectivity is textually and ritually (and so somatically) located. The body becomes the text through the identification with the deities revealed in the revelation and all action is understood as offerings made to the supreme deities Śiva and Śakti, who, as Abhinavagupta and Kṣemarāja tell us, are both contained within absolute I-ness. The circle of deities in the body who animate the cosmos are emanations of the self and also deities who animate the levels of the cosmos as manifestations of pure consciousness. This idealism is at the heart of the Krama system absorbed within the Trika. The Krama categories of creation, maintenance, destruction, the nameless (*anākhya*) and splendour (*bhāsa*) are implicitly contained in the *maṇḍala*, the circle of bliss realised as the true nature of one's own experience.[38] As the self animates the limbs of the body, so the Lord animates the universe.[39] In the last verse of the *Pratyabhijñāhṛdaya* Kṣemarāja explicitly links the deities of the senses with pure subjectivity in that they are expansions of it, represented in the expansion of the term *aham*.[40]

Kuṇḍalinī and the *Cakra*s

The term used for the deities within the body in the text just discussed is 'wheel' or 'circle' (*cakra*), which also refers to a lotus and the heart as a lotus. This sense of *cakra* as lotus is used more generally for locations within the body itself. Indeed the *cakra*s have become part of a common, New Age esotericism in the West, entering from pan-Hindu use of the six or seven *cakra*s in Yoga to indicate centres of power within the body and specifically arranged along the central axis of the trunk. Within Indian medicine this central axis became identified with the spinal column, and there are curious fusions of Western anatomy with yogic esoteric anatomy.[41] While the system of *cakra*s has become synonymous with tantric esoteric anatomy in popular representation, it is important to remember that there are other systems of mapping the cosmos on to the body, as we have already seen, and that these systems of mapping are text- and system-specific; less reified than modern conceptions yet also more text- and tradition-based than some modern exponents would acknowledge.

The term *cakra* as referring to centres of subtle anatomy first occurs in the Tantras, although earlier texts contain *cakra*-like references. David White has argued that probably the earliest Hindu source is the *Bhāgavata-purāṇa* where six sites (*sthāna*) are listed at the navel (*nābhi*), heart (*hṛt*), breast (*uras*), root of the palate (*svatālumūla*), the place between the eyebrows (*bhruvorantara*), and the cranium (*mūrdha*). He goes on to suggest that the earliest Hindu source for the application of the term *cakra* to these centres is the *Kaulajñāna-nirṇaya*.[42] In this text there are eight *cakra*s listed, meditation and worship (*dhyānapūjā*) of each in turn bestowing different magical powers: worship and visualisation of the first *cakra* giving the power of being one with Yoginīs and the yogic powers of becoming minute and so on; visualisation of the second *cakra* giving the powers of attraction and subjugation, the ability to project oneself and break objects at a distance; and so on.[43]

Yet the earliest text that documents the six *cakra*s, known to later Kaulism and yoga traditions, is the eleventh-century CE *Kubjikāmata-tantra*.[44] Here, in chapter 11 and elsewhere, we have the standard list of the *mūlādhāra* (anal region), *svādhisthāna* (genital region), *maṇipura* (navel), *anahāta* (heart), *viṣuddha* (throat) and *ājñā* (between the eyebrows), plus the 'centre' beyond the *cakra*s at the crown (*sahasrāra*), although later chapters only present five *cakra*s, not linked to Kuṇḍalinī, as Padoux has observed, but associated with the five elements.[45] Indeed the humpbacked or crooked Goddess Kubjikā of this text is identified with Kuṇḍalinī.[46] This list of six is unknown to the earlier tradition, where instead we find a variety of terms and text-specific systems of mapping the cosmos on to the vertical axis of the body. Sanderson writes:

> In fact it [the system of six *cakra*s] is found in none of the early traditions mentioned. Instead we find there a great variety in the division of the vertical line of the central power (*suṣumṇā*). There are six 'seasons', five 'knots' (*granthayaḥ*), five voids (*vyomāni*), nine wheels (*cakrāni*), eleven wheels, twelve knots, at least three sets of sixteen loci (*ādhārāḥ*), sixteen knots, twenty-eight vital points (*marmāni*), etc.[47]

By the time of the later Kaulism, especially the Śrī Vidyā associated with the Goddess Tripurasundarī, along with medieval Haṭha yoga and Nāth Siddha texts such as the *Siddhasiddhānta-paddhati* and the famous *ṣaḍcakranirupaṇam*, the term *cakra* refers to points or lotuses (*padma*) with varying numbers of petals, specific letters of the alphabet and colours, located along the central axis of the body.[48] Indeed the *cakra*s are connected by subtle channels (*nāḍī*) along which power or subtle energy (*prāṇa*) flows to animate the body and which needs to be controlled through yogic and tantric practice. But an important point is that there is textual variety in these systems, exhibited not only in the *Netra-tantra* but in other texts as well. The *Lakṣmī-tantra*, for example, cites three centres for visualisation as well as thirty-two located along the body's axis,[49] we have seen systems of subtle anatomy in the JS and Śaiva Siddhānta texts, Aghoraśiva describes visualising the subtle body as an inverted banyan tree, and the *Dehasthadevatācakra-stotra*, discussed above, has the body as a circle of goddesses. The Saiddhāntika *Sārdhatriśatikālottara* devotes a chapter to the circle of channels (*nāḍīcakra*), knowledge of which is necessary to attain supernatural power. The text describes the principal kind of channel and the secondary channels, totalling 72,000 in total. These channels flow upwards and downwards from the navel to all parts of the body, along which flow blood and subtle breath (*prāṇa*).[50] These breaths are classified into ten types in the text, the descending breath (*apāna*) responsible for digestion and excretions, the *udāna* responsible for movement of the eyes, and so on.[51] While there are textual variations, and though the subtle anatomy of visualisation is sometimes conflated with physiological processes, there is a general shared structure of locating a column of power along the body's axis. This structure, however, has some variability in our texts and always occurs within the context of ritual and visualisation. While there are ancient precedents for the idea of a subtle anatomy in the Upaniṣads, especially a focus on the heart,[52] the system of six *cakra*s and three principal *nāḍī*s that pervades medieval and later Hinduism is post-eleventh century.

Let us describe one of these early systems. Probably before the *Kubjikāmata-tantra*, perhaps before the tenth century, the *Netra-tantra* lists six *cakra*s without the *svādhisthāna* or *sahasrāra*, as Padoux has observed,[53] but rather with a *cakra* of the palate (*tālu*) along with the *dvādaśānta*, the point either twelve fingers from the brow centre or twelve above the crown of the head. The *Netra-tantra* presents these six in describing the subtle visualisation of the form of Śiva, Mṛtyunjit, and then connects them to six centres (*adhara*) and twelve 'knots' (*granthi*) and six spaces (*vyoma*) located along the central axis. Although the text does not mention Kuṇḍalinī, it does say that the yogi should visualise Śakti in the central breath (*udāna*) that is manifested between inhalation (*prāṇa*) and exhalation (*apāṇa*). This is similar to the *Vijñānabhairava-tantra*, which refers to the upward movement of *prāṇa* within the body without mentioning the term *kuṇḍalinī*. In other places *kuṇḍalinī* is explicitly linked to *prāṇa*.[54] The practitioner fills this power with his own virile energy (*vīrya*) through identifying the Śakti with mantra. She then arises from the organ of generation (*janmādhāra* or *ānandendriya*) up through the central channel that pervades the body, through the navel (*nābhi*), heart (*hṛt*), throat (*kṛṭtha*), palate (*tālu*) and the centre between the eyebrows (*bhrūmadya*), piercing the twelve knots and voids to the crown of the head where Śiva in the form of Mṛtyunjit is located. She descends from there to the heart, where the body is filled with the elixir of longevity (*amṛta* or *rasāyaṇa*) that flows through the innumerable channels bestowing agelessness and immortality.[55] The basic structure of the rising of energy in the body that we find in later tradition is here, although the details of alignments and terminology are text-specific.[56]

The rising of energy in the body that we see in the *Netra-tantra* is also found in the *Kubjikāmata-tantra* where a serpentine energy is associated with mantra and levels of speech. In many texts this energy is named Kuṇḍalinī, the coiled one, although the 'crooked goddess' Kubjikā is earlier and perhaps a precursor. She sleeps in the lowest *cakra*; once awakened through yogic practice, especially breath control through the two channels from the nostrils that meet the central channel in the *mūlādhāra*, she rises the central channel to Śiva at the crown. According to White, the earliest occurrence of 'this indwelling female serpent' is the *Tantrasadbhāva-tantra*, possibly dated as early as the eighth century CE, where this in-dwelling power is described as *kuṇḍalī*, she who is 'ring shaped'.[57]

Kṣemarāja cites this text, which would appear to be a visualisation in which Kuṇḍalinī is unconscious and appears as if poisoned. Once awakened she rises up and so transforms the poison of ignorance into a force of liberation.[58] Abhinavagupta identifies different levels of Kuṇḍalinī and stresses her cosmological dimension, expanding from *bindu*, the source of manifestation, and shining in all things in the form of energy (*śaktikuṇḍalkā*) and in the form of breath (*prāṇakuṇḍalikā*), then up to the extreme point of emission where she is the supreme Kuṇḍalinī.[59] For Abhinavagupta there are two main forms: an 'upward' Kuṇḍalinī (*urdhva*) associated with expansion, and a 'downward' Kuṇḍalinī (*adha*) linked with contraction; she is the systole and diastole of cosmic expansion and contraction. In his commentary on the *Parātrīśikā*, Abhinavagupta links Kuṇḍalinī with the *kaulikī śakti*, a name for the supreme or highest form of energy, from whom the Lord is inseparable. The *Parātrīśikhā* identifies *kaulikī śakti* with the supreme power of the Lord called the *kulanāyikā*, the Lord of the clan, who resides in the heart. In his commentary Abhinavagupta identifies this goddess with the power that brings into manifestation the body, breath, and experiences of pleasure and pain (*śarīra–prāṇa–sukhādeḥ*), and the energy of the whole circle of deities within the body (Brahmī and the others discussed above). This is also the power within the body and the power of sexuality as the source of reproduction. He furthermore links Kuṇḍalinī to the force of the syllable *ha* in the mantra and the concept of *aham*, the supreme subjectivity as the source of all, with *a* as the initial movement of consciousness and *m* its final withdrawal.[60] Thus we have an elaborate series of associations, all conveying the central conception of the cosmos as a manifestation of consciousness, of pure subjectivity, with Kuṇḍalinī understood as the force inseparable from consciousness, who animates creation and who, in her particularised form in the body, causes liberation through her upward, illusion-shattering movement.

What is significant about the descriptions of the central channel within the body and the power that moves along it are the mercurial nature of the accounts. The texts do not intend to reify the subtle body and its centres; although admittedly Abhinavagupta uses Kuṇḍalinī as an explanation, generally in the texts the bodily centres and the upward movement of energy are intended for visualisation purposes. This is stated in the *Netra-tantra*, where the text presents a list of the centres in the context of the visualisation of Mṛtyunjit, and Śiva explicitly declares that he will speak about the supreme, subtle visualisation (*dhyāna*).[61] This is an important point. The centres of the subtle body are given meaning and form a part of the practice only in the context of ritual and meditative visualisation grounded in text. The Kuṇḍalinī image is complex and claiming that it must be understood within the tradition and within specific forms of practice that intend to eventuate in the 'experience' of Kuṇḍalinī is not to disclaim or reduce these practices, although it is to be suspicious of the claim that Kuṇḍalinī is universal and found in different cultural locations. Abhinavagupta would have regarded the raising of Kuṇḍalinī as an experience, as indicated by his claim that if this rising force should descend, then possession by demons (*piśācāveśa*) would ensue,[62] but such experience can only be understood in the context of the texts and traditions of its occurrence. The body is constrained by text and tradition. Visualising the body as being mapped with these subtle centres is clearly an entextualisation of the body, a mapping of the cosmos and journey of the self to its transcendent source in ways specified within the tradition. Indeed, to seek to understand the *cakra*s outside of this context as if they are intended as extra-textual, ontological structures is incoherent. The rising of *śakti* within the body, the piercing of the centres along a central axis, and the accompanying mantras are part of the practitioner's aligning of himself with tradition and part of the construction of his body in tradition-specific ways to attain the tradition-specific goal.

Finally we must examine the same processes of entextualisation at work in what has sometimes become synonymous with Tantra, its sexualised ritual.

Two Ritual Systems

An important difference between the Trika and Śaiva Siddhānta is that for the Trika the ritual sequence of daily rites, the entextualisation of the body, is not understood as a manipulation of material substance but as action within consciousness. Ritual actions must be understood in terms of cognition and knowledge for the Kashmiri non-dualists, for liberation is the recognition of the subject's identity with absolute consciousness. Given this understanding, the monistic commentators on Śaiva ritual texts had to interpret ritual in term of consciousness and stages of awareness. Apart from the three methods (*upāya*) and sudden awakening in the non-means (*anupāya*),[63] there were two principal forms of rites for the initiate into the Trika tradition: the normative rite of the Trika initiate called the *tantra-prakriyā*, lucidly described by Sanderson,[64] and the esoteric rite called the *kula-prakriyā* for the tantric virtuosi, which involved ritualised sex outside of orthodox, vedic bounds.[65] The normative rite followed the basic pattern we have outlined in the Śaiva Siddhānta of purification of the body, the divinisation of the body through *nyāsa*, mental worship and external worship, although with the transgressive addition of the consumption of meat and wine.

I refer the reader to Sanderson's article, which describes how the initiate installs the mantras of the Trika deities into two wine-filled cups, makes offerings to the guardian deities surrounding the place of worship, performs the purification of the body in the way previously described, although he understands it as the destruction of his public and physical individuality (*dehāntata*), leaving him with the awareness that his identity is 'pure undifferentiated consciousness as the impersonal ground of his cognition and action'.[66] Following his divinisation through *nyāsa*, the initiate visualises a trident maṇḍala (*triśūlābjamaṇḍala*) along the axis of the body, with the three goddesses of the Trika – Parā, Parāparā and Aparā – located at its prongs above the crown of the head. The trident is identified with the *tattva* hierarchy, and Sanderson shows how Abhinavagupta overcodes the rite with terminology and deities derived from other tantric systems, notably the Krama and Kula. The initiate identifies himself with the Goddess Parā located on the central prong and ascends up the trident, through his own body and so through the cosmos, to merge with the transcendent source of the three goddesses, the absolute Kālasaṃkarṣiṇī, the fourth power behind them, of which they are emanations. Kālasaṃkarṣiṇī herself is not visualised in the sequence as she is the ground of consciousness behind all appearance and beyond representation. In the ritual sequence the initiate transcends the usual identification of the 'I' with the subject of first-person predicates, the indexical-I, to construct in his visualisation an expanded sense of 'I' coterminous with the ground of appearance and the goal of practice, an idea, as we have seen above, that Abhinavagupta develops in his commentary on the *Parātrīśikā*.

This normative ritual is assumed by the more esoteric rite for high initiates only, the *kula prakriyā*, the secret rite that involves the ritual consumption of meat, alcohol and fish along with the practice of taboo-breaking sex in a ritual setting. The ritual use of sex, an exceedingly difficult observance (*asidhārāvrata*), is mainly the preserve of the non-Saiddhāntika traditions, although it is not wholly unknown within the Siddhānta.[67] Chapter 29 of Abhinavagupta's *Tantraloka* is probably the clearest description of the rite. It has now become the object of scholarly attention, as has the inquiry into tantric sex. White has written a definitive work on 'tantric sex' and put paid to the connection between Western 'tantric sex' and the ancient traditions of India. I do not intend to attempt to reproduce his very thorough and engaging work but will simply illustrate how sexualised ritual is indeed another example of the entextualisation of the body. But it is necessary to outline White's argument very briefly. Put simply, White argues that originally 'tantric sex' was 'nothing more or less than a means to producing the fluids that Tantric goddesses ... fed upon'.[68] In the quest for power, generally male practitioners courted generally female supernatural beings, such as the Yoginīs, who needed to be appeased (and controlled) through taboo-breaking offerings of meat, alcohol and sexual fluids. Texts in these traditions continued to be composed into fairly modern times; the sixteenth- or seventeenth-century *Yoni-tantra* describes such a ritual. The practitioner (*sādhaka*) needs to procure a woman who is wanton (*pramāda*), free from shame, whom he worships in the centre of a maṇḍala, offering her cannabis (*vijaya*)[69] before performing the sexualised rite (preferably during menses) to produce the *yoni-tattva*, the fluids necessary to offer to the Goddess.[70] Indeed, the basic structure of Hindu ritual worship (*pūjā*) of making an offering to a deity and receiving a blessing, usually in the form of the food that had been offered, consumed as 'grace' (*prasāda*), is followed in tantric rites. But instead of offered rice or fruit, it is meat, alcohol, and above all sexual fluids produced in a ritual context, which, in the Veda-aligned, later tantric tradition of the Śrī Vidyā, may be replaced by substitutes (*pratinidhi*). This sexualised ritual (White's phrase) serves to satisfy the ferocious and dangerous deities of the tantric pantheons and to allow the practitioner to gain control over them, power being the main concern of these practitioners, especially the power of immortality.[71]

Such acts of ritual appeasement, the offering and consumption of mixed sexual fluids to ferocious goddesses, is at the origin of the 'hard' tantric traditions, the more extreme cults of what Sanderson designates the 'left'.[72] Indeed, the Trika in its origins is such a tradition, whose foundation lies in the Kaula religion of cremation-ground asceticism, which worshipped a pantheon of goddesses of the clan or family (*kula*) surrounding a lord and/or his goddess (Kuleśvara and Kuleśvarī), as, for example, the deities of the senses surrounding Ānandabhairava and Ānandabhairavī described above. The Trika added to this the worship of the three goddesses Parā, Parāparā and Aparā in a triangle, within which is the Lord of the Kula. Sanderson writes:

> The worship could be carried out externally, on a red cloth upon the ground, in a circle filled with vermilion powder and enclosed with a black border, on a coconut substituted for a human skull, a vessel filled with wine or other alcohol, or on a *maṇḍala*,. It may also be offered on the exposed genitals of the *dūtī* [female practitioner], on one's own body, or in the act of sexual intercourse with the *dūtī*. Later tradition emphasises the possibility of worshipping the deities in the vital energy (*prāṇa*) – one visualises their gratification by the 'nectar' of one's ingoing breath. We are told that the seeker of liberation may carry out this worship in thought alone (*sāṃvidī pūjā*). However, even one who does this must offer erotic worship with his *dūtī* on certain special days of the year (*parvas*).[73]

This erotic worship was a requirement for those initiated into the Kaula dimension of the Trika tradition, regarded by Abhinavagupta as its esoteric heart, the quintessentially tantric system which regarded vedic injunctions and worship restricted by caste as founded on a restrictive prohibition that prevented the realisation of the spontaneous expansion of consciousness.[74] The feminine is given precedence, and women are to be worshipped and their homes treated as thrones of deities (*pīṭha*).[75] Here ecstasy takes precedence over dharma.

While this rhetoric might seem to go against tradition and established authority, it only goes against a particular kind of tradition and in so doing aims at establishing the superiority of its own revelation. The tantric traditions – including the extreme ones – set themselves against what they perceive to be the restrictive and lower revelation of the Veda (see pp. 55–60). The erotic worship of the pantheon, while being clearly at variance with vedic injunction and purity rules, is nevertheless within a tradition of practice based on a body of texts. The earliest layers of the traditions of the left emphasised the appeasing and control of ferocious deities through the offering and consumption of sexual fluids from around the seventh century CE, but these traditions widened their appeal through time, becoming adapted to householder ways of life. By the time of Abhinavagupta we have the traditions being reinterpreted and a shift of emphasis from the production of sexual fluids in ritual intercourse to sexual experience being an analogue of the bliss of the experience of pure consciousness. The production of sexual fluids for ritual purpose is still important, but, as Sanderson observes, the stress comes to be on sexual experience itself as a method of realising the expansion of consciousness. Sexual experience between the male practitioner and his female partner becomes a reflection of the joy of Śiva and Śakti. The rite becomes aetheticised.[76]

It is in this context that Abhinavagupta composes his chapter on the *kula prakriyā*. The chapter and Jayaratha's commentary show that this was a well winnowed tradition by the tenth and eleventh centuries, with a history of textual transmission and teachings handed down through lineages of masters. While the kula rite in the *Tantrāloka* undoubtedly reflects the earlier tradition of consuming sexual fluids – and this would seem to be a part of the rite – there is also an emphasis on an aesthetic dimension and the realisation of the bliss of the consciousness of Śiva and Śakti in union. In his commentary on the *Parātrīśikā-tantra*, Abhinavagupta writes:

> In the case of both sexes sustained by the buoyancy of their seminal energy, the inwardly felt joy of orgasm (*antaḥsparśa-sukham*) in the central channel induced by the excitement of the seminal energy intent on oozing out at the moment of thrill is a matter of personal experience to everyone. This joy is not simply dependent on the body which is merely a fabricated thing. If at such a moment it serves as a teaching of remembrance of the inherent delight of the divine self, one's consciousness gets entry in to the eternal, unalterable state that is realised by means of the harmonious union with the expansive energy of the perfect I-consciousness which constitutes the venerable supreme divine Śakti who is an expression of the absolutely free manifestation of the bliss of the union of Śiva and Śakti denoting the supreme Brahman.[77]

Sexual experience, specifically orgasm (*kampakāla*), can reflect the divine union of Śiva and Śakti. Ordinarily sexual experience does not, and sexuality only becomes a transpersonal joy once it is a 'teaching of remembrance' (*abhijñānopadeśa*); that is, the remembrance of tradition. Sexual experience can become an embodiment of the memory of tradition[78] if performed in awareness of the truth of revelation. This is true of other emotional experience according to Abhinavagupta, such as the joy of seeing one's wife and son or the delight when two pairs of eyes meet or on hearing a sweet song, all of which stir up energy (*vīrya*)[79] and have the potential to awaken awareness and stir the memory of the supreme I-consciousness. In such experiences the indexical-I can potentially realise its identity with supreme I-ness mediated through the revelation of tradition. Only through the text and tradition can such experience be evoked and such an expansion of the indexical-I take place.

Establishing a connection between human sexual experience and trans-human cosmic forces is not unique to Tantra; it had precedents much earlier in the Indian traditions. Perhaps the most famous example is from the *Bṛhadāraṇyaka Upaniṣad*, where human sexual experience is akin to a person realising the self: 'As a man embraced by a woman he loves is oblivious to everything within or without, so this person embraced by the self (*ātman*) consisting of knowledge is oblivious to everything within or without.'[80] The same is true of the *Chāndogya Upaniṣad*, where the vedic recitation is identified with the sexual act.[81] So the Trika claim is not unusual in the Indian context, although the emphasis on the liturgical use of sexual fluids is unique to the 'hard core' tantric traditions, as White has shown. What I would wish to emphasise is that there is a tradition of understanding human experience in a way that links it to trans-human powers and forces in the cosmos, and that such links are always mediated through the texts. Indeed, the female practitioner in the rite conveys the power of the deity, the power of pure consciousness, to the male practitioner in a process that parallels the consumption of blessed food (*prasāda*) that was previously offered to the deity (she also thereby reflects temple women of the later medieval period).[82] Human sexuality reflects cosmic process because revelation tells us so; the I-consciousness of Śiva can be realised in sexual encounter because the text and tradition tell us that it is so and not because of any properties of an unmediated experience (whatever that could be).

While the expansion of pure consciousness, the filling out of the indexical-I with the I-ness of Śiva, can be realised in ordinary, everyday transactions, it can also be evoked through ritual. The *kula prakriyā* sets up a situation in which the intention is the identification of the practitioner and his partner with Śiva and Śakti and the resulting sexual experience with the joy of their union. This identification can be seen in terms of the remembrance of tradition, always mediated through sacred text or revelation and through the teacher. To undergo the *kula prakriyā* means that the couple need to have the requisite qualification (*adhikāra*),[83] which means having undergone an initiation into the practice but also having certain personal qualities and high levels of receptivity, such as the displaying of signs of possession (trembling, loss of consciousness) during initiation. While I have shown in more detail elsewhere how the *kula prakriyā* enacts the memory of tradition (where I have also discussed the gender implications of the rite),[84] for our purposes we need to describe briefly the ritual process in order to see its relevance for the entextualisation of the body.

The *kula* rite entails the male practitioner (*sādhaka*) performing preliminary purifications that include the visualisation of the rise of Kuṇḍalinī. Once the female partner, called the 'messenger' or *dūtī*, joins him they both perform *nyāsa*, thereby divinising their bodies, before the practice of the 'three *m*s' (*makāratraya*), namely consumption of wine (*madya*), meat (*māṃsa*) and sexual fluids resulting from their union (*maithuna*). According to Jayaratha, sexual substances are actually passed from mouth to mouth in the rite (a practice which, observes Silburn, reflects Kashmiri marriage custom of passing food from mouth to mouth[85]). These three were to become transformed into the famous 'five *m*s' (*pañcamakāra*) or substances (*pañcatattva*) of later Śākta Tantrism, with the addition of fish (*matsya*) and parched grain (*mudrā*), which in the Śrī Vidyā Brahmanical response to the earlier tradition were substituted with 'pure' substances (*pratinidhi*).[86] Abhinavagupta even redefines 'celibacy' or *brahmacarya* as the ritual use of these three substances, forbidden to orthodox Brahmans, while he still accepts the legitimacy of the celibate renouncer whose semen is upturned (*ūrdhvaretas*).[87] The hero (*vīra*) or perfected one (*siddha*) who follows the esoteric path (*kulavartman*) must nevertheless perform the rite with complete detachment and without desire, consuming the probhibited substances as integral to the ritual process, for otherwise the hero would simply remain as a beast (*paśu*). Indeed, later Śākta Tantrism evokes a distinction between three dispositions (*bhāva*): the beast (*paśu*), who does not perform worship with the five *m*s; the hero (*vīra*), who does; and the divine (*divya*), who has realised the goal,[88] although these are not found in Śaiva texts. The bodies of the participants in the *kula* rite are mapped by the textual tradition. For Abhinavagupta and Jayaratha the Siddha and Dūtī have themselves developed to a high level of attainment within the tradition; they have already shaped their lives in accordance with the prescriptions of the tradition, and they reflect Śiva and Śakti in the ritual process. The aim of the rite is perfection in a condensed time period, which, in the rhetoric of the tradition, would otherwise take countless years with floods of mantras;[89] the *kula* practice is a quick path to liberation.

From these examples from non-Saiddhāntika traditions we can see that the same processes are at work as in the Śaiva Siddhānta and Pāñcarātra tantric traditions. The body is structured in accordance with text, and tradition becomes a map of the self by which the practitioner navigates towards the goal. In the case of the Trika this is particularly marked in the recognition of the identity-limited self with the transcendent subjectivity of Śiva, in the hierarchical structure of the body in alignment with the cosmos, in the various pantheons of deities located within the body, and in the sexualised ritual at the Trika's heart.

EIGHT

The Tantric Imagination

SO FAR, we have seen that there is a variety of tantric traditions, practices, terminologies and metaphysics, and that while practices are unique to specific texts there are shared processes and structures filled out with different content across traditions. I have characterised this as the body as text or its entextualisation. The body is central to the tantric *imaginaire*,[1] serving as the focus for the self-enactment of tradition through ritual and asceticism and serving as the focus for the self-declaration of tradition in tantric theology. Indeed, if anything is common to tantric traditions it is the divinisation of the body through the processes we have described: mantra, the *bhūtaśuddhi*, *nyāsa* and so on. The body is the central organising topos or metaphor of the traditions, which structures ideas of power, vision and levels of awakening in our texts. Furthermore, the body entails a corporeal understanding that functions not only as a conceptual scheme but as a lived experience; an experience always within the boundaries of tradition. Through paying close attention to textual detail of the body's representation in ritual and theology, we have seen how the body is encoded in text-specific ways. We can now make some more general remarks about shared processes. Of particular importance is how deixis or metalepsis functions within the texts: that is, how the practitioner becomes identified with the text, how he transgresses the boundaries of the everyday self or everyday indexicality to align himself with the implied 'reader' within the texts. In the technical jargon, the indexical-I becomes identified with the 'I' of discourse, the 'I' of the text. This is also to say that the text becomes the body, becomes entextualised. We have seen this especially in the ritual procedures of vision, gesture and the use of icons.

Vision

There is an inseparable link between body and vision in the tantric traditions. The body, as we have seen, is envisaged and constructed as divine in the ritual imagination. This construction is a corporeal understanding of text and tradition that is enacted not simply through reading the texts but through enacting the texts in ritual procedures that entail a high degree of visual imagination. Indeed, the visionary is of crucial importance in the tantric traditions; there is no connotation of the 'imagined' as unreal. The visions constructed in inner awareness in conformity to the texts, the 'imaginative' construction of the body through visualisation, are not less real for the tantric practitioner than ordinary sense perception; they are more real. The visualisation of deities and the body are not categorised as the mere imagination of the wandering mind based on personal memory that is distracting from the goal of higher awareness, but are the construction of a world that, while being removed from the material realm of everyday transaction, is closer to the source of creation, and so the quality of reality is intensified. The world of everyday transaction for monistic Śaivas (the world wherein the indexical-I operates) is ultimately unreal, although it is real for the Śaiva Siddhāntin, where 'real' means ontologically distinct. The power of visualisation is the realisation of a higher level or deeper world of experience, an intensification of aesthetic experience, and an intensification of the truth of the body; that it is truly divine, and as such can approach and serve the Lord and his or her forms. Visualisation is realisation. Meditation or visualisation is a technique of experiencing a higher reality for the practitioner beyond the imaginatively restricted world of sense experience determined by past actions and ignorance. Through a tradition-constrained imagination, a new world of clarity, light and joy is opened to the practitioner.

One way of speaking about visualisation is that it is a representation of the body within the text, enacted in the inner vision of the practitioner. The representation of the body, the visionary body of tantric ritual imagination, occurs within the texts (as we have seen), within practice, and as objects in the form of icons of deities, paintings, and diagrams used in ritual. There are two aspects to tantric representation and vision. The first is that there is a strong connection between visionary representation and the symbolic order; the symbolic order of the system, text or tradition is envisaged in visionary terms (as in the visualisation of Nārāyaṇa in the heart, supported by a throne whose legs are made up of different aspects of the cosmical hierarchy and the sacred revelation of the Vedas – see pp. 116–17). Second, the lived body, the body of experience, and the visionary representation of the symbolic order are interpenetrated. The lived body experiences the symbolic order as a more intensified level of imagination than the world of everyday transaction bereft of imagination, where the common denominator is merely cultural functionality. The tantric practitioner constructs the world she or he inhabits from the texts, which provide, as it were, the architecture of the building of the imagination he, or indeed she, inhabits. This building is the palace of the deity with whom the practitioner is ritually identified at particular ritual junctures of the day, even in traditions that are metaphysically dualist. The tantric practitioner lives within the *maṇḍala*, lives within the *yantra*, lives within the vision of divinity such that the symbolic world of the text becomes the lived world of the body. Representation in text, icon and rite coalesce in the experience of the lived body. The world of the practitioner becomes a ritually constrained world or, to use Hanks's term, 'frame space',[2] which contains limited options within which the practitioner can operate. This construction of what is seen to be a more real edifice around the practitioner is both the mapping of life's journey from bondage in the cycle of transmigration to power and freedom, and the entextualisation of the body within a text-dependent symbolic order or representation. The practitioner lives within the frame space of the ritual edifice or within the ritual canopy (*vitānaka*) constructed in his visionary imagination.

Vision is therefore suffused with power (*śakti*) in these imaginative constructions, which are also realisations. The verb *smṛ*, 'to remember', is often used for visualisation, a term that has wider connotation than 'memory' and might be better understood as recollection or bringing to mind and evoking the forms of tradition (see below p. 178). The tāntrika lives within 'memory' understood in this way as an edifice of a ritual–visual symbolic order that his body is within and that is also within his body. The lived body reflects the level of representation and symbolic order, or, to put it less passively, acts out and performs that symbolic order. Indeed, the acting out of the particular symbolic order or visionary representation, which is the deification of the self and entextualisation of the body, is a defining feature of tantric culture. The imaginative mental actions of ritual, accompanied by ritual utterances, have illocutionary force. The utterance of the mantra is the making present of the deity; the inhabiting of the visionary universe is making it present as a stronger reality than that of the merely everyday or of the frame space of those who inhabit a lower revelation.

The Tantras and tantric theologians are therefore opposed to the views of the materialist tradition (*carvaka*, *lokāyata*) on the grounds that materialism is in fact moving away from the truth of higher worlds, and to strip imaginative vision away from any account of reality is to strip away the very foundational nature of the world. Without imaginative vision the world is nothing and almost unconscious. In Śaiva Siddhānta theology, without Śiva's enlivening gaze the cosmos is indeed unconscious (*jaḍa*); the practitioner recapitulates this creative vision in his own practice, especially in animating complex visualisations (*dhyāna*) within the ritual and meditative process.

Gesture and Utterance

Inseparably associated with visualisation are the two practices of ritual hand gestures or *mudrās* and the utterance of mantra. There is a variety of *mudrās* that accompany ritual, described in various texts including foundational ritual texts such as the *Mṛgendrāgama*.[3]

The term *mudrā*, 'seal', is rich, with levels of meaning that exceed the primary reference to gesture. Its principal designation is to hand gestures that accompany ritual action; hence it might be seen as the gestural equivalent of mantra. *Mudrā* is the gestural form of the deity. Yet the term can refer not only to ritual gestures that 'seal' and protect the body but to practices that seal power within it in the form of semen: the practice of the *vajroli mudrā* in which mixed sexual fluids are retracted into the penis for the purpose of gaining power,[4] and the *khecarī-mudrā* of *haṭha* yoga, the practice of turning the tongue back above the palate in order to drink the nectar of immortality dripping from the thousand petalled lotus at the crown.[5] The term *mudrā* is even used for levels of the cosmos, perhaps in the sense that one level is sealed off from the next. André Padoux has outlined the meanings and contexts of the term's occurrence, especially with reference to the *Vāmakeśvarīmata-tantra* and to Abhinavagupta.[6] *Mudrā*, explains Abhinavagupta, is of four sorts, done with body, hands, speech or mind and he gives an etymology (*nirukta*) of the word: that it 'is so called in the śāstras because it is that which gives, that which bestows, upon the self, through the body (*dehadvārena*), a bliss which is the attainment of one's real nature'.[7] *Mudrā* is not simply a ritual gesture but a reflection (*pratibimba*) of a deity and energy (*śakti*) that liberates beings from all conditions of existence. The *Yoginīhṛdaya* gives ten kinds of *mudrā* as hand gestures which are aspects of the deity Tripurasundarī, and indeed only discusses their cosmic significance as ten aspects of her energy of action. Padoux observes that the procedure of the *mudrā*s takes place on several levels, the divine–cosmic, the corporeal–mental and the ritual, and 'brings into play, through thought and bodily action, a cosmic, mental and corporeal totality'.[8]

Mantra is connected to *mudrā* in that as *mudrā* is the expression of the deity in the body through gesture, so mantra is the sonic form of the god. It is not within the scope of this work to offer a systematic study of mantras; such study can be seen in the works of André Padoux[9] and the important volume of papers published by Alper,[10] and Gonda's important paper is still germane to the topic.[11] In the tantric traditions mantra is the sound form of the deity empowered by the master and given at initiation. The master, says the *Mālinī*, illuminates the energy of mantra (*mantravīrya*),[12] and Kṣemarāja in his commentary on the *Śiva-sūtras* links the guru with the energy of mantra and *mudrā*.[13] This notion of *mantravīrya* is important in that as the master enlivens the mantra, brings it to life as he would the icon of a deity, so the *mantravīrya* is internalised by the practitioner. Through mantra his body is brought to life as the divine body; the repetition of mantra (*japa*) is clearly an entextualisation of the body. This has to be well taught (*suśikṣita*) says Abhinavagupta. Although the mantra comes through the mouth of the master its real source is pure consciousness, absolute subjectivity (*aham*), which is the greatest mantra.[14] Mantra embodies the energy of the deity, which is activated by the master and through its repetition, thereby enabling the adept, in Gonda's words, 'to exercise power over the potencies manifesting in it, to establish connections between the divinity and himself, or to realise his identity with that divinity.'[15]

In his study of Kṣemarāja's commentary on the *Śiva-sūtras*, Alper shows how mantras must be taken on a number of levels, in a social context (attitudes, expectations, socialisation) and in an epistemological context as 'tools for engendering (recognizing) a certain state of affairs'.[16] They also have illocutionary force in so far as uttering the mantra is the performance of a ritual action, although we must be aware here of the subtlety of the tantric cosmology that links mantras to worlds, sign to function.[17] Different mantras (and therefore different deities) correspond to or have their source in different levels of the cosmical hierarchy, as Padoux has shown.[18] We might say that mantras embody the vibrational energy of a higher level of the cosmos and/or deity. By repeating the mantra the adept is attempting to access or conform to the mantra's source. As this source is textual and revealed, the internalisation of the mantra is making the body conform to the textual revelation. Repeating mantras is entextualising the body.

Icon

We have then, different forms of the tantric deity internalised by the practitioner: the icon of inner vision, the *mudrā* as an expression of the deity, and the sound-form of the deity in mantra in all tantric traditions, including the Buddhist where visions of the body become highly ornate.[19] The inner vision and mantra of the deity also have external correlates in the icon. This is particularly important in external worship which follows divinisation and mental worship. The inner vision of the deity and retinue, which is the *maṇḍala*, has an external correlate installed and empowered as a temporary focus for daily rites or on a more permanent basis as a temple icon. The temple itself is an icon of the deity and the deity's body. The identification of the temple with the deity is a standard idea, well documented in medieval Hindu kingdoms (see pp. 81–3). As vision is to the practitioner's body, so the icon in the temple is to the temple as a whole. The representation of the body of the deity at the heart of the temple is a correlate to the inner vision of the deity by the practitioner, and as the external practice can be seen as an extension of the inner practice of mental worship, so the temple itself can be seen as an extension of the icon at its centre – the extended body of the deity extended in precise ways as laid down in tantric revelation.

The material representation of the deity in the image or icon (*mūrti*, *vigraha*, *bimba*) is the correlate of the deity within the practitioner's body; indeed, the traditions of the left tend to disparage physical manifestations of the deity as inferior. The representations that remain generally follow the descriptions in the texts; material reality follows textual prescriptions. A number of texts contain iconographic descriptions of pantheons of deities, of particular note being the sixteenth century *Tantrasāra* by Kṛṣṇānanda,[20] edited and translated by Pal, and three texts translated by Bühnemann: the *Mantramahodadhi*, also of the sixteenth century, the tenth-century *Prapañcasāra*, and the slightly later *Śāradātilika* by Lakṣmaṇa.[21] Bühnemann observes that these texts, while being tantric, were also Smārta, composed by tantric, orthodox Smārta Brahmans for Brahmans. A discussion of this material, generally much later than the texts that have been our main concern here, would not contribute much to our argument; nevertheless it is significant that the bodies of the deities are represented in plastic form. Within the tantric *imaginaire*, this plastic expression is a physical manifestation of a higher power, at least once made subject to ritual invocation. We have, then, a two-stage process of the forming of the icon in accordance with iconographic texts, followed by the empowering of the image, the bringing down of the deity into it by the qualified tantric priest. The icon is divinised in a way that directly parallels the divinisation of the body; the icon becomes the body of the deity and the mantra energised by the guru becomes the body of the deity, as the human body becomes divinized through the *bhūtaśuddhi* and *nyāsa*.

Indexicality

The practices of vision or visualisation (*dhyāna*), gesture (*mudrā*) and divinizing the icon (*mūrti*, *bimba*, *vigraha*) are shared across the tantric traditions. To establish the idea of variable indexicality more firmly we need to take a short, technical diversion, looking at the language our texts use for ritual meditation or visualisation.[22] The verbs used for ritual meditation or visualisation are from the roots *smṛ, dhyā*, *bhū*. caus., and *cint*. The term *smṛ*, 'to remember', is particularly interesting, having a wider semantic field than simply recalling something past. Although a more thorough study of its occurrences would be needed to substantiate the claim fully, the term seems to refer to the holding of a mental image in imagination.[23] In terms of grammar in the texts we have presented, these verbs are generally used in the third-person optative, the mood expressing a wish, apart from gerundives, which is all-pervasive in these texts and is nothing unusual, but is perhaps significant in supporting our claim about the body becoming inscribed by the text. Let us take three random examples of the use of the optative from the *Jayākhya*.

1. In context of the destruction of the earth element we read: '[The practitioner] should visualize a quadrangular, yellow earth, marked with the sign of thunder'.[24]
2. At the completion of the dissolution of the water element, 'with the inhaled breath he should bring to mind, O twice-born one, the body is its own sacred diagram, completely filled with that [water element].'[25]
3. In the dissolution of the air element 'he should meditate upon [the air element] pervading from the throat to the place of the navel.'[26]

In these examples the main verb, 'he should meditate' ... etc, is in the third-person singular optative, a mood which, according to the famous grammarian Pāṇini, is used in five senses: to denote a command (*vidhi*), a summons (*nimantraṇa*), an invitation (*āmantraṇa*), a respectful command (*adhīṣṭa*), an enquiry (*saṃpraśna*) or a request (*prārthana*).[27] All of these senses have the implication of conditions; that the performance of certain actions will lead to certain future effects. Indeed, the optative implies action and its effects in future time, as it cannot refer to the past or to the actualised present. As used here, the optative corresponds to Pāṇini's analysis in that the Pāñcarātrin's religious discipline (*vrata*) is a command from the lord (*vidhi*, as in 'you must go to the village' – *grāmaṃ bhavān gacchet*), and is also an invitation (*āmantraṇa*, as in 'do sit here' – *iha bhavān āsīta*) or a request from an authoritative source (*prārthana*, 'I would like to study grammar' – *vyakaraṇam adhīyīya*).

The analysis of the optative mood within different schools tended to focus upon the relationship between the person or text uttering the injunction, the receiver, and the action to be performed. According to one commentator on Pāṇini, Nāgeśabhaṭṭa, the first four definitions (*vidhi* etc.) can be included within a fifth, namely *pravartana* or 'instigation', an activity on the part of one person which leads to another's performing an action. There is a sequence of implication in the use of the optative. Namely, that the instigation is uttered by an authoritative person (*āpta*); that there is nothing inhibiting the instigation; and that the 'instigatee' infers that the action he is being asked to perform is something he desires and is achievable.[28] Nāgeśa defines the qualified person as being one who is free from confusion, anger and so on, and who does not perform actions that lead to undesired results. A *vidhi*, he says, is connected with certain properties of an action, the property of being a means to something desired (*iṣṭasādhyatva*), its feasibility (*kṛtisādhyatva*), and the absence of inhibitory factors (*pratibandhakābhāva*).[29] The use of the optative in our texts is therefore consonant with this understanding.

There is therefore an imperative to perform mental action as prescribed in these texts, in the sense that if a certain course of action is undertaken then certain results will follow, a fact that can be inferred from the imperative coming from an authoritative source. Indeed, the terms *smaret* (e.g. at 10.34a), *cintayet* (e.g. at 10.28a), *dhyāyet* (e.g. at 10.54a) and *bhāvayet* (e.g. at 10.46a) are the same grammatical form as terms denoting physical actions, such as imposing or infusing the body with mantra (*nyāset*, e.g. at 10.66b). In this sense, it would seem that the use of the optative in the Tantras is akin to its use in the Vedas, as in the injunction 'one desirous of heaven should perform the *jyotiṣṭoma* sacrifice' (*jyotiṣṭomena svargakāmo yajet*).[30] There is no grammatical distinction within these texts between actions performed 'in the mind' and actions performed 'with the body'. Indeed the grammar points in quite the opposite direction to a mind/body dualism, namely that mental action is directly akin to physical action, and that as physical action has effect in the ritual realm, so too does mental action. This is because the hierarchical cosmology assumed in these ritual operations is a 'magical' cosmology that enables actions (including mental action) to have effects at spatially and temporally distinct locations.

One might speculate further that the use of the optative, with its implication of possible future action, is related to the imagination or the metaphorical space in which events and abstractions are projected; a projection which is permitted by the very structure of languages with at least three tenses.[31] While, as Lakoff and Johnson have shown, all of language is pervaded by metaphor,[32] the use of the optative is particularly suggestive of the possibility of metaphor and of the kinds of mapping and overcoding on to the body that we find in our texts. The terms *kṣipet* and *nyāset* imply that the adept should project the mantra or image into the metaphorical space of his creative imagination. This is indeed a mental action that has effect in that metaphorical space, and will have consequences for the practitioner in terms of liberation at death.

Reading

The use of language and metaphorical space of projected meaning allows for the identification of the self with the implied 'I' of the texts. While I have developed this in relation to scriptural traditions elsewhere,[33] we need briefly to restate this fundamental idea here.

Reading these texts through a dialogical lens, the use of the optative tells us something of the relationship between the 'reader' and the 'text', and tells us something about the nature of the self assumed. In one conception, the fundamental structure of semiotics is an addresser transmitting a message to an addressee, who receives it, almost in a passive fashion, and decodes it. This requires 'contact' between the two, a 'code' in which the message is formulated, and a 'context' that gives sense to the message.[34] In the case of the JS, for example, the addresser, the redactor of the text, sends the message of the text (the ritual representation) to an addresser, the Pāñcarātrin, who receives it. If, however, we look at ritual representation through the lens of dialogism, we are presented with a different picture. The dialogists reject the emphasis on language as a purely abstract system, seeing it rather as constantly changing and adapting to concrete historical situations and not, to use Volosinov's phrase, as 'a stable and always self-equivalent signal'.[35] On this view the meaning of words is governed by the contexts of their occurrence, so utterance can be accounted for only as a social phenomenon. Language is a process generated in the interaction of speakers within social contexts. Turning to our texts, whereas a structuralist reading of the JS and ISP might present the Brahmanical addressee in purely passive terms as the decoder of a message from the text (and from the past), a dialogical reading would see both addresser and addressee as constructing the text's meaning. That is, there is a dialogical relationship between 'sender' and 'receiver' and meaning is constructed between the two rather than passively received and an original meaning decoded. This is more in line with Peircean semiotics, where the basic pattern is threefold, of a sign, that to which it points, and the interpreter.[36]

This general relationship between the 'reader' and the 'addresser' can be more closely analysed and textually instantiated in terms of what might be called a relationship between extra-textual indexicality and intra-textual anaphora. The dialogical relationship is between the implicit (Brahman) reader, a notional 'I', and the 'characters' of the text who yet can function indexically as 'I's. Indeed, we have already encountered deixis or metalepsis in our study, the idea that first- and second-person pronouns and locative and temporal adverbs such as 'here' and 'there' can be contrasted with anaphoric terms which refer to a previous item in a discourse (such as 'he', 'she', 'it' and 'they'). Thus indexicality always refers outside of itself to a context (as would be indicated by 'you' or 'there'), whereas anaphora does not refer outside of the utterance; the term 'he', for example, would refer to a previously named person. The qualities of indexicality are both generalised and referential, inexorably linked to the context of utterance. When we shift to anaphoric terms, to the third person for example, discourse ceases to have the indexical qualities of deixic language. Anaphora is always discourse-internal in that terms such as 'he' or 'her' are substitutes for some previously named person or entity. As has been discussed by Urban in an important paper, a complication arises when apparently indexical terms, particularly the floating signifier 'I', are used anaphorically in direct discourse.[37] 'I' becomes anaphoric when placed in a sentence such as 'the Brahman said "I perform the sacrifice"' where the 'I' does not refer to anything outside of the narrative itself. The 'I' is an empty sign in the sense that it is not referential with respect to a specific reality. This is important in the context of the ritual representations in tantric texts.

The *Jayākhya*, for example, is a dialogue between the Lord (Bhagavān) and the sage Nārada, where Nārada is addressed in the second person. The Lord uses the imperative, 'hear this' (*tac chṛṇu*), which is anaphoric in that the implied *tvam* ('you') refers to the sage often named in the vocative ('O Nārada'). Yet ritual prescriptions are usually in the third-person singular optative, as we have seen above, in phrases such as 'he should visualise' or 'remember' or 'know'. The third person here takes the place of the second person directed to Nārada and indirectly to the reader of the text, but its use serves to formalize and distance the discourse from any direct indexical reference. The ritualist 'reader' of the text is being addressed by the Lord indirectly through Nārada, who stands in for the practitioner. Indeed the Mīmāṃsaka school of philosophy corroborates this general point in claiming that the use of the third person optative in vedic injunction actually refers to 'me', the reader of the text, performing the ritual injunction.[38] We might make a similar claim of the ritual injunction here. This linguistic form, the objectification of the ritual performer, has the effect of controlling the dialogic relations between the characters and the reader, and of allowing their identification in imagination. In the passages cited above, the anaphoric third person is indirectly understood by the text's receiver or reader to be referring to the indexical 'I'. The reader understands that the third person actually refers to 'me' (the indexical 'I') through Nārada. The object of the second-person discourse is also the grammatical subject of the third-person optatives, and moreover indirectly refers outside of the text to the reader.

In this way, the text's meaning is constructed through the identification of the indexical 'I', the tantric Brahmanical reader of the text, with the third person understood as though indexical. Yet being articulated in the third person optative also maintains an impersonal voice concordant with the claimed universality of the revelation. The use of the optative allows for the imaginative identification of the indexical 'I' with the implied 'I' of the text itself. The grammar of the text allows for the imaginative identification of the reader with the representation of the ritual practitioner and the structure of the texts' language, its ritual injunctions, allows for variable indexicality.

Through this kind of analysis we can see how the text achieves the replication of ritual processes, and so the perpetuation of tradition, through the identification of the indexical 'I' with the anaphoric third person in the optative mood. The third-person optative functions as a substitute for an anaphoric 'I' in the text: the anaphoric 'I' is deferred through the third person. The social agent – the tantric Brahmanical reader – wishes to close the gap between the indexical 'I' (himself) and the deferred anaphoric 'I' of the texts through imagination and projection into the metaphorical space allowed by the use of the optative. Imagination provides awareness of the possibility of transformation and the possibility of behaving in a way that allows the goals of the tradition, internalized through the identification of the two 'I's, to be realised. The replication of the text and the truth-value it contains for a community, suggests furthermore that the text, as Urban and Silverstein have argued, is a trope of culture which is constantly decontextualised, or liberated from a specific historical context, and recontextualised in a new context.[39] Texts are the result of continuous cultural processes that create and re-create them over again as meaningful objects or tropes, which are constructed as having de-temporalised and de-spacialised meanings.

By way of conclusion, then, we can see this process occurring in the divinisation of the body in the tantric ritual texts. These texts transcend the boundaries of their production and are reconstituted through the generations, especially through the identification of the reader of the text with the ritualist represented. The textual representation of the *bhūtaśuddhi* is made meaningful both by the content of the texts and by the construction of its meaning in the imagination by the Brahmanical reader. One of the tasks in the study of tantric traditions becomes the inquiry into the ways in which these texts have been transmitted, their internalisation by the individual practitioner, and the function of these texts within the practices of the tradition. Through focusing on the divinisation of the body, it is hoped that this work has made some contribution to this understanding.

Epilogue

We have come a long way in our journey into the tantric body. In many ways this account is preliminary in that there are so many other texts that could be drawn on, critical editions of many texts are still to be made, and the map of historical trajectory of tantric traditions is far from complete. However, I hope to have presented a coherent picture of the processes at work in the development of representation and practice in some tantric material, namely the Śaiva and Pāñcarātra traditions. I also hope to have contributed to a corrective reading through presenting the tantric body in terms of text and tradition rather than in terms of a popular misconception of a dislocated 'experience'. The tantric body that thrived in tantric civilisation for centuries is not that of modernity. I hope to have shown how the tantric body in tradition is less reified than its modernist, literalist rendering, and how the subtle anatomy of the tantric body must be located in text and tradition and seen in terms of the body's divinisation, which is, I have argued, the body being inscribed by the text. This is, second, to show that the tantric body is not only less reified than its modern version but more conservative and tradition-based. The tantric body has been established within traditions of specific revelation, ritual practice and initiatory teachings from which it cannot be separated. Attempts to identify the tantric body with eroticism in the West are distortions of a rich and complex tradition. This distortion has taken two routes, one a laudation of an imagined tantric body as being a way of maximising erotic pleasure, the other a condemnation of the tantric body as being irrational in promoting 'magic' and 'immorality', an attitude found in nineteenth-century scholarship and in Hinduism itself in the trajectory stemming from the Hindu renaissance.

Yet while the tantric traditions are attenuated, the traditions that do remain – in Kerala, for example – will inevitably continue to undergo change and probable erosion. I suspect that the tantric body is at odds with modernity because it can only be understood in relation to a hierarchical cosmology in which the material world is a coagulation of more subtle forces. Although there have been attempts to reconcile or synthesise a hierarchical world-view with an evolutionary perspective (in the work of Aurobindo, for example) the order of being in the tantric universe remains at odds with a materialist, evolutionary understanding of the world. The tantric body of tradition is also at odds with contemporary expectations about gender and a feminist discourse that implicitly questions and critiques the tantric body.

So does the tantric body have anything to say to us today? The answer to this question is complex. Clearly there are elements within the tantric body that have appeal in Western modernity but that have been distorted through their extirpation from their historical and textual locations. This appeal is inevitably linked to the critique of religion as the history of error and the professed liberation of the individual from a straitjacket of conservative, Christian morality. There are, of course, Hindu-based traditions in the West, such as Siddha Yoga, the Nityananda Institute, and the Western inheritors of the Laksman Joo's 'Kashmir Śaivism', which claim to inherit the tantric traditions, and indeed sometimes guru lineages can be traced (as in the case of Laksman Joo), but inevitably these traditions are strongly affected by modernity and the tantric body they promote is not the tantric body of tradition. While all traditions undergo constant reinvention in new generations, traditions in modernity have been particularly susceptible to erosion. But the tantric body does contain resources that could arguably contribute to discourse in late modernity. Because the tantric body is so much a part of the wider cosmos, there are perhaps ecological implications contained within the traditions that those interested can draw upon, and there are transformative implications of tantric practice that could be a resource for those engaged with other traditions such as Christianity. I am sceptical that Hindu tantric traditions could in their richness be transplanted outside of the particular conditions of their past flourishing in South Asia. The Buddhist tantric traditions from Tibet have had considerable success, but the Hindu tantric traditions do not have the infrastructure or institutional history to affect such a successful transfer across cultures. Yet our study of the tantric body reveals a number of important things. The tantric body shows us the importance of text and tradition in the construction of human lives. It shows us a particular way of conceptualising the body distinct from either a Western dualism or materialism, it shows us how subjectivity is formed by tradition, and it shows us that such a tradition-formed subjectivity must be distinguished from Western individuality. There is arguably a wisdom here that has implications across cultures: that subjective transformations occur not through the assertion of individuality but through subjecting self and body to a master and to tradition.

APPENDIX

The Jayākhya-saṃhitā, Chapter 11

Now the procedure for fixing the mantra (Nyāsa)

1–3 The reciter of mantras, whose body is completely pure [due to the purification of the body rite or *bhūtaśuddhi*], should perform the fixing of mantras [on the body]. Only through the imposition of mantras can be become equal to the God of Gods. By this worship he wins power (*adhikāra*) over all outcomes and gains all supernatural powers. He will then be fearless, even in a place crowded with bad people, and attain victory over accidental death.

Making the throne

4–5 Upon the raised plank on the ground previously described [at 10.6], [the practitioner should] set down an ocean and lotus [in his imagination]. He should make effort with his own mantra accompanied by visualisation, then having fixed and visualised Tārkṣya [i.e. Viṣṇu's mount] he should sit down.

Making a protective wall around the throne

6–9 Having repeatedly purged the directions with the Weapon mantra (*astra*) and visualised the wall outside the throne like a web of arrows, the practitioner should cover the wall with the protecting mantra (*kavaca*), whose form is a shining breastplate. Like the perfected ones dwelling in heaven, O twice born one, he can become invisible. He should perform the fixing of mantras on himself. He should perform the protection according to this ordinance, since they [the demons?] take the strength of the mantra-born one who is not protected. Having first fixed mantras on his hands, he should then perform the fixing of mantras on his body.

Fixing mantras on the hand

10 The root (*mūla*) mantra followed by the mantra of form (*mūrti*) is on his thumb, followed by the remaining deities in due order beginning with the forefinger.

11–13 Having fixed all [the deities] ending with the little finger, he should fasten the [other] parts of the body [with mantra]. [He should establish the deities] in due order beginning with the Heart mantra on the little finger and so on. The Weapon mantra is on the thumb, whilst the Eye mantra is on the tips of the fingers. The Man-lion (*nṛiṃha*) should be fixed on the right hand and the sage Kapila on the left. Beginning with the left hand [he should fix] the Boar mantra on the fingers of both [hands]. The Kauṣṭubha mantra is on the right palm and the Vanamālā mantra on the other.

14–16 He should fix the Lotus mantra in the middle of the right palm and the Conch mantra on the left palm. Afterwards, [he should fix] the brilliant, Disc-weapon mantra there as well. He should fix the Club mantra on the right hand, flaming with its own splendour. Beginning from the right thumb to the least part [the little finger] at the end of the left, he should fix the Garuḍa mantra on all ten fingers in due order, followed by the Bond mantra on the palm of the left hand and the Goad mantra on the right.

17 He should establish the Heart [and other mantras] on both hands in due order. [Then he should fix] the secondary mantras, the five Seed mantras, beginning with Satya and ending with Aniruddha.

18–19b Then on both hands, from the fingernails to the end of the wrist, he should fix the Seven Syllable mantra [i.e. the *vyāpaka mantra*], which is laid over all the other mantras. By this ordinance he should perform the fixing of the hands mentioned previously.

Fixing mantras on the body

19c–22b The powerful, supreme Śakti is located in the cave of the heart centre. Her form is the wind and [her power] is established as tenfold. By her will through the current of the path of the hands, [ten channels of power] have gone out [from her]. The fingers are thus regarded as containing the ten channels. So, O best of twice-born ones, having first fixed the horde of mantras in the body of the Lord where they are known as [his] powers (*śakti*), one should then fix the elements.

22c–24b After placing the mass of mantras correctly on the body, the root mantra on the body as before from head to feet, and having fixed [mantras] all over himself from his feet to the end of his head, he should perform the fixing of all parts [of the body] with the mantra of form.

24c–25b [He should fix mantras] on his head, mouth, and left and right buttocks, in due order, then on the heart, on the back, in the navel, on the hips, on the knees, and then on the feet.

25c–29b In succession, beginning with *nā* and ending with *hā* there are twenty-two syllables. After fixing the mantra of form he should then fix the deities. On the left shoulder he should fix Lakṣmī and on the right Kīrtī. Next he should fix Jayā on the right hand and Māyā on the left. Following [that he should fix] the Limb mantras, [namely] the Heart [mantra] and so on. The Heart mantra is placed on the breast and the Head mantra on the head. The Tuft mantra is on the tuft and Breastplate mantra on the shoulders. He should fix the Eye mantra on both eyes and the Weapon mantra on the palms of the hands, O twice-born one.

29c–31c The Man-lion [he should fix] on the right ear and the Kaplila mantra at the throat.[1] Having fixed the chief mantra, Varāha, at the lower part of the left ear, [he should then fix] the Kauṣṭubha mantra in the middle of the chest and the Vanamālika mantra at the throat. Then [he should fix] the Lotus mantra and so on, as before [in the right palm], and, O twice-born one, the great Gāruḍa mantra between the two thighs.

31d–35b Then he should fix the group of secondary mantras beginning with Aniruddha, O best of twice-born ones, in sequence on the feet, between navel and penis, at the navel, at the heart, and at the base of the tuft. He should once more fix the fivefold Satya mantra and so on in succession, at the end of the aperture of Brahma, in the middle of the heart, in the lotus of the navel, between the navel and penis, and on the feet, in correct order. Then he should apply the great mantra of seven syllables of Viṣṇu, the Lord Nārāyaṇa, to the body from the head, like armour.

35c–36. All mantras are located in him and he is in them. He is the supreme power (*karaṇa*) of this group of mantras and stands at their head. Therefore one should fix him over all.

37–39b The circle of powers is variously fixed [in this way] from the heart to the navel, O best of sages, and he establishes their connection through mantra. Having performed the fixing [of mantras] in this way, he should next perform his own hand gesture for the mass of mantras that have been fixed, and for all of the root mantras and so on, on the body and on the hands. [These gestures] are associated with his mantra and how they are fixed [on the body].

39c–40 [The practitioner] should then visualise himself with his body in the form of Viṣṇu, possessing the six great qualities, by means of the visualisation practice previously described.[2] In this way his own form and the form of the universe are imagined as possessing [a single] form.

41–43b I am the Lord Viṣṇu, I am Nārāyaṇa, Hari, and I am Vāsudeva, all pervading, the abode of beings,[3] without taint. Thus having put down the ego [he establishes] a firm form, O sage. The best practitioner speedily becomes absorbed in that [form], due to the fixing of mantras, due to visualisation, and due to being in the midst of contemplation born from yoga.

43c–44b The action of fixing has been concisely taught to you by me. Practising diligently you must guard [this ritual knowledge] against others.

The Mantras Used in these Ritual Sequences

This table is derived from the mantras given by the editor of the *Jayākhya*, Embar Krishnamacharya, pp. 31–7. Rastelli also gives a list of mantra names associated with *nyāsa*, *Philosophisch-theologisch Grundanschaungen der Jayākhyasaṃhitā*, pp. 243–4.

The mūla mantra with the mūrti mantra

oṃ kṣīṃ kṣiḥ namaḥ, nārāyaṇāya viśvātmane hrīṃ svāhā

The Śakti mantras

Lakṣmī mantra oṃ lāṃ lakṣmyai namaḥ, paramalakṣmāvāsthitāyai lāṃ śrīṃ hrīṃ svāhā

Kīrti mantra oṃ kāṃ kīrttyai namaḥ, sadoditānantdavigrahāyai hrīṃ krīṃ svāhā

Jayā mantra oṃ jāṃ jayāyai namaḥ, ajitadhāmāvasthitāyai jāṃ jrīṃ svāhā

Māyā mantra oṃ māṃ māyāyai namaḥ, mohātītapadāśritāyai māṃ mrīṃ svāhā

The aṅga mantras

Hṛt mantra oṃ haṃ namaḥ, oṃ haṃsaḥ śuciṣade hṛdayāya namaḥ
Śiras mantra oṃ hāṃ namaḥ, oṃ parabrahmaśirase svāhā
Śikha mantra oṃ hīṃ namaḥ, oṃ pradyotaniśikhāyai vaṣaṭ
kavaca mantra oṃ huṃ namaḥ, oṃ śāśvataśaraṇyakavacāya huṃ
netra mantra oṃ hauṃ namaḥ, prakāśaprajvalanetrāya vauṣaṭ
astra mantra oṃ haḥ namaḥ, 'dīptodṛptaprabha astrāya phaṭ

The vaktra mantras

Nṛsiṃha mantra oṃ ṭjroṃ ṭj dmruauṃ namaḥ, jvalanāyutadīptaye nṛsiṃhāya svāhā

Kapila mantra oṃ ṭhūm ṭghrūauṃ namaḥ, anantabhāsāya kapilāya svāhā

Varāha mantra oṃ ṭgloṃ ṭsvūṃ namaḥ, kṛṣṇapiṅgalāya parāhāya svāhā

The lāñchana mantras

Kaustubha mantra oṃ ṭhaṃ rhrūṃ ṭhaṃ namaḥ prabhātmane kaustubhāya svāhā

Vanamāla mantra oṃ lsbīṃ namaḥ sthalajalodbhūtabhūṣite vanamāle svāha

Padma mantra oṃ bsuṃ namaḥ śrīnivāsapadmāya svāha
Śaṅkha mantra oṃ hūṃ hūṃ hūṃ namaḥ mahāśaṅkhāya svāha
Cakra mantra oṃ jraḥ kraḥ phaṭ hūṃ namaḥ phaṭphaṭphaḍviṣṇucakrāya svāha

Gadā mantra oṃ gmleṃ jḷṃ namaḥ sahasrāśrigade svāha
Garuḍa mantra oṃ rkṣrūauṃ rkhrūauḥ namaḥ anantagataye garuḍāya svāha

Pāśa mantra oṃ rṇaṃ kaḍhḍha kaḍhḍha ṭhaṭha parapāśāya svāha
Aṅkuśa mantra oṃ lṛṃ kṛṃ niśitaghoṇāya svāha

The upāṅga mantras

Satya bīja mantra oṃ kṣauṃ oṃ
Vāsudeva bīja mantra oṃ hūṃ oṃ
Saṅkarṣaṇa bīja mantra oṃ sūṃ oṃ
Pradyumna bīja mantra oṃ ṣīṃ oṃ
Aniruddha bīja mantra oṃ śāṃ oṃ

Abbreviations and Sources

AD	*Āgamaḍambara* of Jayantha Bhaṭṭa. V. Raghavan and A Thakur (eds.), *Āgamaḍambara, Otherwise called Ṣaṇmatanāṭaka of Jayantha Bhaṭṭa* (Darbhanga: Mithila Institute, 1964).
AG	*Āgamapramāṇya* of Yāmuna. M. Narasimhachary (ed.), *Āgamapramāṇya of Yāmuna* (Baroda: Oriental Institute, 1976). English translation by J.A.B. van Buitenen, *Yāmuna's Āgamaprāmānya or Treatise on the Validity of Pāñcarātra. Sanskrit Text and English Translation* (Madras: Rāmānuja Research Society, 1971).
Ajit	*Arthaśāstra*. R.P. Kangle, *The Kautilya Arthaśāstra* (University of Bombay, 2nd edn, 1969).
Aṣṭ	*Aṣṭādhyāyī of Pāṇini*. Trans. Sumitra M. Katre (Delhi: MLBD, 1989).
Bhut	*Bhūtaśuddhi*. Transcript no. 656 (Pondicherry: Institut Français d'Indologie, n.d.).
DH	*Dehasthadevatācakrastotra*. H. Sri Ragunath Temple Manuscript Library, Jammu, pp. 205–6, 290–92. Copy courtesy of Alexis Sanderson. French translation by L. Silburn, *Hymnes aux Kālī, La Roue des Énergies Divine* (Paris: de Boccard, 1975), pp. 85–6. Source unattributed, but probably from the text published by Pandey which differs slightly from the Ragunath Temple manuscript.
IP	*Īśvarapratyabhijñā-kārikā* by Utpalaseva. Ed. M.S. Kaul (Srinagar: KSTS no. 34, 1921).
IPV	*Īśvarapratyabhijñāvimarśinī* by Abinavagupta, vol.1, ed. M.R. Śāstri (Srinagar: KSTS, no. 22, 1918); vol. 2, ed. M.S. Kaul (Srinagar: KSTS no. 33, 1918). English translation by K.C. Pandey, edited with K.A.S. Iyer, *Bhāskarī*, 3 vols (Delhi: MLBD reprint, 1986 [1938, 1950, 1954]).

ISG *Īśānaśivagurudeva-paddhati*. Ed. M.M.T. Gaṇapati Śāstrī with an introduction by N.P. Unni, *Īśānaśivagurudeva Paddhati of Īśānaśiva Gurudeva*, 4 vols (Delhi and Vārāṇasī: Bharatiya Vidyā Prakashan, 1988).

JS *Jayākhya-saṃhitā of the Pāñcarātra Āgama*. Ed. E. Krishnamacharya (Baroda: Gaekwad's Oriental Series, no. 54, 1931).

KA *Kāmikāgama (Uttara Bhāga)*. Ed. Śrī C. Svaminathasivacarya (Madras: South Indian Archarkar Association, 1988).

Kaul *Kaulajñānanirṇaya and Some Minor Texts of the School of Matsyendranāth*. Ed. P.C. Bagchi (Calcutta Sanskrit Series, 1934). English translation by Michael Magee, *Kaulajñāna-nirṇaya of the School of Matsyendranātha* Tantra Granthamala no. 12 (Varanasi: Prachaya Prakashan, 1986).

KMT *Kubjikāmata-tantra*. Critical edition by T. Goudriaan and J.A. Schoterman, *The Kubjikāmatatantra, Kulalikāmnaya Version* (Leiden: Brill, 1988).

KSTS Kashmir Series of Texts and Studies.

KirT *Kiraṇa-tantra. Bhaṭṭa Rāmakaṇṭha's Commentary on the Kiraṇatantra*, vol. 1 chapters 1–6. Critical edition and annotated translation by Dominic Goodall (Pondicherry: Institut Français d'Indologie, 1998).

KT *Kulārṇava-tantra*. Edited and translated by Arthur Avalon (London: Tantrik Texts vol. 5, 1917).

KumT *Kumāratantra*. Jean Filliozat, *Le Kumāratantra de Rāvaṇa et les textes parallèles Indiens, Tibétains, Chinois, Cambodgien, et Arabe* (Paris: Imprimerie Nationale, 1937).

LT *Lakṣmī-tantra. A Pāñcarātra āgama*. Ed. Pandit V. Krihnamacharya (Madras: Adyar Library and Research Centre, 1959). English translation by Sanjukta Gupta, *The Lakṣmī Tantra* (Leiden: Brill, 1972).

Manu *Mānavadharmaśāstra, the Code of Manu*. Critically edited by J. Jolly (London: Trübner, 1887). *Manuśāstravivaraṇa*. J. Duncan Derrett M. *Bharuci's Commentary on the Manusmṛti (the Manu-śāstra-vivarana, books 6–12)*, text, translation and notes, vol. 1 (Wiesbaden: Franz Steiner, 1975).

MManj *Mahārthamañjari with parimala by Maheśvarānanda*. Ed. M.R. Śāstrī (Srinagar: KSTS, no. 11, 1918). French translation by Lilian Silburn, *La Mahārthamañjari de Maheśvarānanda* (Paris: de Boccard, 1968).

MNPrak *Mahānayaprakāśa* edited by K. Sāmbaśiva Śāstrī, Trivandrum Sanskrit Series 130 (Trivandrum: Government Press, 1937).

Mrg *Mṛgendrāgama (Kriyāpāda et Caryāpāda) avec le commentaire de Bhaṭṭa Nārāyaṇakṇṭha*. Critically edited by N.R. Bhatt (Pondicherry: Institut Français d'Indologie, 1962). French translation by Hélène Brunner-Lachaux, *Mṛgendrāgama: section des rites et section du comportement avec la vṛtti de Bhaṭṭa Nārāyaṇakaṇṭha* (Pondicherry: Institut Français d'Indololgie, 1985). French translation by Michel Hulin, *Mṛgendrāgama: sections de la doctrine et du yoga avec la vṛtti de Bhaṭṭanārāyaṇakantha et la dipika d'Aghorásivācārya*. (Pondicherry: Institut Français d'Indololgie, 1980).

MVT *Mālinīvijayottara-tantra*. Ed. M.S. Kaul (Sringar: KSTS no. 37, 1922).

MVT vart *Mālinīślokavārttika*. Jürgen Hanneder, *Abhinavagupta's Philosophy of Revelation: Mālinīślokavārttika* I, 1–399 (Groningen: Egbert Forsten, 1998).

MTP *Mataṅgaparameśvarāgama*. See below.

MTPVrt *Mataṅgaparameśvarāgama (vidyāpāda), avec le commentaire de Bhaṭṭa Rāmakaṇṭha*. Critically edited by N.R. Bhatt (Pondicherry: Institut Français d'Indologie, 1977).

NeT *Netra-tantra with uddyota by Kṣemarāja*. Ed. M.S. Kaul, 2 vols (Srinagar: KSTS nos 46 and 61, 1926 and 1927).

NJ *Nyāyamañjari of Jayantha Bhaṭṭa*. English translation by V.N. Jha (Delhi: Śrī Satguru publications, 1995).

PH *Pratyabhijñāhṛdaya* by Kṣemarāja. Ed. J.C. Chatterji (Sringar: KSTS no. 3, 1911). English translation by Jaideva Singh, *Pratyabhijñāhṛdaya* (Delhi: MLBD, 1980).

PS *Paramārthasāra* by Abhinavagupta with *vivṛti* by Yogarāja. Ed. J.C. Chatterjee (Srinagar: KSRTS no. 7, 1916). French translation by Lilian Silburn, *La Paramārthasāra* (Paris: de Boccard, 1957).

Ptlv *Parātrīśikālaghuvṛtti* by Abhinavagupta. Edited with notes by Mahamahopadhyaya Pandit Mukunda Rama Shâstrî (Srinagar: KSTS, vol. 18, 1918). French translation by André Padoux, *La Parātrīśikālaghuvṛtti de Abhinavagupta*, Publications de l'Institut de Civilisation Indienne, fasc. 38 (Paris: de Boccard, 1975). English translation by Paul Muller-Ortega, *The Triadic Heart of Śiva: Kaula Tanrism of Abhinavagupta in the Non-dual Shaivism of Kashmir* (Albany: SUNY Press, 1989), pp. 205–32.

Ptv *Parātrīśikāvivaraṇa*. Jaideva Singh, *Abhinavagupta: A Trident of Wisdom*, Text and translation (Delhi: MLBD, 1989).

RA *Rauravāgama*. Critical edition by N.R. Bhatt, 3 vols (Pondicherry: Institut Français d'Indologie, 1988).

RAot *Rauravottarāgama*. Critical edition by N.R. Bhatt (Pondicherry: Institut Français d'Indologie, 1983).

Sard *Sārdhatriśatikālottarāgama avec le commentaire de Bhaṭṭa Rāmakaṇṭha*. Critical edition by N.R. Bhatt (Pondicherry: Institut Français d'Indologie,1979).

SP *Śilpaprakāśa, a Medieval Orissan Sanskrit Text on Temple Architecture* by Rāmacadra Kaulācāra. English translation by Alica Boner and Sadāśiva Rath Śarma (Leiden: Brill, 1966).

Spand *Spandapradīpikā* by Utpalācārya. Ed. Mark S.G. Dyczkowski, *The Spandapradīpikā, a Commentary on the Spandakārikā* (Varansi: private publication, 1990).

SSP *Somaśambhupaddhati*. Ed. and French trans. by Hélène Brunner-Lachaux, 4 vols (Pondicherry: Institut Française d'Indologie, vol. 1, 1963; vol. 2, 1968; vol. 3, 1977; vol. 4, 2000).

SSV *Śiva-sūtra-vimarśinī* by Kṣemarāja. Ed. Jagadisha Chandra Chatterji (Srinagar: KSTS, vol. 1, 1911). English translation by Jaideva Singh (Delhi: MLBD, 1979).

SVT *Svacchandabhairava-tantra* with *uddyota* by Kṣemarāja. Ed. M.S. Kaul, 7 vols (Srinagar: KSTS, 1921–55); reprinted in 4 vols (Delhi: Sanskrit Gian Sansthan, 1986).

TA *Tantrāloka* by Abhinavagupta with *viveka* by Jayaratha, 12 vols. Ed. by M.S. Śāstrī (vol. 1) and M.S. Kaul (vols 2–12) (Srinagar: KSTS, 1918–38). Edition by R.C. Dwivedi and N. Rastogi, 8 vols (Delhi: MLBD, 1987). Italian translation by R. Gnoli, *La Lucce delle Sacre Scritture* (Torino: Boringheri, 1972). French translation by Lilian Silburn and André Padoux, *La Lumière sur les Tantras: La Tantrāloka d'Abhinavagupta chapitres 1 à 5* (Paris: de Boccard, 1998).

TatPrak *Tattvaprakāśa Siddhāntaśaiva darśanam by Bhojadeva with tātparya-dīpikā and vṛtti Commentaries by Śrī Kumāradeva and Aghoraśivācharya.* Ed. Kameshwar Nath Mishra (Vārāṇasī: Chaukhamba Orientalia, 1976).

TS *Tantrasāra* by Abhinavagupta. Ed. M.S. Kaul (Srinagar: KSTS no. 17, 1918).

TSam *Tantrasamuccaya* by Nārāyaṇa with the commentary vimarśinī of Śaṇkara. Ed. M.T. Gaṇapati Śāstrī with an introduction by B.P. Unni (Delhi: Nag Publishers, 1990 [1921].

TSG *Tantra Sāra Saṅgraha* with commentary, critcially edited by M. Duraiswami Aiyangar (Madras: Government Oriental Manuscripts Library, 1950).

VK *Vākyapādiya* by Bhartṛhari. Ed. with English translation by K.A.S. Iyer, 3 vols (Delhi: Motilal Banarsidass, 1983).

YH *Yoginīhṛdaya.* A. Padoux, *Le coeur de la yogini: Yoginīhṛdaya avec le commentaire Dīpikā D'Amṛtānanda* (Paris: de Boccard, 1994).

YT *Yoni-tantra.* J.A. Schoterman, *The Yoni Tantra Critically Edited with Introduction* (Delhi: Manohar, 1980).

Notes

Chapter 1

1. M. Monier-Williams, *Hinduism* (London: Society for the Promotion of Christian Knowledge, 1880), p. 129.
2. M. Monier-Williams, *Brāhmanism and Hinduism or Religious Life and Thought in India* (London: John Murray, 1891 [1883]), p. 190. It is, of course, easy to take pot shots at texts from the colonial past that reflect very different values to those of late modernity. This is not my intention. I wish, rather, to point to one important way in which Tantrism has been represented. Monier Williams is in many ways an exemplary scholar. His value judgements aside, his comments on the texts are remarkably accurate considering the limited knowledge of these traditions available to him.
3. Bhagavan Shree Rajneesh, *The Book of Secrets 1: Discourses on the Vigyan Bhairav Tantra* (Poona: Rajneesh Foundation, 1974), pp. 3–4.
4. I take 'first-order discourse' to be the texts of tradition or tradition itself; second-order discourse is the application of methods (such as critical reading, text editing and so on) to the first-order discourse; and third-order discourse is metatheoretical reflection that assumes the second-order discourse but wishes to go beyond this in establishing interpretations and theories that exceed the texts themselves. We might say that a third-order discourse allows reflection on a first-order discourse through its being embedded in that third order, through the second-order discourse. Translated to a terminology of phenomenology, the *noema* is linked to the *noesis* through the second-order discourse. To use a different kind of terminology, we have a dialogical process of constantly shifting readers; the dialogical process mediated through the structures of reading.
5. I am aware that these are Western, and so contentious, categories to use in

the context of Tantra. I tend not to put such terms in scare quotes. For now I shall simply say that we have to use some categories and some language in which to describe these traditions on to which terminologies of the traditions can be mapped. As will become clear, I do not hold to a strong incommensurability thesis.

6. Inden substitutes this phrase for 'ritual'. R. Inden, 'Introduction: From Philological to Dialogical Texts', in R. Inden, Jonathan S. Walters, and Daud Ali, *Querying the Medieval: Texts and the History of Practices in South Asia* (Oxford: Oxford University Press, 2000), pp. 3–28; p. 22.
7. I am indebted to James Gentry for this felicitous phrase. On my understanding of subjectivity, see G. Flood, *The Ascetic Self: Subjectivity, Memory and Tradition* (Cambridge: Cambridge University Press, 2004), pp. 16–19.
8. One particularly pervasive Western reification is 'tantric sex'. See, for example, Val Sampson, *Tantra: The Art of Mind Blowing Sex* (London: Vermilion, 2000), although many others could be cited. White has argued against this Western appropriation: D. White, *The Kiss of the Yoginī: 'Tantric Sex' in its South Asian Contexts* (Chicago: University of Chicago Press, 2003), pp, xii–xv, 258.
9. Northrop Frye, *Fearful Symmetry: A Study of William Blake* (Boston MA: Beacon Press, 1947), p. 9.
10. See Hugh Urban, *Tantra* (California University Press, 2003), especially pp. 203–81. On the pioneer of tantric studies, John Woodroffe, see Kathleen Taylor, *Sir John Woodroffe, Tantra and Bengal: 'An Indian Soul in a European Body'?* (Richmond: Curzon Press, 2001).
11. Alexis Sanderson, 'Śaivism and the Tantric Traditions', in S. Sutherland et al. (eds), *The World's Religions* (London: Routledge, 1988), pp. 660–704; pp. 660–61. For an account of the structure of the Śaiva tantric canon founded on Sanderson's work, see Mark Dyczkowski, *The Canon of the Śaivāgama and the Kubjikā Tantras of the Western Kaula Tradition* (Albany NY: SUNY Press, 1988).
12. Sanderson, 'Śaivism and the Tantric Traditions', p. 661.
13. Gavin Flood, 'Introduction: Establishing the Boundaries', in G. Flood (ed.), *The Blackwell Companion to Hinduism* (Oxford: Blackwell, 2003), pp. 1–19; p. 3.
14. Alexis Sanderson, 'Śaivism: Its Development and Impact' (incomplete draft, 2002), p. 4. Note 5 gives full references to the use of the term by the historian Śrīvāra, who was at the court of Sultan Zain-ul-abidin (r. 1420–70). For the use of the term in Bengal, see J.T. O'Connell, 'The Word "Hindu" in Gaudiya Vaiṣṇava Texts', *Journal of the American Oriental Society* 93/3 (1973), pp. 340–44. Also see Julius Lipner, 'Ancient Banyan: An Inquiry into the Meaning of "Hinduness"', *Religious Studies* 32 (1996), pp. 109–26.
15. Inden, 'Introduction', p. 22.
16. Alexis Sanderson, 'Vajrayāna: Origin and Function', in Mettanando Bhikkhu et al. (eds), *Buddhism into the Year 2000* (Bangkok and Los Angeles: Dhammakaya Foundation, 1991), pp. 87–102; 'History Through Textual Criticism in the Study of Śaivism, the Pāñcarātra and the Buddhist Yoginītantras', in François Grimal (ed.), *Les sources et le temps* (Pondicherry:

École Français de'Extrême Orient, 2001), pp. 1–47; D. Snellgrove, *Indo-Tibetan Buddhism: Indian Buddhists and Their Tibetan Successors* (London: Serindia Publications, 1987), pp. 152–56.

17. For a stimulating and insightful discussion of the problem of internal and external definitions, see André Padoux, 'Concerning Tantric Traditions', in G. Oberhammer (ed.), *Studies in Hinduism II: Miscellenea to the Phenomenon of Tantras* (Vienna: Der Österreichischen Akademie der Wissenschaften, 1998), pp. 9–20.
18. Sanderson, 'Śaivism and the Tantric Traditions', p. 660; 'Purity and Power Among the Brahmans of Kashmir', in Michael Carruthers, Steven Collins and Steven Lukes (eds), *The Category of the Person* (Cambridge: Cambridge University Press, 1985), pp. 190–216.
19. Padoux, 'Concerning Tantric Traditions', p. 10.
20. White, *The Kiss of the Yoginī*, p. 16.
21. Padoux, 'Concerning Tantric Traditions', p. 10.
22. E.g. the generally excellent early study by T. Goudriaan, S. Gupta and D. van Hoens, *Hindu Tantrism* (Leiden: Brill, 1979), pp. 7–9, although the list of eighteen characteristics is not exclusively tantric.
23. André Padoux, 'Tantrism', in M. Eliade (general ed.), *The Encyclopaedia of Religions* (New York: Macmillan, 1986), vol. 14, pp. 272–6; p. 273.
24. White, David 'Introduction', in D. White (ed.), *Tantra in Practice* (Princeton: Princeton University Press, 2000),p. 9: 'Tantra is that Asian body of beliefs and practices which, working from the principle that the universe we experience is nothing other than the concrete manifestation of the divine energy of the godhead that creates and maintains that universe, seeks to ritually appropriate and channel that energy, within human microcosm, in creative and manipulative ways.'
25. R.M. Davidson, *Indian Esoteric Buddhism: A Social History of the Tantric Movement* (New York: Columbia University Press, 2002), p. 121. Tantra as a quest for power has also been emphasised by Brunner in her focusing on the figure of the sādhaka. See 'Le sādhaka, personnage oublié de l'Inde du Sud', *Journal Asiatique*, 1975, pp. 411–43. See also the discussion by Phylis Granoff, 'Other People's Rituals: Ritual Eclectism in Early Medieval Indian Religious [*sic*]', *Journal of Indian Philosophy* 28 (2000), pp. 399–424; p. 419.
26. Sanderson, 'Purity and Power', pp. 198–202; TA 37.10–12b, ref. in ibid., p. 211, n61.
27. Davidson, *Indian Esoteric Buddhism*, p. 119, developing Douglas Brooks, *The Secret of the Three Cities* (Chicago: University of Chicago Press, 1990), pp. 52–3.
28. Brooks, *The Secret of the Three Cities*, p. 53.
29. Perhaps the most popular and influential presentation of prototype effects in language is George Lakoff *Women, Fire and Dangerous Things: What Categories Reveal about the Mind* (Chicago: University of Chicago Press, 1987), pp. 58–90. Lakoff draws on and develops the prototype theory of Eleanor Rosch, 'Prototype Classification and Logical Classification: The Two Systems', in E. Scholnick (ed.), *New Trends in Cognitive Representation:*

Challenges to Piaget's Theory (Hillsdale NJ: Lawrence Erlbaum Associates, 1981), pp. 73–86; discussed in Lakoff, *Women, Fire and Dangerous Things*, pp. 39–57.

30. Lakoff, *Women, Fire and Dangerous Things*, pp. 21–2, 26–30, 138–42.
31. A.M. Hocart, *Kings and Councillors: An Essay in the Comparative Anatomy of Human Society*, edited by Rodney Needham (Chicago: University of Chicago Press, 1970 [1936]), pp. 93–94.
32. Tsong-ka-pa, *Tantra in Tibet: The Great Exposition of Secret Mantra*, trans. and ed. J. Hopkins, vol. 1 (London and Sydney: Unwin Hyman, 1980 [1977]), pp. 64–6. Thanks to Suzanne Besenger for alerting me to Tsong-ka-pa's understanding.
33. A reference in the *Śatapatha Brāhmaṇa* 1.1.1.4–5 about the self becoming divine, passing from men to the gods, does not seem to refer specifically to the divinisation of the body. Julius Eggeling (trans.), *The Śatapatha Brāhmaṇa*, vol. 1, Sacred Books of the East, vol. 12 (Oxford: Clarendon Press, 1882). Thanks to Craig Danielson for this reference.
34. I have argued this point in *The Ascetic Self*, pp. 223–6 and *passim*.
35. See Granoff, 'Other People's Rituals' p. 399.
36. A. MacIntyre, *Three Rival Versions of Moral Enquiry: Encyclopedia, Genealogy and Tradition* (Notre Dame: University of Notre Dame Press, 1990), pp. 60–61.
37. W.D. Whitney, *Sanskrit Grammar* (Cambridge MA: Harvard University Press, 1889), p. 448. Rajneesh is insightful here when he claims that 'tantra is pure technique'. Rajneesh, *The Book of Secrets*, p. 12. The suffix *trā* has also been taken to be from the root *tṝ*, to cross over; thus Tantra would be that which enables the crossing over the ocean of birth and death.
38. J. Gonda, 'The Indian Mantra', *Oriens* 16 (1963), pp. 244–97; pp. 249–50.
39. S. Pollock, 'The Sanskrit Cosmopolis, 300–1300 CE: Transculturation, Vernacularization, and the Question of Ideology', in Jan E.M. Houben (ed.), *Ideology and Status of Sanskrit: Contributions to the History of the Sanskrit Language* (Leiden: Brill, 1996), pp. 197–247.
40. G. Flood, *Body and Cosmology in Kashmir Śaivism* (San Francisco: Mellen Research University Press, 1993), pp. 238–39; Sanderson 'Purity and Power', p. 203.
41. Abhinavagupta TAV, vol. 3, pp. 27, 10–13, 277–8; Sanderson, 'Purity and Power, p. 205 and n130. The idea is echoed in later texts such as the *Yonitantra* 4.20: 'Privately a Śākta, outwardly a Śaiva, among people a Vaiṣṇava, bearing various outward appearances the followers of the Kula system spread over the earth' (*Antaḥ śāktāḥ bahiḥ śaivaḥ sabhāyām vaiṣṇavāḥ matāḥ/ nānārūpadharāḥ kaulāḥ vicaranti mahītale*). Translated and discussed by J.A. Schoterman, *The Yoni Tantra, Critically Edited with Introduction* (Delhi: Manohar, 1980), p. 16.
42. Weston La Barre, *The Ghost Dance: Origins of Religion* (London: Allen & Unwin, 1972), pp. 404–6. There are spiritual practices, such as breathing techniques, in both East and West that may share a common heritage and probably reach back into prehistory. See Mircea Eliade, *Yoga: Immortality and Freedom*, trans. W.R. Trask (Princeton NJ: Princeton University Press,

1969), pp. 104–7. On archaic ideas in Greek thought, see E.R. Dodds, *The Greeks and the Irrational* (Berkeley: University of California Press, 1951), pp. 134–78. J.-P. Vernant, *Mythe et pensée chez les Grecs: études de psychologie historique* (Paris: La Découverte, 1985), pp. 94ff, 108f.

43. Robert Mayer, 'The Origins of the Esoteric Vajrayāna', *The Buddhist Forum*, October 1990, pp. 1–57.
44. Bernard Sergent, *Genèse de l'Inde* (Paris: Payot & Rivages, 1997), p. 10.
45. Richard Gombrich, *How Buddhism Began: The Conditioned Genesis of the Early Teachings* (London: Athlone, 1996), pp. 158–9.
46. White, *The Kiss of the Yoginī*, pp. 27–32.
47. Sergent, *Genèse de l'Inde*, p. 113.
48. MacIntyre, *Three Rival Versions*, p. 42.
49. MacIntyre puts this strongly: 'The notion of a single neutral non-partisan history is one more illusion engendered by the academic standpoint of the encyclopedist; it is the illusion that there is the past waiting to be discovered, *wie es eigentlich gewesen*, independent of characterisation from some particular standpoint' (ibid., p. 151).
50. E. Blondel, *Nietzsche: The Body and Culture. Philosophy as Philological Genealogy*, trans. Sean Hand (Stanford CA: Stanford University Press, 1991), p. 99.
51. Inden, 'Introduction: From Philological to Dialogical Texts', pp. 3–28.
52. Peter Ochs, *Peirce, Pragmatism and the Logic of Scripture* (Cambridge: Cambridge University Press, 1998), pp. 4–5.
53. See Oliver Davies and Gavin Flood, *Religion as Reading: Text, Ritual, Asceticism* (forthcoming).
54. D. Goodall, *Bhatta Ramakantha's Commentary on the Kiranatantra* vol. 1, chs 1–6 (Pondicherry: Institut Français de Pondichéry, 1998), p. cxix.
55. Greg Urban, 'The "I" of Discourse', in Benjamin Lee and Greg Urban (eds), *Semiotics, Self and Society* (Berlin and New York; Mouton de Gruyter, 1989), pp. 27–51.
56. For a further elaboration of this theory of religious reading and textual reception, see Davies and Flood, *Religion as Reading*. See also G. Flood, *Beyond Phenomenology: Rethinking the Study of Religion* (New York and London: Cassell, 1999), pp. 185–91.
57. M. Silverstein and G. Urban (eds), *Natural Histories of Discourse* (Chicago: University of Chicago Press, 1996), pp. 1–3.
58. On this see M.L. Lyon and J.M. Barbalet, 'Society's Body: Emotion and the "Somatization" of Social Theory', in Thomas J. Csordas (ed.), *Embodiment and Experience: The Existential Ground of Culture and Self* (Cambridge: Cambridge University Press, 1994), pp. 48–66.
59. Csordas, 'Preface', *Embodiment and Experience*, p. xi.
60. Brian Turner, 'The Body in Western Society: Social Theory and Its Perspectives', in Sarah Coakley (ed.), *Religion and the Body* (Cambridge: Cambridge University Press, 1997), pp. 15–41. See also his review article 'What is the Sociology of the Body?', *Body and Society* 3/1 (1997), pp. 103–7.

61. Thomas Csordas, 'Introduction: The Body as Representation and Being in the World', in *Embodiment and Experience*, pp. 1–24.
62. M. Mauss, 'Les techniques du corps', in *Sociologie et Anthropologie* (Paris: Presses Universitaires de France, 1950).
63. Robert Hertz, 'The Pre-eminence of the Right Hand: A Study in Religious Polarity', trans. Rodney Needham, in R. Needham (ed.), *Right and Left, Essays on Dual Symbolic Classification* (Chicago: University of Chicago Press, 1973), pp. 3–31. Translation of Hertz 'La prééminence de la main droit: étude sur la polarité religieuse', *Revue Philosophique* 68 (1909), pp. 553–80.
64. The literature here is vast, but important points of reference are the volumes edited by M. Feher et al., *Fragments for a History of the Human Body*, 3 vols (New York: Urzone, 1989); P.A. Mellor and C. Shilling, *Re-forming the Body: Religion, Community and Modernity* (London: Sage, 1997). There is also a journal *Body and Society* dedicated to exploring the links between body and culture, and *Cultural Values* and *Theory, Culture and Society* are important in giving the body central place in cultural discourse.
65. Paul Schilder, *The Image and Appearance of the Human Body* (New York: International University Press, 1968 [1950]).
66. Turner, 'The Body in Western Society', p. 17.
67. D. Haraway, 'Investment Strategies for the Evolving Portfolio of Primate Females', in Mary Jacobus, Evelyn Fox Keller, and Sally Shuttleworth (eds), *Body/Politics: Women and the Discourse of Science* (New York: Routledge, 1990), pp. 11–28. Discussed by Csordas, 'Introduction', in *Embodiment and Experience*, pp. 2–3.
68. Sarah Coakley, 'Introduction', in *Religion and the Body*, p. 4.
69. I say inappropriate because critical theory originally and more usefully referred to the Frankfurt School, the powerful, recent expression being Habermas's work, which looks to the completion of the Enlightenment project. But the term in recent years has come to refer to almost any theoretical, genealogical critique. In some ways this is ironic as there is fundamental tension between the critical theory of the Frankfurt School, with its universalist aspirations, and the genealogists such as Foucault, whose thinking is generally opposed to such aspirations, although still aligned with the political left. See Michael Kelly (ed.), *Critique and Power: Recasting the Foucault/Habermas Debate* (Canbridge MA: MIT Press, 1994). I would wish to restrict the term 'critical theory' much more usefully to Habermas and the Frankfurt School in contrast to the 'genealogy' of Foucault and others drawing on Nietzsche rather than Marx.
70. See for example, the interesting collection of essays by Londa Schiebinger (ed.), *Feminism and the Body* (Oxford: Oxford University Press, 2000).
71. M. Foucault, *The Order of Things: An Archaeology of the Human Sciences* (London: Routledge, 1970), p. 313.
72. A. MacIntyre, *After Virtue: A Study in Moral Theory* (London: Duckworth, 1985), p. 213.
73. For references and for an illuminating essay on the subject of experience in religion, see Robert H. Scharf, 'Experience', in Mark C. Taylor (ed.),

Critical Terms for Religious Studies (Chicago: University of Chicago Press, 1998), pp. 94–116.

74. S. Katz, 'Language, Epistemology and Mysticism', in S. Katz (ed.), *Mysticism and Philosophical Analysis* (London: Sheldon Press, 1978), pp. 22–74.
75. Robert R. Desjarlais, *Body and Emotion the Aesthertics of Illness and Healing in the Nepal Himalayas* (Philadephia: University of Pennsylvania Press, 1992), p. 16.
76. On experience as narrative see the important work by Oliver Davies, *A Theology of Compassion: Metaphysics of Difference and the Renewal of Tradition* (London: SCM Press, 2001), pp. 24–46.
77. Csordas, 'Introduction', p. 5.
78. Drew Leder, *The Absent Body* (Chicago: University of Chicago Press, 1990), p. 91; cited by Csordas, 'Introduction', p. 8.
79. Geoffrey Samuel, *Civilized Shamans: Buddhism and Tibetan Societies* (Washington DC and London: Smithsonian Institution Press, 1993), p. 8.
80. On my understanding of ritual (which draws on Rappaport), see *The Ascetic Self*, pp. 214–16.
81. Paul Griffiths, *Religious Reading: The Place of Reading in the Practice of Religion* (Oxford: Oxford University Press, 1999), pp. 42, 44–5.
82. Granoff, 'Other People's Rituals'.
83. RA, vol. III, supplement 63.18–22.
84. My use of the terms 'image', 'icon', 'representation' and 'metaphor' are not being used here in a technical sense, although the Sanskrit equivalents of 'icon' or 'image', namely *mūrti*, *bimba*, *vigraha* and so on share the sense of the term 'icon' of participation and sharing in. In this sense my use of 'icon' is quite distinct from Peirce.
85. Stephan Beyer, *The Cult of Tārā: Magic and Ritual in Tibet* (Berkeley: California University Press, 1973), pp. 33–6.
86. G. Oberhammer, 'Beobachtungen zur "Offenbarungsgeschicte" der Paramasaṃhitā', in G. Oberhammer (ed.), *Studies in Hinduism II: Miscellanea to the Phenomenon of Tantras* (Vienna: Der Österreichischen Akademie der Wissenschaften, 1998), pp. 21–41.

Chapter 2

1. On this, see A. MacIntyre, *Three Rival Versions of Moral Enquiry: Encyclopedia, Genealogy and Tradition* (Notre Dame: University of Notre Dame Press, 1990), pp. 65–66.
2. Alexis Sanderson, 'Purity and Power among the Brahmans of Kashmir', in Steven Lukes, Michael Carrithers, and Steven Collins (ed.), *The Category of the Person* (Cambridge: Cambridge University Press, 1985), pp. 190–216.
3. Ronald M. Davidson, *Indian Esoteric Buddhism, A Social History of the Tantric Movement* (New York: Columbia University Press, 2002), p. 27.
4. Ibid., p. 74.
5. B. Stein, *Peasant State and Society in Medieval South India* (Delhi: Oxford University Press, 1980), pp. 340–43.

6. S. Gupta and R. Gombrich, 'Kings, Power and the Goddess', *South Asia Research* 6/2 (1986), pp. 123–38.
7. Davidson, *Indian Esoteric Buddhism*, p. 85. See also David N. Lorenzen, *Kāpālikas and Kālāmukhas: Two Lost Śaivite Sects*, 2nd edn (Delhi: MLBD, 1991), pp. 24–30, who documents epigraphic evidence for the royal patronage of groups linked to the Pāśupatas.
8. Romila Thapar, public lecture, University of Virginia, April 2004.
9. Mark Dyczkowski, *The Canon of the Śaivāgama and the Kubjikā Tantras of the Western Kaula Tradition* (Albany NY: SUNY Press, 1988), pp. 11–12.
10. Wilhelm Halbfass, *India and Europe: An Essay in Understanding* (Albany NY: SUNY Press, 1988), pp. 172–96.
11. These three are somewhat paraphrasing MacIntyre but they convey his general point. MacIntyre, *Three Rival Versions*, pp. 196–7.
12. Sanderson, 'Purity and Power', p. 204, citing reference to MTPVrt pp. 150–51.
13. MacIntyre, *Three Rival Versions*, p. 197.
14. Charles Malamoud, 'Semantics and Rhetoric in the Hindu Hierarchy of the "Aims of Man"', in *Cooking the World: Ritual and Thought in Ancient India*, trans. D. White (Delhi: Oxford University Press, 1996), pp. 109–29.
15. J. Duncan and M. Derrett, *Bharuci's Commentary on the Manusmrti (the Manu-sastra-vivarana, books 6–12)*, text, translation and notes, vol. 1 (Wiesbaden: Franz Steiner, 1975), p. 21.
16. Werner F. Menski, *Hindu Law: Beyond Tradition and Modernity* (Delhi and Oxford: Oxford University Press, 2003).
17. J. Duncan M. Derrett, 'A Juridical Fabrication of Early British India: The *Mahānirvāṇa-Tantra*', *Essays in Classical and Modern Hindu Law*, vol. 2, *Consequences of the Intellectual Exchange with Foreign Powers* (Leiden: Brill, 1977), pp. 197–242.
18. Gudrun Bühnemann, 'On Puraścaraṇa: Kulārṇavatantra, Chapter 15', in Teun Goudriaan (ed.), *Ritual and Speculation in Early Tantrism* (Albany NY: SUNY Press, 1992), verse 57, pp. 78 and 89.
19. JS 25.40.
20. E.g. Wendy Doniger, 'The Body in Hindu Texts', in Sarah Coakley (ed.), *Religion and the Body* (Cambridge: Cambridge University Press, 1997), pp. 167–84.
21. Richard Roberts, 'Religion and the Body in Comparative Perspective', *Religion* 30 (2000), pp. 55–64; p. 59.
22. Manu 6.76–77, cited by Doniger, 'The Body in Hindu Texts', pp. 169–70.
23. Manu 6.75–76; Derrett, *Bharuci's Commentary*, p. 23.
24. Patrick Olivelle, *The Āśrama System: The History and Hermeneutics of a Religious Institution* (Oxford: Oxford University Press, 1993), pp. 207–8.
25. The relationship between Brahmanical values and renunciate values is, of course, a huge topic. Broadly speaking, on the one hand Dumont has argued for the divergence of the two ideologies, while on the other Heesterman has argued for their proximity. (For a brief summary of the debate, see my *Introduction to Hinduism* (Cambridge: Cambridge University Press, 1996), pp. 72–4).

26. *Yajñavalkya-smṛti* 1.15–27 on morning ablution rituals and so on. *Yajñavalkyasmṛti with the commentary of Vijñāneśvara called the Mītaksara*, Book 1, trans. Rai Bahadur Srisa Chandra Vidyārṇava (Allahabad: Pāṇini Office, Bhuvaneśwari Aśrama, 1918).
27. Ludo Rocher, *Jīmūtavāhana's Dāyabhāga: The Hindu Law of Inheritance in Bengal* (Oxford: Oxford University Press, 2002), pp. 177–80. Hindu law is not equal in this respect. Duncan J. Derrett, *Studies in Hindu Law* (Turin: Indologica Taurinensia, 1994), p. 78.
28. Rocher, *Jīmūtavāhana's Dāyabhāga*, pp. 186, 195.
29. Manu 5.147–48. See Julia Leslie, *The Perfect Wife: The Orthodox Hindu Woman According to the Strīdharma-paddhati of Tryambakayajvan* (Oxford: Oxford University Press, 1989), pp. 305–16.
30. Manu 9. 33. See Doniger, 'The Body in Hindu Texts', pp. 170–73.
31. P.V. Kane, *History of Dharmaśāstra*, vol. 3 (Poona: Bhandarkar Oriental Research Institute, 1973) p. 8.
32. Kāma Sūtra 1.20. Alain Danielou, *The Complete Kāma Sūtra: The First Unabridged Modern Translation of the Classic Indian Text* (Rochester NY: Park Street Press, 1994).
33. E.g. Arth. 4.8.1–4; 4.12.32–35.
34. In a European context the classic here is, of course, E.H. Kanotorowicz, *The King's Two Bodies* (Princeton NJ: Princeton University Press, 1957).
35. Arth. 6.1. R.P. Kangle, *The Kautilya Arthaśāstra* (University of Bombay, 2nd ed., 1969). See Kane, *History of Dharmaśāstra*, pp. 17–20.
36. Jīvānanda *Śukranītisāra* 1.61–62. Reference from Kane, *History of Dharmaśāstra*, p. 18. For full textual references to the seven elements, see ibid., p. 19.
37. Richard A. Shweder and Edmund Bourne, 'Does the Concept of Person Vary Cross-culturally?', in R A Shweder and R LeVine (eds), *Culture Theory: Essays on Mind, Self and Emotions* (Cambridge: Cambridge University Press, 1984), p. 191.
38. Puruṣa Sukta *Ṛg-veda* 10.90.
39. Manu 9. 296–97.
40. Arth. 9.2.1: *rājā rajyamiti prakṛtisaṃkṣepaḥ*.
41. Arth. 1.6.1–1.7.1. The vices are listed as *kāma-krodha-lobha-māna-mada-harṣa*.
42. Manu 7.4–5, 5.96.
43. Manu 7.27–28. For a discussion and references, see Kane, *History of Dharma-śāstra*, pp. 25–7.
44. McKim Marriott, 'Hindu Transaction, Diversity without Dualism', in Bruce Kapferer (ed.), *Transaction and Meaning* (Philadelphia: Institute for the Study of Human Issues, 1976), pp. 109–42.
45. Arth. 2.3.23.
46. E.g. Gloria Goodwin Raheja, *Poison in the Gift: Ritual, Prestation and the Dominant Caste in an Indian Village* (Chicago: University of Chicago Press, 1988), pp. 26, 118–19, 239–42; Arjun Appadurai 'Is Homo Hierarchicus?', review article, *American Ethnologist* 13 (1986), pp. 745–61; 'Putting Hierarchy in Its Place', in G. Marcus (ed.), *Rereading Cultural Anthropology* (Durham

NC: Duke University Press, 1992). See also R. Inden, *Imagining India* (Oxford: Blackwell, 1990), pp. 201–3. A. Beteille, 'Reply to Dumont', *Current Anthropology* 28 (1987), pp. 672–6; Pauline Kolenda, 'Seven Kinds of Hierarchy in Homo Hierarchicus', *Journal of Asian Studies* 35 (1976), pp. 581–96. For a good summary of the debates and positions, see Steven M. Parish, *Hierarchy and Its Discontents* (Philadelphia: University of Pennsylvania Press, 1996), pp. 71–95.

47. F.A. Marglin, *The Wives of the God King: The Rituals of the Devadāsis of Puri* (Oxford: Oxford University Press, 1985), pp. 285–99.
48. Raheja, *Poison in the Gift*, especially pp. 93–292.
49. Michael Witzel, 'The Vedas and Upaniṣads', in G. Flood (ed.), *The Blackwell Companion to Hinduism* (Oxford: Blackwell, 2003), pp. 68–101; pp. 82–7.
50. R.C. Zaehner, *Hinduism* (Oxford: Oxford University Press, 1962), pp. 114–17.
51. Simon Brodbeck, 'Asakta Karma in the Bhagavad Gītā', Ph.D. thesis (London: SOAS, 2002).

Chapter 3

1. NJ , p. 562.
2. Bhaṭṭa, AD. Alexis Sanderson, 'Purity and Power among the Brahmans of Kashmir', in Micheal Carrithers, Steven Collins, and Steven Lukes (eds), *The Category of the Person: Anthropology, Philosophy, History* (Cambridge: Cambridge University Press, 1985), pp. 190–216; p. 208 n3.
3. Gerhard Oberhammer, 'Bemerkungen zum Phänomen religiöser Tradition', in G. Oberhammer (ed.), *Studies in Hinduism: Vedism and Hinduism* (Vienna: Österreichischen Akademie der Wissenschaften, 1997), pp. 1–42; p. 28.
4. E.g. MVT 1.7; KirT. 1.11c-12.
5. E.g. RA vol. I, vidyāpāda chapter 3.
6. R.J.S. Inden, 'Imperial Purāṇas: Kashmir as Vaiṣṇava Center of Words', in R.J.S. Inden, Jonathan Walters and Daud Ali, *Querying the Medieval: Texts and the History of Practices in South Asia* (Oxford: Oxford University Press, 2000), pp. 29–98; p. 51.
7. Inden, 'Introduction: From Philological to Dialogical Texts', in Inden et al., *Querying the Medieval*, pp. 3–28; p. 11.
8. Francis X. Clooney, 'Why the Veda has No Author: Language as Ritual in Early Mīmāṃsā and Post-Modern Theology', *Journal of the American Academy of Religion* 55/4 (1988), pp. 659–84; p. 674.
9. NJ p. 484.
10. NJ p. 562; Sanskrit text pp. 648–9.
11. NJ pp. 550–51.
12. AD, p. 40: *aho batāpūrvam idam tapaḥ.*
13. AD p. 42: *viplavate varṇāśramasamācāraḥ.* See also NJ, pp. 562–63.
14. Although Jayantha praises the king, this was not a universal sentiment among intellectuals of the time. Kalhaṇa, for example, is scornful of Śaṇkaravarman's ignorance of Sanskrit. Cited by D.H.H. Ingalls, 'Introduction',

in Ingalls et al. (eds), *The Dhvanyālocana of Ānandavardhana with the Locana of Abhinavagupta* (Cambridge: Harvard University Press, 1990), p. 28.
15. AD, pp. 45–9; NJ, p. 556.
16. Mark Dyczkowski, *The Canon of the Śaivāgama and the Kubjikā Tantras of the Western Kaula Tradition* (Albany NY: SUNY Press, 1988), p. 5.
17. Alexis Sanderson, 'Śaivism and the Tantric Traditions', in S. Sutherland, L. Houlden, P. Clarke, and F. Hardy (eds), *The World's Religions* (London: Routledge, 1988), pp. 660–704.
18. AG, p. 33.
19. AG, pp. 40–41.
20. Dennis Hudson, 'Vāsudeva Kṛṣṇa in Theology and Architecture: A Background to Śrīvaiṣṇavism', *Journal of Vaiṣṇava Studies* 2/1 (1993), pp. 139–70.
21. G. Colas, 'Sectarian Divisions According to the Vaikhānasāgama', in T. Goudriaan (ed.), *Sanskrit Tradition and Tantrism* (Leiden: Brill, 1990), p. 24.
22. Detailed textual work and translation has been done by others. For example: H. Dan Smith, *A Descriptive Bibliography of the Printed Texts of the Pañcaratrāgama* (Baroda: Oriental Institute: 1975-1980); Sanjukta Gupta, *The Laksmā Tantra* (Leiden: Brill, 1972); Marion Rastelli, *Philosophisch-theologische Grundanschauungen der Jayakhyasamhita* (Vienna: Österreichen Akademie der Wissenschaften, 1999); Andreas Bock-Raming, 'Untersuchungen zur Gottesvortstellung in der äleren Anonymliteratur des Pāñcarātra', *Beiträge zur Indologie* 34 (Wiesbaden: Harraossowitz, 2002); Gérard Colas, *Visnu, ses images et ses feux: les métamorphoses du dieu chez les vaikhanasa* (Paris: Presses de l'Ecole Française d'Extrême-Orient, 1996).
23. See Dan Smith, 'The Three Gems of the Pāñcarātra Canon: A Critical Appraisal', *Studies in the History of Religions*, supplement to *Numen* 22 (1972), pp. 40–49. On the contents of the texts, see Otto Schrader, *Introduction to the Pāñcarātra and the Ahirbudhnya Saṃhitā* (Madras: Adyar Library, 1973 [1916]), pp. 2–30.
24. This complexity is becoming clear, especially through the work of the Oxford scholars Alexis Sanderson and his students (such as D. Goodall, J. Todzok, A. Watson, S. Vasudev, J. Hanneder and others), by scholars in Paris and Pondicherry (such as André Padoux, Hélène Brunner, N.R. Bhatt) and in Rome (especially Raffaela Torella).
25. See Robert Mayer, *A Scripture of the Ancient Tantra Collection: The Phurpa bcu-gnyis* (Oxford: Kiscadale Publications, 1996), pp. 82–90. Mayer points to the parallels between the Buddhist and Śaiva material here, particularly texts that have yet to have wider public dissemination such as the *Jayadrathayāmala* researched by Alexis Sanderson.
26. Jürgen Hanneder, *Abhinavagupta's Philosophy of Revelation: Mālinīśloka-vārttika* I, 1–399 (Groningen: Egbert Forsten, 1998), p. 33. Also see Alexis Sanderson, 'The Doctrine of the Mālinīvijayottaratantra', in T. Goudriaan (ed.), *Ritual and Speculation in Early Tantrism* (Albany NY: SUNY Press, 1992), pp. 281–312; p. 282 n7.
27. Sanderson, 'The Doctrine of the Mālinīvijayottara', pp. 294–7.

28. MVT vart. 374–91; Hanneder, *Abhinavagupta's Philosophy of Revelation*, pp. 26–7.
29. For the twenty-eight dualist Āgamas, see Dominic Goodall (ed. and trans.), *Bhaṭṭa Rāmakaṇṭha's Commentary on the Kiraṇatanra*, vol. 1 (Pondicherry: Institut Français d'Indologie, 1998) Appendix III, pp. 402–17.
30. Hanneder, *Abhinavagupta's Philosophy of Revelation*, p. 16, quoting Abhinavagupta's TA 15.203cd–206ab.
31. Given by H. Brunner 'Les Membres de Śiva', *Etudes Asiatiques* 40/2 (1986), pp. 89–132; p. 93. Cited by Hanneder, *Abhinavagupta's Philosophy of Revelation*, p. 13.
32. I have derived this list, which is a fusion of two sets of identification, from those given by Hanneder, *Abhinavagupta's Philosophy of Revelation,* pp. 14–15.
33. Ibid., p. 15.
34. Again, the list is derived from Hanneder, *Abhinavagupta's Philosophy of Revelation*, p. 18. Also see Dyczkowski, *The Canon of the Śaivāgama*, pp. 31–2.
35. Hanneder, *Abhinavagupa's Philosophy of Revelation*, p. 26.
36. Ibid., p. 19.
37. TA 37.1.
38. TA 37.4–6. Verse 5 repeated at 11c-12b.
39. TA 37.7–9 and commentary.
40. TA 37.14.
41. Sanderson, 'Śaivism and the Tantric Traditions', p. 668.
42. TA 37.17–25. 17–24, translated by Sanderson, 'The Doctrine of the Mālinīvijayottara', p. 292.
43. MVT 1.11. For an exposition of the text and its place in Śaiva revelation, along with an exposition and translation of Abhinavagupta's commentary, see Hanneder, *Abhinavagupta's Philosophy of Revelation*.
44. Sanderson, 'Śaivism and the Tantric Traditions'. See also Dyczkowski, *The Canon of the Śaivāgama*, pp. 4–19.
45. Sanderson, 'Śaivism and the Tantric Traditions', p. 664; Dyczkowski *The Canon of the Śaivāgama*, pp. 19–26; Flood, 'The Śaiva Traditions', in *The Blackwell Companion to Hinduism* (Oxford: Blackwell, 2003), pp. 200–28; pp. 206–8.
46. Ronald M. Davidson, *Indian Esoteric Buddhism: A Social History of the Tantric Movement* (New York: Columbia University Press, 2002), pp. 218–24.
47. Manu 11.73.
48. David N. Lorenzen, *The Kāpālikas and Kālāmukhas: Two Lost Śaivite Sects* (Delhi: MLBD, 2nd edn, 1991 [1972]), pp. 74–5. Diana Eck, *Banares, City of Light* (London: Routledge, 1984), p. 119. There are different versions of this myth. In the *Skanda Purāṇa*, chapter 5, during a quarrel between Brahmā and Sacrifice about dominance, Veda interferes declaring Mahādeva to the source of all (including Brahmā and Sacrifice). A great sound arises and a disc, like the sun. Brahmā falls to earth and a fifth head issues above his other four to behold the disc. Mahādeva then cuts off the head with his

thumbnail and Brahmā realises his greatness and praises him. R. Adriansen, H.T. Bakker, and H. Isaacson *The Skanda Purāṇa volume 1, Critically Edited with a Prolegomena and English Synopsis* (Groningen: Egbert Forsten, 1998), 5.31–45.

49. Sanderson, 'Purity and Power among the Brahmans of Kashmir' p. 201. To quote Sanderson's highly evocative description: 'Smeared with the ashes of funeral pyres, wearing ornaments of human bone, the initiate would carry in one hand a cranial begging-bowl and in the other a *khaṭvāṅga*, trident-topped staff on which was fixed beneath the prongs a human skull adorned with a banner of blood-stained cloth. Having thus taken on the appearance of the ferocious deities of his cult, he roamed about seeking to call forth these gods and their retinues in apocalyptic vision thereby to assimilate their superhuman identities and powers.' On the Kāpālikas, see Lorenzen, *The Kāpālikas and Kālāmukhas*, pp. 73–95; Dyczkowski, *The Canon of the Śaivāgama*, pp. 26–31. On modern Aghorīs, see J.P. Parry, *Death in Benares* (Cambridge: Cambridge University Press, 1994), pp. 251–92.
50. André Padoux, *Le Coeur de la Yoginī: Yoginīhṛdaya avec le commentaire Dīpikā d'Amṛānanda* (Paris: de Boccard, 1994), pp. 9–10; Dyczkowski, *The Canon of the Śaivāgama,* pp. 68–85.
51. On the Śrīvidyā, see Douglas Brooks, *The Secret of the Three Cities* (Chicago: University of Chicago Press, 1990).
52. Sanderson, 'The Doctrine of the Mālinīvijayottaratantra', p. 282 n7.
53. E.g. Abinavagupta's commentary on *Īśvarapratyabhijñāvimarśinī*, *Jñānādhikāra* V.7. See David Peter Lawrence, *Rediscovering God with Transcendental Argument: A Contemporary Interpretation of Monisitic Kashmiri Śaiva Philosophy* (Albany NY: SUNY Press, 1999), especially on the relation between the Pratyabhijñā and Buddhism, pp. 67–84.
54. KT, p. 176.
55. KT, p. 180.
56. KT, p. 165.
57. Sat 1.2.
58. MTP 1.11–12, 28c-33b. Cf. RA Vidyāpāda 3.11–28.
59. SardhVrt. 1.4ab.
60. MVT 1.2–14.
61. JS 1.70–72.
62. Jaideva Singh, *Abhinavagupta: A Trident of Wisdom* (Delhi: MLBD, 1989), p. 16. See Natalia Isayeva, *From Early Vedānta to Kashmir Shaivism: Gaudapda, Bhartrhati, and Abhinavagupta* (Delhi: Śrī Satguru, 1997 [1995]), p. 135.
63. Sardh. 1.5ab: *nādākhyaṃ yatparaṃ bījaṃ sarvabhūṣvavasthitam.*
64. Mrg 1.2.
65. PH sūtra 2 plus auto-commentary.
66. TA 35.39.
67. PH sūtra 8, commentary.
68. Sanderson, 'The Doctrine of the Mālinīvijayottara', pp. 293–308.
69. Ibid., p. 297.
70. Ibid., p. 308.
71. Īśvarakṛṣṇa, *Sāṃkhya-kārikās* 4; 20; 21. Summarised by Karl H. Potter

and G. Larson in G.J. Larson and Ram Shankar Bhattacharya (eds), *Encyclopedia of Indian Philosophies* vol. IV *Sāṃkhya, a Dualist Tradition in Indian Philosophy* (Princeton NJ: Princeton University Press, 1987), pp. 152, 156–7.

Chapter 4

1. For a useful overview, see 'Civilization, concept of', in Neil J. Smelser and Paul B. Baltes (editors in chief), *International Encyclopaedia of the Social and Behavioural Sciences* (Oxford: Elsevier, 2001), vol. 3, pp. 1903–14.
2. Wilhelm Halbfass, *India and Europe: An Essay in Understanding* (Albany NY: SUNY Press, 1988), p. 177.
3. Sheldon Pollock, 'The Sanskrit Cosmopolis, 300–1300 CE: Trasculturation, Vernacularization, and the Question of Ideology', in Jan E.M. Houben (ed.), *Ideology and Status of Sanskrit: Contributions to the History of the Sanskrit Language* (Leiden: Brill, 1996), pp. 197–247.
4. Sheldon Pollock, 'The Cosmopolitan Vernacular', p. 10. *Journal of Asian Studies* vol. 57, 1998, pp. 6–37.
5. Ibid., pp. 14–15.
6. Ibid., pp. 6–7.
7. Rich Freeman, 'The Literature of Hinduism in Malayalam', in Gavin Flood (ed.), *The Blackwell Companion to Hinduism* (Oxford: Blackwell, 2003), pp. 159–81.
8. David White, *The Kiss of the Yoginī: 'Tantric Sex' in its South Asian Contexts* (Chicago: University of Chicago Press, 2003), p. 3.
9. R. Freeman, 'Formalised Possession Among the Tantris and Teyyams of Malabar', *South Asia Research* 18/1 (1998), pp. 74–98.
10. Bruno Dagens, *Mayamata. Traité Sanskrit d'architecture*, critical edition, translation and notes, Parts 1 and 2 (Pondicherry: Institut Français d'Indologie, 1970 and 1976). See also B. Dagens, *Les Enseignements architecturaux de l'Ajitāgama et du Rauravāgama, Etudes sur les āgama śivaites*, vol. 1 (Pondicherry: Institut Français d'Indologie, 1977).
11. Marie-Luce Barazer-Billoret, Bruno Dagens and Vincent Lefevre (eds), *Dīptāgama*, vol. 1, chs 1–21 (Pondichéry: Institut Français d'Indologie, 2004).
12. *Śilpaprakāśa: A Medieval Orissan Sanskrit Text on Temple Architecture* by Rāmacadra Kaulācāra, trans. Alica Boner and Sadāśiva Rath Śarma (Leiden: Brill, 1966).
13. RAot, chs 1 to 6. Bhatt provides a lucid description in his introduction to the text, pp. vii–xlv.
14. Ronald Inden, *Imagining India* (Oxford: Blackwell, 1990), pp. 214, 228–44.
15. R. Davidson, *Indian Esoteric Buddhism: A Social History of the Tantric Movement* (New York: Columbia University Press, 2002), p. 68. On these developments generally, see ibid., pp. 28–74.
16. Harald Tambs-Lynche, *Power, Profit, and Poetry: Traditional Society in Kathiawar, Western India* (Delhi: Manohar, 1997), p. 260.

17. Davidson, *Indian Esoteric Buddhism*, p. 57.
18. T. Goudriaan and S. Gupta, *Hindu Tantric and Śākta Literature in Sanskrit*, History of Indian Literature, vol. II (Wiesbaden: Otto Harrassowitz, 1981), p. 16. Mark S.G. Dyczkowski, *The Canon of the Śaivāgama and the Kubjikā Tantras of the Western Kaula Tradition* (Albany NY: SUNY Press, 1988), p. 36. On the importance of a particular tantric text in Southeast Asia, see Max Nihom, *Studies in Indian and Indo-Indonesian Tantrism: The Kuñjarakarṇadharmakathana and the Yogatantra*, de Nobili Research Library vol. 21 (Vienna: Institute of Indology, 1994). On inscriptions as evidence of the presence of Hindu traditions in Cambodia, see Richard Salomon, *Indian Epigraphy: A Guide to the Study of Inscriptions in Sanskrit, Prakrit, and Other Indo-Āryan Languages* (New York and Oxford: Oxford University Press, 1998), pp. 155–7. See also O.W. Wolters, 'Khmer "Hinduism" in the Seventh Century', in R.B. Smith and W. Watson (eds), *Early South East Asia: Essays in Archaeology, History and Historical Geography* (New York: Oxford University Press, 1979).
19. Alexis Sanderson, 'Meaning in Tantric Ritual', in Ann-Marie Blondeau and Kristofer Schipper (eds), *Essais sur le rituel*, vol. III (Louvain and Paris: Peeters, 1995), pp. 15–95; p. 16.
20. Davidson, *Indian Esoteric Buddhism*, p. 26.
21. A.M. Hocart, *Kings and Councillors: An Essay in the Comparative Anatomy of Human Society*, ed. Rodney Needham (Chicago: University of Chicago Press, 1970 [1936]), pp. 97, 183–5. See also Louis Dumont, 'La conception de la royauté dans l'Inde ancienne', *Contributions to Indian Sociology* 6 (1962), pp. 48–77. Also M. Biardeau, 'The Salvation of the King in the Mahābhārata', *Contributions to Indian Sociology* 15 (1981), pp. 75–97.
22. Inden, *Imagining India*, p. 229.
23. Gérard Tofflin, *Le Palais et le Temple, la function royale das la vallée du Nepal* (Paris: CNRS, 1993), p. 12.
24. Burton Stein, *Peasant, State and Society in Medieval South India* (Delhi: Oxford University Press, 1980), pp. 22, 264.
25. C.J. Fuller, *The Camphor Flame: Popular Hinduism and Society in India* (Princeton NJ: Princeton University Press, 1992), pp. 115–16.
26. Manu 7.35.
27. Tofflin, *Le Palais et le Temple*, p. 222.
28. Manu 7.5–7.
29. Freda Matchet, 'The Purāṇas', in Flood (ed.), *The Blackwell Companion to Hinduism* (Oxford: Blackwell, 2003), pp. 129–43; pp. 134–6.
30. Inden, 'Imperial Purāṇas', pp. 48–55.
31. Davidson, *Indian Esoteric Buddhism*, pp. 118–53.
32. White, *Kiss of the Yoginī*, pp. 123–47.
33. R.C. Hazra, *Studies in the Purāṇic Records on Hindu Rites and Customs*, 2nd edn (Delhi: MLBD, 1975). Particularly the *Agni-purāṇa*, see Marie-Thérèse de Mallmann, *Les Enseignements Iconographiques de l'Agni Purāṇa* (Paris: Presses Universitaires de France, 1963), pp. 4, 6–10.
34. White, *Kiss of the Yoginī*, p. 136. This idea of the transmission of divine power to king and people through sex is ancient in India. The vedic horse

sacrifice entailed the king symbolically sleeping with the dead stallion, thereby ensuring the flow of divine power to the people. See Wendy O'Flaherty, *Women, Androgynes and Other Mythical Beasts* (Chicago: University of Chicago Press, 1980), p. 168.

35. White, *Kiss of the Yoginī,* p. 127.
36. Tofflin, *Le Palais et le Temple,* pp. 53, 94; White, *Kiss of the Yoginī,* p. 127.
37. Davidson, *Indian Esoteric Buddhism*, pp. 123–31. See also White, *Kiss of the Yoginī,* pp. 133–6.
38. JS 18.34–35.
39. Sanjukta Gupta and Richard Gombrich, 'Kings, Powers and the Goddess', *South Asia Research* 6/2 (1986), pp. 123–38.
40. Tofflin, *Palais et temple*, pp. 220–22. Tofflin documents in some detail the case of King Pratap Malla, who stepped down in 1768. The king derives his power especially from the tantric Goddess Taleju (p. 51).
41. NeT 12.6–8, 17.5–7, 19.88–115. References from Brunner, 'Un Tantra du Nord: le *Netra* Tantra', *Bulletin de l'École Française d'Extrême-Orient* 61 (1974), pp. 125-97; pp. 156, 166, 178–79.
42. ISG Mantrapāda 2.52.17: *bālaḥ kumāro rājā ca vṛddhaḥ svargata eva ca/ bhuktir yānaṃ ca rājyaṃ ca karma suptis tathā mṛtiḥ.*
43. ISG Mantrapāda 2.52.124. Such magical conceptions have a long pedigree in Sanskrit literature going back to the Brāhmaṇas.
44. The classic study is, of course, E.H. Kantorowicz, *The King's Two Bodies* (Princeton NJ: Princeton University Press, 1957).
45. Tofflin, *Le palais et le temple.* On the centrality of the king in Hindu ritual generally, see Chris Fuller, *The Camphor Flame: Popular Hinduism and Society in India* (Princeton NJ: Princeton University Press, 1992), pp. 106–27.
46. RAot, chapters 1–4 on different kinds of temples, chapter 5 on the rites of installation, chapters 9–13 on the installation of specific deities. Also Ajit, chapters 39, 40, 46–54; ISG Kriyāpāda 31–32; starting from the groundplan and working out, the most important text of tantric architecture is the SP 1.90–106. For details on the *Mayamata* and SP, see notes 9 and 10. For an interesting discussion of the *kāmakalā* in the text, see White, *Kiss of the Yoginī*, pp. 94–99. On Śākta temples and mātṛkā imagery in Orissa, see K.S. Behera and Thomas Donaldson, *Sculpture Masterpieces from Orissa* (New Delhi: Aryan Books, 1998), pp. 32, 91–2.
47. RA Kriyāpāda, chapters 30, 31 and 32 respectively. There is some variation in the Āgamas, but in the RA the dvārapālas are Nandin and Kāla in the east, Daṇḍin and Muṇḍin in the south, Vijaya and Bhṛṅgi to the west, and Gopati and Ananta to the north. RA kriyāpāda 32.1–7.
48. N.P. Unni, 'Introduction', *The Tantrasamuccaya of Nārāyaṇa with the commentary vimarśinī of Śaṅkara*, ed. M.T. Gaṇapati Śāstrī with an elaborate introduction by N.P. Unni (Delhi: Nag Publishers), pp. 1–75; pp. 5–33. For a brief, clear, internal description of Kerala temple worship see D.Appukuyttain Nair, 'Śiva Temple Worship in Kerala', in S.S. Janaki (ed.), *Śiva Temple and Temple Rituals* (Madras: Kupuswami Research Institute, 1988), pp. 1–21. We await Rich Freeman's forthcoming study of the Kerala

Tantrāgama tradition. On the Kerala 'tantric' Goddess Bhagavatī see Sarah Caldwell, *Oh Terrifying Mother: Sexuality, Violence, and the Worship of the Goddess Kālī* (New Delhi and Oxford: Oxford University Press, 1999).

49. White, *Kiss of the Yoginī*, pp. 136–7.
50. On theology practised at Cidamabaram, especially Umāpati's work, see David Smith, *The Dance of Śiva: Religion, Art, and Poetry in South India* (Cambridge: Cambridge University Press, 1996).
51. KT 2.24.
52. Dermot Killingley, 'Enjoying the World: Desire (*kāma*) and the *Bhagavadgītā*', in Julius Lipner (ed.), *The Fruits of Our Desiring: An Inquiry into the Ethics of the Bhagavadgītā for Our Times* (Calgary: Bayeux, 1997), pp. 67–79; p. 67.
53. E.g. Daṇḍin, *The Tale of Ten Princes*; Charles Malamoud, 'Seduction in an Indian Light', in *Cooking the World, Ritual and Thought in Ancient India*, trans. David White (New Delhi and Oxford: Oxford University Press, 1996), pp. 130–43.
54. Louis Dumont, 'World Renunciation in Indian Religions', in *Homo Hierarchicus: The Caste System and Its Implications*, revised English edition (Chicago: University of Chicago Press, 1980), pp. 267–86.
55. Also a practice witnessed in Tibetan Buddhist texts. David Germano, personal communication, 2004.
56. C.S. George, *The Caṇḍamahāroṣaṇatantra*, chs I–VIII. Sanskrit and Tibetan texts with English translation (New Haven CT: Oriental Society, 1974), pp. 56, 64.
57. Kaul, 11.11.
58. Richard A. Darmon, '*Vajrolī mudrā*. La retention séminale chez les yogis *vāmācārī*', in Véronique Boullier and Gilles Tarabout (eds), *Images du corps dans le monde hindou* (Paris: CNRS, 2002), pp. 213–40. Also attested in Buddhist Tibetan texts (David Germano, personal communication, 2004).
59. KT 5.48ab.
60. D.D. Shulman, *Tamil Temple Myths: Sacrifice and Divine Marriage in the South Indian Śaiva Tradition* (Princeton NJ: Princeton University Press, 1980), pp. 261–62. Cited by J.P. Parry, *Death in Benares* (Cambridge: Cambridge University Press, 1994), p. 256.
61. Friedhelm Hardy, *The Religious Culture of India: Power, Love, and Wisdom* (Cambridge: Cambridge University Press, 1994), p. 156.
62. Ibid., pp. 83–4.
63. White, *Kiss of the Yoginī*, p. 137.
64. Devagana Desai, *Erotic Sculpture of India: A Socio-Historical Study* (New Delhi: McGraw Hill, 1975), pp. 86, 118–20.
65. Discussed in White, *Kiss of the Yoginī*, pp. 94–9.
66. SP 1.498–9.
67. SP 1.548.
68. KT 8.57–75, trans. Alexis Sanderson, cited in R.C. Zaehner, *Our Savage God* (London: Collins, 1974), pp. 102–3. There are also 'orgistic' representations, including drinking scenes and the drinking of female sexual fluids (*rajapāna*), depicted on temple walls, for example in Orissa. Behera and

Donaldson, *Sculpture Masterpieces from Orissa*, p. 99–100. See White, *Kiss of the Yoginī*, p. 99.

69. Gavin Flood, 'Techniques of Body and Desire', *Religion* 22 (1992), pp. 47–62.
70. R. Freeman, 'The Teyyam Tradition of Kerala', in Flood (ed.), *The Blackwell Companion to Hinduism* (Oxford: Blackwell, 2003), pp. 307–26; p. 308.
71. Again, see Freeman's important publications here. I do not have space to discuss his thesis of ritual possession as the model for other forms of religious formation in South Asia but this is clearly highly germane to all work in this area. My reading of his work would be to see possession in terms of entextualisation. See also Frederick Smith, *Friendly Acquisitions, Hostile Takeovers: Deity and Spirit Possession in South Asian Civilization* (Berkeley: University of California Press, forthcoming).
72. Freeman, 'The Teyyam Tradition of Kerala', p. 314.
73. Ibid., p. 315.
74. Some work on intertextuality has been done here on the interconnections between the ISG and *Tantrasāra-saṃgraha*. See Gudrun Bühnemann, 'Buddhist Deities and Mantras in the Hindu Tantras: II, The Tantrasārasaṃgraha and the Īśānaśivagurudevapadhati', *Indo-Iranian Journal* 42 (1999), pp. 303–34.
75. NT 19.68 and commentary pp. 167–8.
76. NT 19.63c–65. 'If an aggrieved man should be somewhat afflicted by them [the terrible vināyakas] then he should worship Vighneśa, the chief Vināyaka. He should worship with the practice of visualisation and offerings from another Tantra, with many kinds of sweetmeats, various greedy offerings, with strong drink, meat, and the perfume of red flowers.' *yadi tair vighnitaḥ kaścid abhibhūto bhaven naraḥ// tatrādhidaivataṃ pūjyo vighneśas tu vināyakaḥ/ anyatantropacāreṇa dhyānayogena pūjayet// modakair vividhaiś citrair valibhir ghasmarais tathā/ bhūrimadyais tathā māṃsairraktapuṣpavilepanaiḥ.*
77. NT 19. 55–56: 'Whenever the boundless mothers, situated near, desire to destroy (one), then one should worship the eternal great mothers, the seven mothers Brāhmī, Māheśvarī, kaumārī, vaiṣṇavī, Vārāhī, Indrāṇī, and Cāmuṇḍā.' *Yadā hy anantās tatrasthā mātaraḥ saṃnidhānataḥ/ jighāṃsanti tadā sadyo mahāmātṛḥ prapūjayet// brāhmī māheśvarī caiva kaumārī vaiṣṇavī tathā/ vārāhī ca tathendrāṇī cāmuṇḍā saptamātaraḥ.*
78. NT 19.60c.
79. Filliozat, Jean *Le Kumāratantra de Rāvaṇa et les textes parallèles Indiens, Tibétains, Chinois, Cambodgien, et Arabe* (Paris: Imprimerie Nationale, 1937), p. 20.
80. Ibid., text pp. 4–11; translation pp. 11–19.
81. Ibid., text p. 7; translation p. 15.
82. ISG Mantrapāda 2.43.54–55. Cf. the description in the later *Śāradātilakatantra*, Gudrun Bühnemann, *The Iconography of Hindu Tantric Deities*, vol. II (Groningen: Egbert Forsten, 2001), pp. 275–6.
83. ISG Mantrapāda 2.41. The chapter refers to itself as the 'therapy for children of Khaḍgarāvaṇa'. Discussed in Filliozat, *Le Kumāratatra*, pp. 68–9.
84. Filliozat, *Le Kumāratantra*, pp. 84–109. Teun Goudriaan points to two

traditions of Rāvaṇa in the Sanskrit sources, the one more familiar as the demon king, the other as a an exorcist deity, 'Khaḍga-Rāvaṇa and his Worship in Balinese and Indian Tantric Sources', *Weiner Zeitschrift für die Kunde Südasiens* 21 (1977), pp. 143–69.

85. ISG Mantrapāda 2.42.1
86. TSG 12.9–11.
87. ISG Mantrapāda 2.42. 3b-8.
88. Kaul. 23.2–11.
89. ISG Mantrapāda 2.42. 26–29b.
90. TSG 12.1–2.
91. ISG Mantrapāda 2.42. 15–16b.
92. ISG Mantrapāda 2.42. 35d.
93. ISG Mantrapāda 2.43. 1–8. *hṛdayaṃ bhagavacchabdo ṣudrāśagatā phacuta m andarakusumaṣaṭpadavajratuṇḍa nīlāñjanasamaprabha idaṃ bhūtaṃ hana vilipantaṃ kha kha huṃ phaṭ ṭhaṭha/ anena māṣakṛsarair jāpitvā grastatāḍanāt/ taṃ muñcanti grahāḥ svaikhyaṃ rudradhyānena tat kṣanāt//1// hṛdayānte bhagavate phaveścāṣāśa namaḥ kāsaśa maheśvarāya bhramari bhrāmaya sūkari bhakṣaya ṭhaṭha/ māṣānnanena saṃmantrya bhakṣaṇān muñcati grahaḥ/ namo bhagavate ṣudrāśa mahābhairava devāya nartaya moḍaya balgaya kroḍaya bhrūṃ graham caṇḍa huṃ phaṭ ṭhaṭha/ bhūtapretapiśācādiñ japādyair mocayen manuḥ//2// tāraṃ hṛdccaṇḍaśabdaśca krodharudrāya dūṣu puṣu bhūtasamaye tiṣṭha ṭhaṭha/ saptavāraṃ japitvemaṃ śikhāṃ grastasya bandhayet/ grahas tu samaye tiṣṭhed vahnivāyupuraṃ punaḥ//3// likhitvā bhasmanā tasmin grastaṃ saṃsthāpya mantrataḥ/ anenāṣṭottaraśataṃ japitvāmbho mukhe'sya vai//4// prakṣipec ca japan kruddho graha āviśya muñcati/ rajjvā japitayānena stambhaṃ badhudhvā sa badhyate//5// piṣṭapratikṛtiṃ kṛtvā tatrāvāhya tu graham/ prāṇapratiṣṭhāṃ kṛtvā tu kṣureṇainaṃ vidārayet//6// chedayec ca triśūlena marmasu kṣatajaṃ sravet/ etāvatā grahagrastān na muñcati yadā tadā //7// chinnāṃ pratikṛtiṃ rājiyuktāṃ kuṇḍe juhotu ca/ sahasraṃ sa graho dagdhaḥ parityajya palāyati//8//*
94. ISG Mantrapāda 2.42.36ab; 2.43.3; 2.43.11–12.
95. ISG Mantrapāda 2.43.14–15.
96. ISG Mantrapāda 2.43.28.
97. Freeman, 'The Teyyam Tradition', p. 324.
98. ISG Mantrapāda 2.43.31
99. David L. Haberman, *Acting as a Way of Salvation: A Study of Rāgānuga Bhakti Sādhana* (New York and Oxford: Oxford University Press, 1988), pp. 31–5, 65–76.
100. On the Sahajiyas, see S.N. Dasgupta, *Obscure Religious Cults* (Calcutta: Firma K. Mukhopadhyay, 1962 [1946]), pp. 113–22; Edward Dimock, *The Place of the Hidden Moon: Erotic Mysticism in the Vaishnavasahajiya Cult of Bengal* (Chicago: University of Chicago Press, 1966), p. 83.

Chapter 5

1. G. Oberhammer, 'Beobachtungen zur "Offenbarungsgeschicte" der Paramasaṃhitā', in G. Oberhammer (ed.), *Studies in Hinduism II. Miscellanea to*

the Phenomenon of Tantras (Vienna: Der Österreichischen Akademie der Wissenschaften, 1998), pp. 21–41; p. 36.

2. Natalia Isayeva, *From Early Vedānta to Kashmir Shaivism: Gaudapda, Bhartrhati, and Abhinavagupta* (Delhi: Śrī Satguru, 1997 [1995]), p. 28.
3. For an interesting account of cosmology in the *Paramasaṃhitā* see Marzenna Czerniak-Droździowicz, 'Sṛṣṭikrama – Order of Creation in the *Paramasaṃhitā*', in G. Oberhammer (ed.), *Studies in Hinduism II*, pp. 43–54.
4. *Spand*, pp. 6–7, 12, 56. The passages quoted are JS 20.233–39, 10.69, and 1.63c-64b.
5. For an excellent summary of Pāñcarātra cosmology, see Otto Schrader, *Introduction to the Pāñcarātra and the Ahirbudhnya Saṃhitā* (Madras: Adyar Library, 1973 [1916]), pp. 31–98.
6. JS 4.3–9. All translations to the JS are my own, although there is a German translation of five chapters in M. Rastelli, *Philosophisch–theologische Grundanschauungen der Jayakhyasamhita* (Vienna: Österreichen Akademie der Wissenschaften, 1999), and also in Andreas Bock-Raming, *Untersuchungen zur Gottesvorstellung in der älteren Anonymliteratur des Pāñcarātra,* Beiträge zur Indologie 34 (Weisbaden: Harrassowitz, 2002), pp. 261–3. For an extended discussion of cosmology in the *Jayākhya*, see pp. 257–74.
7. These deities are known to the parallel, orthodox tradition of the Vaikhānasa. See Gerard Colas, 'History of Vaiṣṇava Traditions', in Gavin Flood (ed.), *The Blackwell Companion to Hinduism* (Oxford: Blackwell, 2003), pp. 229–70; p. 242. G. Colas, *Viṣṇu, ses images et ses feux. Les métamorphoses du dieu chez les vaikhānasa* (Paris: de Boccard, 1996).
8. The term *vyūha* is from the Sanskrit root *ūh*, 'to remove', and *vi*, 'asunder'. Schrader speculates that the term refers to the pushing asunder of six qualities of God into three pairs (*Introduction to the Pancaratra and the Ahirbudhnya Samhita*, Madras: Adyar Library 1973 [1916], p. 40). However, the term may be derived from Buddhism, where its occurrence is earlier. The *Sukhāvatī-vyūha* is an early Mahāyāna text about the manifestation of a pure Buddha land called the land of contentment. We must surely take *vyūha* here to mean something like appearance or manifestation, as the *tat puruṣa* compound surely cannot mean the shoving away of the pure land. Rather it is suffering that is removed and the pure land takes its place. Indeed, there are dimensions to this text, its meditative and visionary dimensions, the idea of a happy place beyond the world, that echo the Pāñcarātra idea of Viṣṇu's heaven (*vaikuṇṭha*).
9. Schrader, *Introduction to the Pāñcarātra*, pp. 1–107, although since then there have, of course, been developments in locating the sources of the *vyūhas*. See Andreas Bock-Raming, *Untersuchungen zur Gottesvorstellung in der äleren Anonymliteratur des Pāñcarātra Beiträge zur Indologie* 34 (Weisbaden: Harraossowitz, 2002). For a thorough account of the cosmology of the *Jayākhya-saṃhitā*, see Rastelli, *Philosophisch-theologische Grundanschauungen*, pp. 39–73.
10. Bock-Raming shows remarkable early icons of the *vyūha*s and a pillar representing the *tattva* hierarchy. Bock-Raming, *Untersuchungen zur*

Gottesvortstellung, Plates 7–9.
11. *Ahirbudhnya Saṃhitā* 6.33c-34. Quoted by Rastelli, *Philosophisch-theologische Grundanschauungen*, p. 50, n120. Rastelli seems, reasonably, to suggest that the concept of the Puruṣa in the JS is not dissimilar to the *kutasthā puruṣa* of other texts. While the details of different texts vary, the principles remain constant.
12. LT 7.11–12. See Schrader, *Introduction*, pp. 69–70.
13. See Schrader, *Introduction*, pp. 79–90.
14. See ibid., pp. 80–81. On the origins of the *vyūha* ways of thinking in the *Chāndogya Upaniṣad*, see Bock-Raming, *Untersuchungen zur Gottesvorstellung*, p. 301.
15. Although Schrader claims that the *buddhi* is the individual aspect of the cosmic *mahat*. *Introduction*, pp. 83–4.
16. It has even been rendered as 'instinct' by J. Pereira, *Hindu Theology: Themes, Texts, and Structures* (New York: Doubleday Image, 1976), p. 59. In his discussion of the term, Larson suggests that the psychoanalytic notion of the unconscious 'might be somewhat helpful in describing the *buddhi*, in so far as it is our Western equivalent to a dimension of man which is not self-conscious but yet determines basic human strivings'. G. Larson, *Classical Sāṃkhya: An Interpretation of Its History and Meaning* (Delhi: MLBD, 1969), p. 200. One can see why scholars have arrived at this understanding as the *buddhi* contains the impulses that limit the self as the empirical experiencer. But these renderings do not appreciate fully enough the hierarchical nature of this cosmology, that limiting constraints are derived from a higher cosmic level.
17. *Sāṃkhya-kārikā* 23rd *ārya*. These are found not only in the Pāñcarātra but in the Śaiva Siddhānta also. See the Mrg. 11.2–3, 74–77; 10.29.
18. See Gavin Flood, *Body and Cosmology in Kashmir Śaivism* (San Francisco: Mellen Research University Press, 1993), pp. 179–81.
19. For a thorough account of this development in the JS, see Rastelli, *Philosophisch-theologische Grundanschauungen*, pp. 56–60.
20. For a discussion of this, see Karl H. Potter, *Presuppositions of India's Philosophies* (Westport: Greenwood Press, 1976), pp. 107–14.
21. Rastelli, *Philosophisch-theologische Grundanschauungen*, pp. 49–50, 188–91.
22. JS 4. 110a.
23. JS 4. 60b-66
24. The material on the *bhūtaśuddhi* in this chapter recapitulates much of my article 'The Purification of the Body in Tantric Ritual Representation', *Indo-Iranian Journal* 45 (2002), pp. 25–43.
25. See S. Gupta, 'Yoga and *Antarayāga* in Pāñcarātra', in Teun Goudriaan (ed), *Ritual and Speculation in Early Tantrism: Studies in Honour of André Padoux* (Albany NY: SUNY Press, 1992), pp. 175–208; p. 177; Gavin Flood, 'Ritual, Cosmos and the Divine Body in the *Jayākhyasaṃhitā*', *Wiener Zeitschrift für die Kunde Südasiens* 36 (supplement) (1992), pp. 167–77.
26. See Alexis Sanderson, 'Vajrayāna: Origin and Function', in Mettanando Bhikkhu et al. (eds), *Buddhism in the Year 2000* (Bangok: Dhammakaya Foundation, 1991), pp. 152–60.

27. *Bṛhadāraṇyaka Upaniṣad* 6.3.3, in Patrick Olivelle (trans.), *The Early Upaniṣads* (New York and Oxford: Oxford University Press, 1996), p. 151.
28. Cf. Puruṣa-sūkta, *Ṛg-veda* 10.90. For the Indo-European ancestry of the symbolic identification of body and cosmos, see Bruce Lincoln, *Myth, Cosmos and Society: Indo-European Themes of Creation and Destruction* (Cambridge MA: Harvard University Press, 1986).
29. Brian K. Smith, *Classifying the Universe: The Ancient Indian Varṇa System and the Origins of Caste* (New York and Oxford: Oxford University Press, 1994), pp. 11–13 and *passim.*
30. Buddhaghosa, *Visuddhimagga*. 4.123–26; 5.170–72. Translated by Pe Maung Tin, *The Path of Purity* (London: Pāli Text Society, 1975), pp. 143–6, 196–8.
31. *Majjhima-nikāya* 2.14. Translated by I.B. Horner, *The Middle Length Sayings* vol. 2 (London: Pāli Text Society, 1972). *Dīgha-nikāya* 3.268. Translated by T.W. and C.A.F. Rhys Davids, *Dialogues of the Buddha*, part 3 (London: Pāli Text Society, 1971). *Aṅguttara-nikāya* III.5.46,60. Translated by F.L. Woodward, *The Book of Gradual Sayings* vol. 5 (London: Pāli Text Society, 1972).
32. Although the actual sequence is as follows: earth, water, fire, air, blue, yellow, red, white, light and space.
33. For a discussion of the *kasiṇas,* see H.V. Guenther, *The Philosophy and Psychology of the Abhidharma* (Berkeley CA and London: Shambala, 1976), pp. 116–20. On early Buddhist meditation, see Lance Cousins, 'Vittaka/ Vitarka and Vicāra: Stages of Samādhi in Buddhism and Yoga', *Indo-Iranian Journal* 35 (1992), pp. 137–57. Lance Cousins, 'Śamatha-yāna and vipassana-yāna', in G. Dhammapala, R. Gombrich and K.R. Norman (eds), *Buddhist Studies in Honour of Hammalava Saddhatissa* (Nugegoda: University of Jayewardenepura, 1984), pp. 56–68.
34. KA 3.4ff. The text follows the pattern of Śaiva Siddhānta worship with a system of *kalā*s, using thirty-one identified with the body (3.6).
35. NT 5.2.
36. SSP, vol. 2, p. xxi.
37. Bhut, pp. 13–20. This text in the manuscript collection of the French Institute at Pondicherry follows the Śaiva Siddhānta model as articulated by Somaśambhu.
38. See David White, *The Alchemical Body: Siddha Traditions in Medieval India* (Chicago: University of Chicago Press, 1996), pp. 150, 180, 270–72.
39. See SSP vol. 3, pp. xii–xxii. André Padoux, *Vāc, the Concept of the Word in Selected Hindu Tantras*, trans. J. Gontier (Albany NY: SUNY Press, 1990), pp. 330–71.
40. TatPrak 1.8.
41. Flood, 'Ritual, Cosmos, and the Divine Body', pp. 167–77.
42. See T. Goudriaan, 'Vaikhānasa Daily Worship', *Indo-Iranian Journal* 12 (1970), pp. 161–215; p. 209.
43. G. Colas, 'Sectarian Divisions According to the Vaikhānasāgama', in T. Goudriaan (ed.), *Sanskrit Tradition and Tantrism* (Leiden: Brill, 1990), p. 25.

44. See Gupta, 'Yoga and *Antarayāga*', p. 178. There are some passages in the Sat (e.g. 6.163f.; 17.142–7) that prescribe these rites without calling them *brahmayajña* etc.
45. See SSP, vol. 1, pp. xxiv–xxvi.
46. Alexis Sanderson, 'Meaning in Tantric Ritual', in Anne-Marie Blondeau (ed.), *Essais sur le rituel*, vol. 3 (Paris: Ecole Pratique des Haute Etudes, 5th section, 1996), pp. 15–95.
47. JS 18.20–33.
48. This pattern is directly paralleled by the Śaiva classification of *samayin, putraka, ācārya* and *sādhaka*. See H. Brunner, 'Le Sādhaka, personnage oublié de l'Inde du Sud', *Journal Asiatique* 263 (1975), pp. 411–43. See also R. Davis, *Ritual in an Oscillating Universe: Worshipping Siva in Medieval India* (Princeton NJ: Princeton University Press, 1991), pp. 89–100.
49. Katherine K. Young, 'Om, the Veda, and the Status of Women with Special Reference to Śrīvaiṣṇavism', in Laurie L. Patton (ed.), *Jewels of Authority: Women and Textual Tradition in Hindu Law* (Oxford: Oxford University Press, 2002), pp. 84–121.
50. For an English translation of this chapter see my 'The Purification of the Body', in David White (ed.), *Tantra in Practice* (Princeton NJ: Princeton University Press, 2000), pp. 509–20.
51. JS 10.2–7.
52. JS 10.9–13.
53. JS 10.16.
54. The six qualities possessed by Nārāyaṇa are *jñāna, aiśvarya, śakti, bala, vīrya* and *tejas*. See LT 2.26–36; Schrader, *Introduction to the Pāñcarātra*, pp. 36–40.
55. JS 10.1–3.
56. JS 10.18a–21.
57. JS 10.26–30ab.
58. JS 10.31–36.
59. JS 10.39–42.
60. JS 10.43–48.
61. JS 10.49–57.
62. This echoes the *Chāndogya-upaniṣad* 8.1.2, which speaks of the space within the heart containing earth and sky, fire and wind, sun and moon, and lightning and stars. Also 8.6.4, where the deceased rises to the crown of the head and reaches the sun.
63. JS 10.58–68.
64. JS 10.69.
65. JS 10.71a.
66. JS 10.72–77.
67. JS 10.81–82.
68. JS 10.85–86.
69. JS 10.103.
70. M. Monier-Williams, *Sanskrit–English Dictionary* (Oxford: Clarendon Press 1899), p. 572.
71. JS 11.1–3. See the Appendix for a translation of this chapter on *nyāsa*.

72. JS 11.10–17. Rastelli gives an extremely helpful list of the names of the mantras and their corresponding body parts in the text, *Philosophisch-theologische Grundanschauungen*, pp. 241–4.
73. JS 11.22c–36.
74. JS 11.26c–27b.
75. JS 11.35b–36.
76. JS 11.39c–40.
77. JS 11.41: *ahaṃ sa bhagavān viṣṇur ahaṃ nārāyaṇo hariḥ/ vāsudevo hyahaṃ vyāpī bhūtāvāso nirañjanaḥ.*
78. M. Rastelli, 'The *āsana* According to the Parameśvarasaṃhitā or A Method of Writing a Saṃhitā', in G. Oberhammer and M. Rastelli (eds), *Studies in Hinduism* III: *Pāñcarātra and Viśiṣṭādvaita* (Vienna: Der Österreichischen Akademi der Wissenschaften, 2002), pp. 9–59.
79. JS 12; LT 36.2–34. For a lucid account of the inner worship in the JS, the visualisation that pervades the body, the construction of the throne, the inner worship of the deity along with the mantras, see Rastelli, *Philosophisch-theologische Grundanschauungen*, pp. 246–71. Rastelli presents a helpful diagram of the visualisation ('The *āsana* according to the Paramesvaradamhita…', p. 12.) See also Flood, 'Ritual, Cosmos and the Divine Body', pp. 167–77; Sanjukta Gupta 'Yoga and *Anta yāga* in Pāñcarātra', and Sanjukta Gupta's translation, *The Lakṣmī Tantra* (Leiden: Brill, 1972), ch. 36.
80. Rastelli, *Philosophisch-theologische Grundanschauungen*, pp. 118, 247.
81. JS 12.1–15.
82. JS 13.4b.
83. LT 37.2–3.
84. JS, chapter 14. See A. Padoux, 'Un rituel hindou du rosaire (*Jayākhyasaṃhitā*, ch. 14)', *Journal Asiatique* 225 (1987), pp. 115–29.
85. JS, chapter 15. See Gudrun Bühnemann, *Pūjā: A Study in Smārta Ritual* (Vienna: Publications of the de Noblili Research Library, 1988).

Chapter 6

1. The JS is quoted by the Kashmiri Utpalācārya along with other Pāñcarātra texts. See Otto Schrader, *Introduction to the Pāñcarātra* (Madras: Adyar Library, 1973 [1918]), pp. 20–22.
2. H. Brunner-Lachaux, 'Introduction', SSP, vol. 1, pp. xli–xlii.
3. The location of the ISG within the history of south Indian traditions is open to dispute, although it is likely to be from Kerala, as all the manuscripts from there are in Malayalam script, and the text is still used by some Nambuthiri families of the Taranallur clan in the Alwaye region. The text contains a synthesis of deities and traditions characteristic of Kerala Tantrism, with material on possession and exorcism, which are strong concerns of 'folk' religion in the Malabar region. A detailed study of the text, its influences, the history of the tradition and the influence of the ISG upon the *Tantrasamuccaya* would help to clarify its origins. This work has yet to be done.

4. Abhinavagupta, Ptlv 19a–21. André Padoux (trans.), *La Parātrīśikālaghuvṛtti de Abhinavagupta*, Publications de l'Institut de Civilisation Indienne, fasc. 38 (Paris: de Boccard, 1975). English translation by Paul Muller-Ortega, *The Triadic Heart of Śiva: Kaula Tantrism of Ahinavagupta in the Non-dual Shaivism of Kashmir* (Albany NY: SUNY Press, 1989), pp. 205–32.
5. H. Brunner-Lachaux 'Introduction', *Mṛgendrāgama: section des rites et section du comportement avec la vṛtti de Bhaṭṭa Nārāyaṇakaṇṭha* (Pondicherry: Institut Français d'Indologie, 1985), pp. vii–xlvii; pp. xvii–xviii.
6. A number of works present this tripartite metaphysics. See SSP, vol. 1, pp. ix–xx; Jorg Gengnagel, *Māyā, Puruṣa und Śiva: Die dualistische Traditions des Śivaismus nach Aghoraśivācārya*. Beiträge zur Kenntnis südasiatischer Sprachen und Literaturen 3 (Wiesbaden: Harrasowitz, 1996); Rohan A. Dunuwila, *Śaiva Siddhānta Theology: A Context for Hindu–Christian Dialogue* (Delhi: MLBD, 1985), pp. 101–3.
7. On Bhojadeva and his dates, see Gengnagel, *Māyā, Puruṣa und Śiva*, pp. 18–21.
8. TatPrak 5.
9. Kumāradeva, in TatPrak, *Tātparyadīpikā*, p. 21. On the five powers of Śiva, see also Mrg Vidyāpāda, chapter 5.
10. TatPrak 6; Mrg Vidyāpāda 6.7. KirT 20cd-22ab.
11. Goodall, *Kiraṇa-tantra,* p. 185, note 79.
12. TatPrak 8–9.
13. KirT 1.13 commentary. Goodall observes that the first use of these terms is Sadyojyoti's *Svāyambhuvavṛtti* 1:2 and 2:26. Furthermore he cites Sanderson as proposing that the source for the new terminology is in fact the non-Saiddhāntika *Mālinīvijayottara*. Goodall, *Kiraṇa-tantra*, pp. 184–5, n71.
14. KirVrt. 1.13; Goodall, *Kiraṇa-tantra*, p. 184.
15. On *kalā* see Rāmakaṇṭha commentary on 1.16ab. Goodall, *Kiraṇa-tantra*, p. 199–201. On the cosmic *kalās* see André Padoux, *Vāc: The Concept of the Word in Selected Hindu Tantras*, trans. J. Gontier (Albany NY: SUNY Press, 1990), pp. 345–7, 357–64.
16. TatPrak. 10.
17. MTP 8.2; 8.17; 9.24ab.
18. TatPrak 10; *vṛtti,* p. 36. RA Vidyāpāda 3.29–31b.
19. KirT 3.27ef; Goodall, *Kiraṇa-tantra*, p. 299.
20. KirT 4.7cd; Goodall, *Kiraṇa-tantra*, p. 304.
21. TatPrak 11.
22. TatPrak 13; *vṛtti* p. 36. See also KirT Vidyāpāda 1.20cd-22ab and Goodall's explicatory note 171, *Kiraṇa-tantra*, pp. 215–16.
23. TatPrak 13.
24. E.g. the monist Kṣemarāja seems to regard Mantras, Mantreśvaras and Mantramantreśvaras as being higher than the Vijñānakalās, whom he places above *māyā* but below the Mantras. PH, p. 7f. He posits seven kinds of experient (*pramatṛ*), Śiva, the three groups of Mantra Lords and then the three types of soul of the Siddhānta (Vijñānakala, Śūnyakala, Sakala).
25. Mrg Vidyāpāda 5.3cd.

26. TatPrak 15; *Tātparyadīpikā*, p. 42.
27. KirT 2.7; Mrg *vṛtti*, Vidyāpāda 6.1: the soul is the raison d'être for the universe.
28. TatPrak 16.
29. Mrg Vidyāpāda 7.18.
30. KT 2.7cd-8ab.
31. E.g. MTP 16.3d; RA Vidyāpāda 3.28cd.
32. Davis has called this 'the oscillating universe'. He describes the process well, as one in which the universe 'oscillates between moments of creation and destruction, evolution and involution, activity and quietude, expansion and contraction.' R. Davis, *Ritual in an Oscillating Universe: Worshipping Śiva in Medieval India* (Princeton NJ: Princeton University Press, 1991), p. 42.
33. See Raffaela Torella, 'The *Kañcukas* in the Śaiva and Vaiṣṇava Tantric Tradition: A Few Considerations between Theology and Grammar', in G. Oberhammer (ed.), *Studies in Hinduism II: Miscellania to the Phenomenon of Tantras* (Vienna: Der Österreichischen Akademie der Wissenschaften, 1998), pp. 55–86.
34. TatPrak 19.
35. KirT 2.15cd; Goodall, *Kiraṇa-tantra*, p. 241.
36. TatPrak 19; *Tātparyadīpikā*, p. 46.
37. TatPrak 21–3. For an account of the *tattva*s in the Śaiva Siddhānta, see Brunner-Lachaux, 'Introduction', SSP vol. 1, pp. xvi–xx. On the definition of *māyā*, see Mrg 9.2–5.
38. MTP 2.14–17b.
39. For details, see N.T. Bhatt, 'Introduction', in MTPVrt, pp. xxii–xxiv.
40. Abhinavagupta, IPV 2.3.13, p. 128–9. See my *Body and Cosmology in Kashmir Śaivism* (San Francisco: Mellen Research University Press, 1993), pp. 46–50.
41. E.g. RA Kriyāpāda 47.38–42, described 60–86b; these are supplementary chapters. N.R. Bhatt (ed.), *Rauravāgama*, vol. III (Pondicherry: Institut Français d'Indologie, 1988).
42. SSP, pp. xiii–xiv.
43. On the six ways, see SSP, vol. 3, pp. xiii–xxii. There are extremely helpful plates in vol. 3 illustrating the parallels between each of the ways (especially plate 5). See also Padoux, *Vāc*, pp. 330–71.
44. RA Kriyāpāda, supplementary chapter 47.62–77.
45. For a comparative table, see SSP vol. 3, Pl. VIIA.
46. MVT 5.5.
47. Alexis Sanderson, 'The Doctrine of the Mālinīvijayottaratantra', in Teun Goudriaan (ed.), *Ritual and Speculation in Early Tantrism: Studies in Honour of André Padoux* (Albany NY: SUNY Press, 1992), pp. 281–312.
48. For an excellent account of the *ṣaḍadhvan*, see Padoux, *Vāc*, pp. 330–71.
49. RA Kriyāpāda 25.61c-62b.
50. MVT 14.2; *vṛtti*.
51. RA, vol. III. 63. 24–28: *śivasaṃskārasaṃbandhād bhasmarudrākṣamiśraṇāt/ śikhāyajñopavītaṃ tu dhṛtvā dīkṣita ucyate//24// jaṅgamaḥ śuddhaśaivaṃ tu tattattantre praveśayet/ śāstrasya saṃpradānena śāsrtadīkṣeti cocyate//25//*

jaḍī vā muṇḍako vāpi śivācāryaḥ praveśakaḥ/ sthāvaraṃ liṅgam ity āhur jaṅgamas tu maheśvaraḥ//26// maheśvarapadāviṣṭaṃ sthānaṃ yat saṃpadāṃ padam / brāhmaṇo vāpi caṇḍālaḥ suguṇo durguṇo 'pi vā//27// bhasmarudrākṣasaṃmiśraḥ śiva eva na saṃśayaḥ/ ity etac chaiva utpanne paścāc chaivaṃ sammācaret//28//. I have followed the alternative reading given by Bhatt for 26d as *jaṅgamaṃ tu maheśvaram*. The term *jaṅgama* could be a proper name for a Śaiva sect. Also Mrg Caryapāda 1.1–2.

52. Hélène Brunner, 'The Sexual Aspect of the *Liṅga* Cult According to the Saiddhāntika Scriptures', in Oberhammer (ed.), *Studies in Hinduism II*, pp. 87–103.
53. SSP, vol. 1; Davis, *Ritual in an Oscillating Universe*, pp. 89–111.
54. Jorg Gengnagel, 'The Śaiva Siddhānta Ācārya as Mediator of Religious Identity', in Vasudha Dalmia, Angelika Maninar, and Martin Christof (eds), *Charisma and Canon: Essays on the Religious History of the Indian Subcontinent* (New Delhi and Oxford: Oxford University Press, 2001), pp. 77–92.
55. SSP, vol. 3, pp. xxvii–xxx.
56. Thus in vol. 3 of the SSP she corrects her earlier reading of the material. Brunner-Lachaux, SSP, vol. 3, p. xxxi.
57. RA Kriyāpāda, supplement 48.
58. See H. Brunner, 'Le *sādhaka*, un personnage oublié du śivaisme du Sud', *Journal Asiatique*, 1975, pp. 411–16.
59. Brunner, 'Le sādhaka', p. 416.
60. Alexis Sanderson, 'Maṇḍala and Āgamic Identity in the Trika of Kashmir', in *Mantras et Diagrammes Rituels dans l'Hindouisme* (Paris: CNRS, 1986), pp. 169–214.
61. Brunner, 'Le sādhaka', p. 418, n21. Mrg Caryāpāda, 1.8–10 and commentary. On the identification of the *bubhukṣu* with the householder and the mumukṣu with the ascetic (*tapasvin*), see C. Caillat, 'Le Sādhaka Śaiva à la Lumière de la Discipline Jaina', in Klaus Brun and Albrechy Wezler (eds), *Studien zum Jainismus und Buddhismus: Gedenkschrift für Ludwig Alsdorf* (Wiesbaden: Franz Steiner, 1981), pp. 51–9.
62. SSP, vol. 3, 1.95–115. For a clear account that summarises much of the detail found in Siddhānta texts such as the SSP, see Davis, *Śiva in an Oscillating Universe*, pp. 94–9.
63. SSP, vol. 3, chapter 2.
64. SSP, vol. 3, chapter 3; described by Brunner-Lachaux in summary form, pp. xxxviii–xliii. My account here generally follows hers.
65. Brunner-Lachaux, 'Introduction' p. xxxix: 'La cordelette ainsi préparée est l'image du disciple, avec son *ātman* emprisonné de liens (d'où son nom *paśusūtra*, "cordelette des liens")'.
66. These Lords of the *kalā*s, the 'cause deities', Kāraṇeśvaras or Kāraṇas, are Brahman, Viṣṇu, Rudra, Īśvara, and Sadāśiva. Listed by Brunner-Lachaux, SSP, vol. 3, p. 118 n7.
67. SSP, vol. 3.4.93–104: *brahmaṃs tavādhikāre 'smin mumukṣuṃ dīkṣayāmy aham/ bhāvyaṃ tvayānukūlena vidhiṃ vijñāpayed iti//93// āvāhayet tato devīṃ raktāṃ vāgīśvarīṃ hṛdā/ icchājñānakriyārūpāṃ ṣaḍvidhād-*

hvaikakāriṇīm//94// pūjayet tarpayed devīṃ prakāreṇamunā tataḥ/ vāgīśvaraṃ ca niḥśeṣayonivikṣobhakāraṇam//95// hṛtsaṃpuṭātmabījādihuṃphaḍantaśarāṇunā/ tāḍayedd hṛdayaṃ tasya prafiśec ca vidhānauit// 96/tataḥ viṣyasya caitanyaṃ hṛdi vahnikaṇopamam/ nivṛttisthaṃ yutaṃ pāśair jyeṣṭhayā vibhajed yathā//97// oṃ hāṃ haṃ hāṃ haḥ huṃphaṭ/ oṃ hāṃ haṃ hāṃ svāhā/ ity anenātha pūrakeṇāṅkuśamudrayā tadākṛṣyātmamantreṇa gṛhītvātmani yojayet/ oṃ hāṃ haṃ hāṃ ātmane namaḥ/ pitror vibhāvya saṃyogaṃ caitanyaṃ recakena tat/ brahmādikāraṇatyāgakramān nītvā śivās padam//98// garbhādhānārthamādāya yugapatsarvayoniṣu/ kṣiped vāgīśvarīyonau vāmayodbhavamudrayā//99// yathā – oṃ hāṃ haṃ hāṃ ātmane namaḥ/ pūjaed apy anenaiva tarpayed api pañcadhā/ asya yoniśu sarvāsu dehasiddiṃ hṛdācaret//100// nātra puṃsavanaṃ stryādiśarīrasyāpi saṃbhavāt/ sīmantonnayanaṃ cāpi daivād andhādidehataḥ//101// śirasā janma kurvīta yugapat sarvadehinām / tathaiva bhāvayed eṣām adhikāraṃ śikhāṇunā //102// bhogaṃ kavacanmantreṇa śastreṇa viṣayātmanoḥ/ moharūpam abhedaṃ ca layasaṃjñaṃ vibhāvayet//103// śivena srotasāṃ śuddhiṃ hṛdā tattvaviśodhanam/ pañcapañcāhutir dadyād garbhādhānādiṣu kramāt//104//

68. SSP, vols 3, 4; Brunner-Lachaux notes, pp. 261–96.
69. KirT 4.18–21, and commentary; Goodall, *Kiraṇa-tantra,* pp. 382–5.
70. For an excellent, full account of Śaiva ritual see Brunner-Lachaux, 'Introduction', SSP, vol. 1, pp. xx–xxxii.
71. RA Kriyāpāda 10.12cd on the *pañcaśuddhi* or *bhūtaśuddhi*; 30–34 on the visualisation of Sadāśiva. On ritual procedures of purification of the place, inner worship, purification of ritual implements, purification of the body, of mantra, of the *liṅga*, inner worship of Śiva and purification of the subtle body before external worship, see Ajit Kriyāpāda 20.108cd–174ab. Invocation, sprinkling the icon, and making offerings of incense, flowers and so on follows this. 20.174.cd–211.
72. MTP 17.24–27b; *vṛtti*. With seven of its attributes the buddhi enchains the soul in transmigration and with the eighth (*jñāna*) liberates it.
73. RA, vol. III, supplement 59.3–7b. On the distinction see H. Brunner, '*Ātmārthapūjā* versus *parārthapūjā* in the Śaiva Tradition', in T. Goudriaan (ed.), *Sanskrit Tradition and Tantrism* (Leiden: Brill, 1990), pp. 1–23. Brunner makes the important point that the distinction does not map directly on to private and public worship. Temple worship is not 'public' in the sense that it makes no difference whether there are witnesses or not (p. 7).
74. RA Vidyāpāda 12.1–5.
75. SSP, vol. 1, p. 4 n5; RA, chs 5 and 6.
76. For details of seven kinds of bath, see Mrg Kriyāpāda 2.
77. SSP, vol. 1, 1.4.
78. SSP, vol. 1, 1.65.
79. SSP, vol. 1,1.93.
80. SSP, vol. 1, III.8
81. SSP, vol. 1, III.14–15.
82. ISG Sāmānya-pāda 10.1–8.

83. ISG Sāmānya-pāda 10.4–5.
84. ISG Sāmānya-pāda 10.6–8.
85. ISG Sāmānya-pāda 10.9–12. This image of the subtle body as an inverted banyan tree is found in the manual of Aghoraśiva. The text is given by Brunner-Lachaux, SSP, vol. 1, Appendix 4, pp. 328–9.
86. ISG Sāmānya-pāda 10.14–15.
87. On the two cosmological systems, see Davis, *Ritual in an Oscillating Universe*, pp. 53–7.
88. SSP, vol. 1, p. 154, n1 and plate 5.
89. SSP, vol. 1, III.57–60.
90. Ajit Kriyāpāda 2.28ab, 32; 29.110.
91. SSP, vol. 1, section iv; see also Ajit Kriyāpāda, chapter 21.
92. E.g. RA Kriyāpāda, chapters 16, 18; SSP, vol. 4.
93. Mrg Caryāpāda 1.18–19.
94. Mrg Caryāpāda 1.2–4.
95. Mrg Caryāpāda 1.11–12, n4.
96. Mrg Caryāpāda 1.67–69.
97. Mrg Caryāpāda 1.78–84.
98. Mrg Caryāpāda 1.119c–120 and commentary.

Chapter 7

1. For an important systematic overview, see Sanderson 'Śaivism and the Tantric Traditions', in S. Sutherland et al. (eds), *The World's Religions* (London: Routledge, 1988), pp. 660–704. For good introductions to doctrine and practice, see Mark Dyczkowski, *The Doctrine of Vibration: An Analysis of the Doctrines and Practices of Kashmir Shaivism* (Albany NY: SUNY Press, 1987); P. Muller-Ortega, *The Triadic Heart of Śiva: Kaula Tantrism of Abhinavagupta in the Non-Dual Shaivism of Kashmir* (Albany NY: SUNY Press, 1989).
2. IPV 1.1: *nirābhāsāt pūrṇād aham iti purā bhāsayati.*
3. TA 3. 203cd–204b: *Anuttaravisargātmaśivaśaktyadvayātmani// parāmarśo nirbharatvād aham ity ucyate vibhoḥ/* I have been guided by Padoux's translation: 'La prise de conscience de l'Ominprésent dans la non-dualité de Śiva et de l'Énergie, c.-à-d. de l'Incomparable et de l'émission [cosmique], est, en raison de tout ce qu'elle contient, appelée le "Je".' Padoux, '*aham*', in H. Brunner, G. Oberhammer and A. Padoux (eds), *Tantrābhidhānakośa* I. *Dictionnaire es termes techniques de la littérature hindoue tantrique* (Vienna: Der Österreichischen Akademie der Wissenschaften, 2000), pp. 166–7.
4. Utpala, *Ajaḍapamātṛsiddhi* quoted by Jayaratha 3.204ab. Padoux's translation, Lilian Silburn and André Padoux, *La Lumière sur les Tantras: La Tantrāloka d'Abhinavagupta chapitres 1 à 5* (Paris: de Boccard, 1998), p. 188.
5. TA 3.204c-208b: *anuttarādyā prasṛtir hāntā śaktisvarūpiṇī//204// pratyyāhṛtāśeṣaviśvānuttare sā nilīyate/ tadidaṃ viśvamantaḥsthaṃ śaktau sānuttare pare//205// tattasyāmiti yatsatyaṃ vibhunā saṃpuṭikṛtiḥ/ tena*

śrītrīśikāśāstre śakteḥ sampuṭitākṛtiḥ//206// saṃvittau bhāti yadviśvaṃ tatrāpi khalu saṃvidā/ tadetatritayaṃ dvandvayogātsaṃghātatāṃ gatam//207// ekam eva paraṃ rūpaṃ bhairavasyāhamātmakam. I have been guided by Padoux's translation *La Lumière sur les Tantra*, pp. 188–9. On the identification of Bhairava with other terms in the process called *nirvacana*, see Eivind Kahrs, *Indian Semantic Analysis: The Nirvacana Tradition* (Cambridge: Cambridge University Press, 1998), pp. 57–66.

6. TA 4.191c–193; Padoux, *La Lumière sur les Tantras*, p. 246.
7. TA 4.193.
8. TA 3.200c–202b and commentary.
9. Jaideva Singh, *Abhinavagupta: A Trident of Wisdom: Translation of Parātrīśikā Vivaraṇa* (Albany NY: SUNY Press, 1989), p. 9.
10. Kerry M. Skora, 'Consciousness of Consciousness: Reflexive Awareness in the Trika Śaivism of Abhinavagupta', Ph.D. thesis (University of Virginia, 2001).
11. Singh, *Abhinavagupta*, p. 9.
12. SSV 1.14, p. 32.
13. See Gavin Flood, *Body and Cosmology in Kashmir Śaivism* (San Francisco: Mellen Research University Press, 1993), chs 1 and 2.
14. PTV 3 and 4, commentary pp. 70–71.
15. PTV p. 71.
16. PH auto commentary on sūtra 12, p. 27. *tathā hi citprakāśāt avyatiriktā nityoditamahāmantrarūpā pūrṇāhamvimaraśamayī yā iyaṃ parā vākśaktiḥ ādikṣāntarūpāśeṣaśakticakragarbhiṇī sā tāvat paśyantīmadhyamādikrameṇa grāhakabhūmikāṃ bhāsayti/ tatra ca parārūpatvena svarūpam aprathayantī māyāpramātuḥ asphuṭāsādhāraṇārthāvabhāsarūpāṃ pratikṣaṇa navnavāṃ vikalpakriyāmullāsayati śuddham api ca avikalpabhūmim tadācchāditām eva darśayati.*
17. On the Goddess Parā and the alphabet deities of Trika, see Alexis Sanderson, 'The Visualisation of the Deities of the Trika', in André Padoux (ed.), *L'image divine, culte et méditation dans l'Hindouisme* (Paris: CNRS, 1990), pp. 31–88.
18. For the standard account of this, see André Padoux, *Vāc: The Concept of the Word in Selected Hindu Tantras*, trans. J. Gontier (Albany NY: SUNY Press, 1990), pp. 147–65.
19. See ibid, pp. 166–222; also Muller-Ortega, *The Triadic Heart of Śiva*, pp. 132, 172.
20. This additional level is a significant difference between the Pratyabhijñā and the Grammarians. Somānanda objects to Bhartṛhari's identification of the absolute with the third level of speech, *paśyantī*, on the grounds that *paśyantī* is from a transitive verb coming from the root *dṛś*, to see, and therefore implies an object. The absolute is beyond all subject–object differentiation and so there must be a supreme level beyond *paśyantī*. *Śivadṛṣṭi* 2.45–48. See K.C. Pandey, *Abhinavagupta, An Historical and Philosophical Study*, 2nd edition (Banaras: Chowkhamba Sanskrit Series Office, 1963), pp. 626–30; D.S. Ruegg, *Contributions á l'histoire de la philosophie linguistique indienne* (Paris: de Boccard, 1959), p. 113.

21. PH sūtra 5: *citireva cetanapadādavararuḍhā cetyasaṃkocinī cittam.*
22. PH p. 2: *asyām hi prasarantyām jagat unmiṣati vyavtiṣṭhe ca, nivṛttaprasarāyāṃ ca nimiṣati.*
23. For a fuller treatment, see my *Body and Cosmology*, pp. 32–44. For the idea of stages of awakening in the *Svacchanda-tantra*, see T. Goudriaan 'The Stages of Awakening in the Svacchanda-tantra', in Teun Goudriaan (ed.), *Ritual and Speculation in Early Tantrism: Essays in Honour of André Padoux* (Albany NY: SUNY Press, 1992), pp. 139–73.
24. PH 20: *tadā prakāśānandasāramahāmantravīryātmakapūrṇāhantāveśāt sadā sarvasargasaṃhārakārinijasaṃviddevatācakreśvaratāprāptir bhavatīti śivam.* Also *Spanda-kārikā*s III.19.
25. See references in Dyczkowski, *The Doctrine of Vibration*, p. 140.
26. Pandey, *Abhinavagupta*, p. 465. Silburn, L. *Hymnes aux Kālī, La Roue des Énergies Divine* (Paris: de Boccard, 1975), pp. 83–96.
27. DH. Sri Ragunath Temple Manuscript Library, Jammu, pp. 205–6, 290–92; text courtesy of Alexis Sanderson. This text slightly differs from that published by Pandey, which is reproduced by Silburn for her translation. In that text verses 2 and 3 are transposed – the present manuscript probably has the correct ordering which makes more sense – and for *śabda* in verse 9 read *śruti* in our text. In the transliteration below I have retained the manuscript's use of the *anusvāra* for most nasals.
28. Sanderson, 'Meaning in Tantric Ritual', pp. 45–7. Rastogi does not think that this text is explicitly from the Krama tradition. N. Rastogi, *The Krama Tantrism of Kashmir* (Delhi: MLBD, 1979), p. 165.
29. Silburn, *Hymnes aux Kālī*, p. 91: 'L'homme ordinaire est broyé par le cercle infernal de ses propres énergies formant pur lui la roue du temps st de l'angoisse dont le movement ne s'arrête jamais.'
30. DH, p. 205: *svaśāntaṃ nirmalaṃ śuddhaṃ sarvavyāpiniraṃjanam cidbodhānaṃdagaha[na?]tejas sarvāśrayaṃ bhajet.*
31. *Oṃ śrī gaṇeśāya namaḥ oṃ śrī asurasuravṛṃdavaṃditam abhimatavaravitaraṇe nirataṃ darśanaśatāgryapūjyaṃ prāṇatanuṃ gaṇapatiṃ vaṃde//1// varavīrayoginīgaṇasiddhāvalipūjitāṃghriyugalaṃ apahṛtavinayijanārtiṃ vaṭukam apānābhidhaṃ vaṃde//2// yo dhībalena viśvam bhaktānāṃ śivapathaṃ bhāti tam aham avadhānarūpaṃ sadgurum amalaṃ sadā vaṃde//3// ātmīyaviṣayabhogair iṃdriyadevyaḥ sadā hṛdaṃbhoje abhipūjaṃti yaṃ taṃ cinmayam ānaṃdabhairavaṃ vaṃde//4// udayāvabhāsacarvaṇalīlāṃ viśvasya yā karoty aniśaṃ ānaṃdabhairavīṃ tāṃ vimarśarūpāṃ ahaṃ vaṃde//5// arcayati bhairavaṃ yā niścayakusumaiḥ sureśapatrasthā praṇamāmi buddhirūpāṃ brahmāṇīṃ tāṃ ahaṃ satatam//6// kurute bhairavapūjām analadalasthābhim ānakusumair yā nityam ahamkṛtirūpāṃ vaṃde tāṃ śāṃbhavīṃ ambām//7// vidadāti bhairavārcāṃ dakṣiṇadalagā viśeṣakusumair yā nityaṃ manāḥsvarūpāṃ kaumārīṃ tām ahaṃ vaṃde//8// nain[r]ṛtadalagā bhairavam arcayate śabdakusumair yā praṇamāmi śrutirūpāṃ nityāṃ tāṃ vaisn[ṣṇ]avīṃ śaktīm//9// paścimadigdalasaṃsthā hṛdayaharaiḥ sparśakusumair yā toṣayati bhairavaṃ tāṃ tvagrūpadharāṃ namāmi vārāhīm//10// varatararūpaviśeṣair mārutadigdalaniṣasma[ṇṇa?]dehā yā pūjayati bhairavaṃ tām iṃdrāṇīṃ dṛktanuṃ vaṃde//11// dhanapatikisala(ya)nilayā nityaṃ vividhaṣaḍrasāhāraiḥ pūjayati*

bhairavaṃ tāṃ jihvābhikhyāṃ namāmi cāmuṃdām// 12// īśadalasthā bhairavam arcayate parimalair vicitrair yā praṇamāmi sarvadā tāṃ ghrāṇābhikhyāṃ mahālakṣmīṃ// 13// ṣaḍdarśaneṣupūjyaṃ ṣaḍtriṃśattattvasaṃvalitaṃ ātmābhikhyaṃ satataṃ kṣetrapatiṃ siddhidaṃ naumi// 14// saṃsphurad anubhavasāraṃ sarvāṃtaḥ satatasaṃnihitaṃ naumi sadoditam itthaṃ nijadehagadevatācakra m// 15// iti śrīdehasthadevatācakrastotraṃ saṃpūrṇaṃ samāp[an]nam.

32. David Kinsley, *Tantric Visions of the Divine Feminine: The Ten Mahāvidyās* (University of California Press, 1997), p. 32.
33. Marie-Thérèse de Mallmann, *Les Enseignements Iconographiques de l'Agni-Purāṇa* (Paris: Presses Universitaires de France, 1963), pp. 150–59. Here they are Brāhmī, Śaṇkarī, Kaumarī, Lakṣmī, Vārāhī, Aindrī and Cāmuṇḍā. Mahālakṣmī is sometimes added.
34. NeT 12. 3–4. Here their names are Brāhmī, Māheśvarī, Kaumarī, Vaiṣṇavī, Vārāhī, Māhendrī, Cāmuṇḍā and Bahurūpiṇī, and they are ordered from the east. Kṣemarāja in his commentary gives an alternative arrangement. H. Brunner, 'Un Tantra du Nord: Le *Netra Tantra*', *Bulletin de l'École Française d'Extrême-Orient* 61 (1974), pp. 125–97; p. 155.
35. TA 29.52–53 and commentary.
36. ISG Kriyāpāda 12.71–77. The seven are Brāhmī, Māheśvarī, Kaumarī, Vaiṣṇavī, Vārāhī, Aindrī and Cāmuṇḍā. For example, the boar-headed goddess Vārāhī is to be visualised as having boar's tusks, mounted on a ram, holding a plough, discus and lotus, terrible yet splendid. Vārāhī, like Cāmuṇḍā, appears as a distinct deity, although this visualisation does not correspond to that in a later text, the *Mantramahodadhi*. Gudrun Bühnemann, *The Iconography of Hindu Tantric Deities* (Gronigen: Egbert Forsten, 2000), pp. 120–21.
37. TAV 29.4, p. 4. John R. Dupuche, *Abhinavagupta: The Kula Ritual as Elaborated in Chapter 29 of the Tantrāloka* (Delhi: MLBD, 2003), p. 182.
38. MNPrak 5.13ab. The arising of circle of bliss is revealed as the true nature of one's own experience: *ānandacakrasya yathopapatti padarśigtaṃ svānubhavasvarūpam.*
39. See references in Dyczkowski, *The Doctrine of Vibration*, p. 140. See Chapter 6 of this book for a general account of the circle of the senses and its interface with the divine body.
40. PH 20 and auto-commentary.
41. See, for example, Dominik Wujastyk, 'Interpréter l'image du corps humain dans l'Inde pré-moderne' in Véronique Boullier and Gilles Tarabout, *Images du corps dans le monde hindou* (Paris: CNRS, 2002), pp. 71–99.
42. D. White, *The Kiss of the Yoginī: 'Tantric Sex' in its South Asian Contexts* (Chicago: University of Chicago Press, 2003), pp. 224–5.
43. Kaul 8.32–44.
44. Sanderson, 'Saivism and the Tantric Traditions', p. 687; D. Heiligjers-Seelen, *The System of Five Cakras in the Kubjikāmatatantra 14–16* (Groningen: Egbert Forsten, 1994). White locates an earlier origin for the system. D. White, *The Alchemical Body: Siddha Traditions in Medieval India* (Chicago: University of Chicago Press, 1996), p. 73. One of the earliest descriptions is in the *Kaulajñāna-nirṇaya*.

45. See André Padoux, 'Corps et cosmos: l'image du corps du yogin tantrique', in Boullier and Tarabout *Images du corps*, pp. 163–87; p. 174. For a full account see Heiligjers-Seelen, *The System of Five Cakras*.
46. On Kubjikā, see Mark Dyczkowski, 'Kubjikā, the Erotic Goddess. Sexual Potency, Transformation and Reversal in the Heterodox Theophanies of the Kubjikā Cult', *Indologica Tauinensia* 21–22 (1995–96), pp. 123–40.
47. A. Sanderson, 'Maṇḍala and Āgamic Identity in the Trika of Kashmir', p. 164. In *Mantras et Diagrammes Rituels dans l'Hindouisme* (Paris: CNRS, 1986), pp. 169–214.
48. See David White, 'Le Monde dans le corps du siddha: microcosmologie dans les traditions médiévale indiennes', in Boullier and Tarabout, *Images du corps*, pp. 189–212. The standard text through which Kuṇḍalinī and the *cakra*s became famous in the West is John Woodroffe, *The Serpent Power, Being the Ṣaṭ-Cakra-Nirūpana and Pāduka-Pañcaka* (Madras: Ganesh and Co., 1973 [1918]), a translation of Puṇyānanda's *ṣaṭcakranirupanam*. See Lilian Silburn, *Kuṇḍalinī, Energy of the Depths: A Comprehensive Study Based on the Scriptures of Nondualistic Kaśmir Śaivism*, trans. J. Gontier (Albany NY: SUNY Press, 1988), pp. 25–35.
49. LT 43.37–48. The text does have the usual six of *ādhāra*, *nābhi, hṛt, kaṇṭha, tālu* and *bhrūmadhya*, along with the *dvādaśānta* and *lalatā* between there and the *bhrūmadhya*. Between these are other centres that the text names.
50. Sardh 10.1c–3b. For an account of recent conflations of subtle, tantric anatomy with modern physiology see Dominik Wujastyk, 'Interpréter l'image du corps humain dans l'Inde pré-moderne', in Boullier and Tarabout, *Images du corps*, pp. 71–99.
51. Sardh. 10.5–6; 9–13.
52. E.g. *Bṛhadāraṇyaka Upaniṣad* 2.1.19. 'There are seventy two thousand veins named Hitā that run from the heart to the pericardium.' Patrick Olivelle (trans.), *The Early Upaniṣads, Annotated Text and Translation* (New York and Oxford: Oxford University Press, 1998), p. 63.
53. Padoux, 'Corps et cosmos', p. 174.
54. See Silburn, *Kuṇḍalinī*, pp. 38–40.
55. NeT 7.1–4; Brunner 'Un Tantra du Nord', pp. 142–3.
56. See Brunner, 'Un Tantra du Nord', p. 142 n1. Here Brunner gives a table showing the correlation between centres of the body, *vyomani*, *cakrani*, *granthayaḥ* and *sthānāḥ*.
57. White, *Kiss of the Yoginī*, p. 230.
58. SSV, pp. 52f. Passage translated and discussed in Flood, *Body and Cosmology*, pp. 263–4.
59. TA 3.137c–141b; Padoux, 'Corps et cosmos', p. 170.
60. PTV 1 and 2; pp. 54–62 of Singh's translation.
61. NeT 7.1.
62. TA 29.238–239b.
63. For a description of the *upāyas*, see Flood, *Body and Cosmology*, pp. 245–6.
64. Sanderson, 'Maṇḍala and the Āgamic Identity in the Trika of Kashmir', pp. 169–214.
65. For an account of this rite as described by Abhinavagupta, see Dupuche, *Abhinavagupta: The Kula Ritual*.

66. Sanderson, 'Maṇḍala and Āgamic Identity', p. 174.
67. E.g. MTV Kriyāpāda 11.41–53, discussed by Alexis Sanderson, *BSOAS* 48 (1985), pp. 564–68. Reference from Hélène Brunner 'The Sexual Aspect of the *Liṅga* Cult According to the Saiddhāntika Scriptures', in G. Oberhammer (ed.), *Studies in Hinduism II. Miscellania to the Phenomenon of Tantras* (Vienna: Der Österreichischen Akademie der Wissenschaften, 1998), pp. 87–103.
68. White, *Kiss of the Yoginī*, p. 73.
69. The use of cannabis (*vijaya*) is sometimes documented in tantric texts accompanying the use of alcohol. See A. Bharati, *The Tantric Tradition* (London: Rider, 1965), pp. 250–53.
70. *Yoni-tantra* 1.15, 6.5. J.A. Schotermann, *The Yoni-tantra Critically Edited with an Introduction* (Delhi: Manohar, 1980), pp. 19–22.
71. White, *Kiss of the Yoginī*, especially chs 3 and 4.
72. Sanderson, 'Meaning in Tantric Ritual', pp. 43–7.
73. Sanderson, 'Śaiva and Tantric Traditions', p. 681.
74. On the degrees of distance from orthodoxy and corresponding intensification of antinomian elements in ritual see Sanderson, 'Meaning in Tantric Ritual', pp. 78–9.
75. TA 29.58, 66. KMT 25.107, 152. Reference from T. Goudriaan and J.A. Schoterman, 'Introduction', *The Kubjikāmatatantra, Kulalikāmnaya Version* (Leiden: Brill, 1988), pp. 1–115; p. 24.
76. Sanderson, 'Śaiva and Tantric Traditions', p. 680.
77. PTV 1 p. 16–17. *tathāhi tanmadhyanāḍīrūpasya ubhayaliṅgātmano 'pi tadviryotsāhabalalabdhāvaṣṭambhasya kampakāle sakala viryakṣobhojjigamiṣātmakam antaḥsparśasukhaaṃ svasaṃvitsākṣikameva/ na ca etatkalpitaśarīraniṣṭhatayaiva kevalaṃ tadabhijñānopadeśadvāreṇa iyati mahāmantravīryavisargaviśleṣaṇāvāptadhruvapadeparabrahmayaśivaśaktisaṃghaṭṭānandasvātantryasṛṣṭiparābhaṭṭārikārūpe 'nupraveśaḥ/*. Singh's translation, pp. 44–5.
78. On the idea of the memory of tradition see Gavin Flood, *The Ascetic Self: Subjectivity, Memory and Tradition* (Cambridge: Cambridge University Press, 2004), pp. 8–13.
79. PTV pp. 43–44 , Singh's translation.
80. *Bṛhadāraṇyaka Upaniṣad* 4.3.21; translated by Olivelle, *The Early Upaniṣads*, p. 115.
81. *Chāndogya Upaniṣad* 2.13.1–2; translated by Olivelle, *The Early Upaniṣads*, pp. 191–2.
82. Leslie C. Orr, *Donors, Devotees, and Daughters of God: Temple Women in Medieval Tamilnadu* (New York and Oxford: Oxford University Press, 2000). On temple women as *prasāda*, see p. 16. As were all initiates, male and female, temple women were branded with the mark of affiliation to their deity (p. 249).
83. On the important term *adhikāra*, see Brunner, Oberhammer and Padoux (eds), *Tāntrikābhidhānakośa* I, pp. 105–6.
84. Flood, *The Ascetic Self*, pp. 105–14. See also the account and translation of the text by Dupuche, *Abhinvagupta, The Kula Ritual*; Silburn, *Kuṇḍalinī*, pp. 177–204; Flood, *Body and Cosmology*, pp. 295–301.

85. Silburn, *Kuṇḍalinī*, p. 224. On this practice and in connection with betel chewing, see White, *Kiss of the Yoginī*, p. 116.
86. On the five *ms*, see Bharati, *The Tantric Tradition*, pp. 228–38.
87. TA 29.97–99 and commentary. For a useful account see Dupuche, *Abhinavagupta, The Kula Ritual*, pp. 125–7.
88. Bharati, *The Tantric Tradition*, pp. 236–7.
89. TA 29.1–3.

Chapter 8

1. The term *imaginaire* is from Castoriadis, who claims that the forms of cultural life are created within a particular *imaginaire*. It does not denote a deficient or secondary mode of being. C. Castoriadis, 'The Imaginary: Creation in the Socio-Historical Domain', in C. Castoradis, *World in Fragments: Writings on Politics, Society, Psychoanalysis, and the Imagination*, ed. and trans. D.A. Curtis (Stanford University Press, 1997), pp. 3–18; p. 5.
2. This term is from William F. Hanks, 'Exorcism and the Description of Participant Roles', in M. Silverstein and Greg Urban (eds), *Natural Histories of Discourse* (Chicago: University of Chicago Press, 1996), pp. 160–200; p. 170.
3. Mrg Kriyāpāda, ch. 5.
4. See Richard A. Darmon, '*Vajroli mudrā*. La retention seminale', in Véronique Boullier and Gilles Tarabout (eds), *Images du corps dans le monde hindou* (Paris: CNRS, 2002), pp. 213–40.
5. For the most thorough treatment of this practice, including critical edition and translation of the *Khecarīvidyā*, accompanied by notes that draw both on other texts and on fieldwork among yogins, see James Mallinson, *The Khecarīvidyā of Adinātha: A Critical Edition and Annotated Translation* (London: Routledge, 2006).
6. André Padoux, 'The Body in Tantric Ritual: The Case of the Mudrās', in T. Goudriaan (ed.), *Panels of the VIIth World Sanskrit Conference*, vol. 1: *The Sanskrit Tradition and Tantrism* (Leiden: Brill, 1990), pp. 66–75.
7. Abhinavagupta TA, vol. 12, p. 305: *mudaṃ svarūpalābhākhyaṃ dehadvāreṇa cātmanām/ rāty arpayati yat tena mudrā śāstreṣu varṇitā*. Quoted by Padoux, 'The Body in Tantric Ritual', p. 72.
8. Padoux, 'The Body in Tantric Ritual', p. 68.
9. André Padoux, 'Contributions a l'Étude du Mantraśāstra', I, II, III, *Bulletin de l'École Française d'Extrème Orient* 65 (1978), pp. 65–85; 67 (1980), pp. 59–102; 76 (1987), pp. 141–54.
10. Harvey Alper (ed.), *Understandng Mantras* (Albany NY: SUNY Press, 1989).
11. J. Gonda, 'The Indian Mantra', *Oriens* 16 (1963), pp. 244–97.
12. MVT 2.10.
13. SSV 2.6, p. 8.
14. IPV 1.5.13
15. Gonda, 'The Indian Mantra', p. 67.

16. Alper, *Understandng Mantras*, p. 258.
17. For an interesting reading of mantra that links Sliverstein's semiotics to structuralism, see Robert A. Yelle, *Explaining Mantras: Ritual, Rhetoric and the Dream of a Natural Language in Hindu Tantra* (New York and London: Routledge, 2003), pp. 71–3.
18. Padoux, *Vāc*, p. 380.
19. See Stephan Beyer, *The Cult of Tārā: Magic and Ritual in Tibet* (Berkeley: University of California Press, 1973), pp. 127–43.
20. Pratapaditya Pal, *Hindu Religion and Iconology According to the Tantrasāra* (Los Angeles: Vichitra Press, 1981).
21. Gudrun Bühnemann, *The Iconography of Tantric Deities*, 2 vols (Groningen: Egbert Forsten, 2002). Bühnemann gives an excellent survey of tantric iconographic literature, vol. 1, pp. 1–5.
22. The following material is taken from Gavin Flood, 'The Purification of the Body in Tantric Ritual Representation', *Indo-Iranian Journal* 45 (2002), pp. 25–43; pp. 34–7.
23. This usage is not dissimilar to that of medieval Europe, where the term 'memory' had the double implication of storing information (inventory) and creation through the imagination (invention). See Mary Carruthers, *The Book of Memory* (Cambridge: Cambridge University Press, 1992).
24. JS 10.26.
25. JS 10.33b–34a.
26. JS 10.46a.
27. Aṣṭ 3.3.161. The same also applies to the imperative (*loṭ*).
28. See Jayashree A. Gune, *The Meaning of Tenses and Moods: The Text of Kauṇḍabhaṭṭa's Lakārāsrthanirṇaya with Introduction, English Translation and Explanatory Notes* (Pune: Deccan College, 1978), p. 17.
29. See ibid., pp. 19–20.
30. Quoted in ibid., p. 19.
31. See Benjamin Whorf, 'The Relation of Habitual Thought to Language', in John B. Caroll (ed.), *Language, Thought and Reality* (Cambridge MA: MIT Press, 1991 [1956]), pp. 147, 152.
32. G. Lakoff and M. Johnson, *Metaphors We Live By* (Chicago: University of Chicago Press, 1980).
33. G. Flood, *The Ascetic Self: Subjectivity, Memory and Tradition* (Cambridge: Cambridge University Press, 2004), pp. 218–20.
34. Roman Jacobsen, 'Closing Statement: Linguistics and Poetics', in Thomas A. Sebeok (ed.), *Style in Language* (Cambridge MA: MIT Press, 1960), pp. 350–77, especially p. 353. See also A.J. Greimas, *Structural Semantics: An Attempt at Method*, trans. S. McDowell Schleifer and A, Velie (Lincoln: University of Nebraska Press, 1983), pp. 177–6; 195–6.
35. V.N. Volosinov, *Marxism and the Philosophy of Language*, trans. L. Matejka and I.R. Titunik (Cambridge MA: Harvard University Press, 1973), p. 68.
36. K. Oehler, 'An Outline of Peirce's Semiotics', in Martin Krampen, Klaus Oehler, Roland Posner, Thomas A. Seboeok and Thure von Uexkull (eds), *Classics of Semiotics* (New York: Plenum Press, 1987), p. 6.
37. Greg Urban, 'The "I" of Discourse', in Benjamin Lee and Greg Urban

(eds), *Semiotics, Self and Society* (Berlin and New York: Mouton de Gruyter, 1989), pp. 38–9. See also G. Urban, *A Discourse-centred Approach to Culture* (Austin: University of Texas Press, 1991).

38. The use of the optative means that 'he is impelling me to action; he is engaging in an operation which is conducive to my action.' Apadeva, *Mīmāṃsā Nyāya Prakāśa*, trans. Frankin Edgerton (Cambridge MA: Harvard University Press, 1929), p. 40.
39. M. Silverstein and G. Urban (eds), 'Introduction', *Natural Histories of Discourse* (Chicago: University of Chicago Press, 1996), p. 1.

Appendix

1. I have followed Rastelli and taken *kṛvāṭike* to be *kṛkāṭake*. Rastelli, *Philosophisch-theologische Grundanschauungen*, p. 244.
2. Namely at 6.73–76. Ref from Rastelli, *Philosophisch-theologische Grundanschauungen*, p. 245.
3. The term *bhūtāvāsa* could also be rendered as 'body', the abode of the elements.

Suggested Further Reading

Boullier, Véronique and Gilles Tarabout (eds), *Images du corps dans le monde hindou* (Paris: CNRS, 2002).

Davis, R., *Ritual in an Oscillating Universe: Worshipping Śiva in Medieval India* (Princeton NJ: Princeton University Press, 1991).

Flood, Gavin (ed.), *The Blackwell Companion to Hinduism* (Oxford: Blackwell, 2003).

Goudriaan, Teun, S. Gupta and D. van Hoens, *Hindu Tantrism* (Leiden: Brill, 1979).

Padoux, André, 'Tantrism', in M. Eliade (general ed.), *The Encyclopaedia of Religions* (New York: Macmillan, 1986), vol. 14, pp. 272–6.

——— *Vāc: The Concept of the Word in Selected Hindu Tantras*, trans. J. Gontier (Albany NY: SUNY Press, 1990).

Sanderson, Alexis, 'Power and Purity among the Brahmans of Kashmir', in Michael Carruthers, Steven Collins and Steven Lukes (eds), *The Category of the Person* (Cambridge: Cambridge University Press, 1985), pp. 190–216.

——— Śaivism and Tantric Traditions', in S. Sutherland et al. (eds), *The World's Religions* (London: Routledge, 1988), pp. 660–704.

Schrader, Otto, *Introduction to the Pāñcarātra and the Ahirbudhnya Saṃhitā* (Madras: Adyar Library, 1973 [1916]).

White, David, *The Kiss of the Yoginī: 'Tantric Sex' in its South Asian Contexts* (Chicago: University of Chicago Press, 2003).

Index

Halbfass, W. 35
Hanks, W.F. 173
Hanneder, J. 57–8
Haraway, D. 21
Hardy, F. 85
Hertz, R. 21
Hindu, as term 7
Hinduism 82, 99, 159, 186
history 6, 33, 35, 44
Hocart, A.M. 11, 77
Holi 85
householder 39, 40
Huxley, A. 24

I, the 5, 13, 18, 89, 147–54, 163, 172, 180, 181, 183
  indexical 26, 66, 115, 119, 149, 151, 163, 167, 172, 183
I-maker 103, 104
I-ness/I-consciousness 66, 157, 167, 168
icon 4, 11, 29, 75, 79, 132, 172, 173, 176–8
iconography 82
ideology 82, 83
  Hindutva 15
  of kingship 73, 77
  of universal ruler 33
  of warfare 76
  tantric 6, 14
imagination 6, 29, 30, 106, 112, 113, 130, 141, 142, 143, 171–84
immanence 154
impurity 40, 44, 45, 123, 152
Inden, R. 8, 16, 33, 50, 75, 77, 78
indexiality 18, 66, 89, 149, 172, 178–80, 182
  variable 5, 12, 113, 178, 183
India, medieval 5, 7, 12, 13, 14, 33, 34, 35, 38, 43, 44, 45, 73, 77, 79, 85, 95, 164
  scripture in 49
individuality 12, 187
Indology 3, 16
Indra 83
Indus civilisation 14
initiation 9, 17, 36, 53, 61, 64, 69, 78, 99, 109, 110, 125, 131–43, 168, 175
  Śaiva Siddhānta 63
  Trika 63
inner worship 116–18, 121
interiority 5, 12, 25
intertextuality 18
Īśāna 57–8, 61
Īśānaśivagurudeva 120–21, 143
Īśānaśivagurudeva-paddhati 80, 90, 91, 92, 108, 120, 140, 141, 142, 156, 181
Isayeva, N. 101
Īśvarapratyabhijñā-kārikās 147
Islam 12, 77, 83

Java 76, 77
Jayākhya-saṃhitā 30, 38, 54, 55, 65, 79, 101–3, 105, 106, 107, 108, 110, 111, 113, 119, 120, 132, 137, 139, 140, 141, 142, 143, 159, 178, 181, 182
  translation of chapter 11, 188–93
Jayaratha 148, 156, 166, 169
Jayantha Bhaṭṭa 43, 48–9, 50–53, 54, 55, 80
Jayavarman II 77
Jīmūtavāhana 41
Jīvānanda 42
Johnson, M. 180
Judaism 12, 16
jurisprudence 38

kaivalya 69
kalā/s 109, 123, 124, 129, 130, 135, 136, 142
Kālāgni 130
Kālāmukhas 52
Kālasaṃkarṣiṇī 63, 163
Kālī 61
kāma 9, 36, 37, 45, 81, 83–5, 86
Kāma-śāstra 37, 83, 84, 85, 86–7
Kāma-sūtra 83
Kāmikāgama 57, 107, 108, 121
Kannada 73
Kāpālikas 52, 61
karma 36, 122, 124, 126, 138
Kārtikeya 64
Kashmir 7, 13, 34, 48, 49, 77, 80, 108, 145, 147
Kashmir Śaivism 55, 146, 186
Katz, S. 24
kaula 154, 156